COACH EDUCATION AND DEVELOPMENT IN SPORT

Global interest in quality sport coaching is at an all-time high, but until now, there hasn't been a go-to resource to help national governing bodies, sport organizations, or coach educators within universities to structure coach education, learning, and development. *Coach Education and Development in Sport* fills that gap, offering a comprehensive guide of instructional strategies used by world leaders in coach education.

Each chapter is written by experienced scholar-practitioners, seamlessly integrating personal experience and insight with current research to show how and why to use an instructional strategy in a specific context that can be adopted or adapted to fit many sport contexts. Covering essential topics such as reflective practice, social learning, online technology, diverse populations, and more, the book provides the fundamentals of tried and trusted instructional strategies to develop coaches from youth, club and collegiate sport to elite, professional, and Olympic levels. It is a complete resource for fostering coaching excellence in small- and large-scale programming, and from volunteer to part-time or full-time coaches.

Designed to stimulate ideas and provide flexible, practical tools, this book is an essential read for anybody working in sport, including coach developers, sport managers, coaches, mentors, athletic directors, sport psychology consultants, and teachers or professors.

Bettina Callary is Canada Research Chair in Sport Coaching and Adult Learning, and Associate Professor in Sport and Physical Activity Leadership, at Cape Breton University in Nova Scotia, Canada. She is Editor-in-Chief of the *International Sport Coaching Journal*, and a trained coach developer through the International Council for Coaching Excellence (ICCE), as well as the National Coaching Certification Program and Alpine Canada.

Brian Gearity is Founding Director and Assistant Professor in the Master of Arts in Sport Coaching program at the University of Denver, USA. He has coached multiple youth sports and been a strength, conditioning, and speed coach for athletes from 6 to 60+. His scholarly interests include coach learning and development and the sociology of sport coaching. A Fellow of the National Strength and Conditioning Association, he is also Editor-in-Chief of their practitioner journal *NSCA Coach* and Associate Editor-in-Chief of *Strength and Conditioning Journal*. He serves on the editorial boards of several journals, including the *International Sport Coaching Journal*, *Sport Coaching Review*, and *Qualitative Research in Sport, Exercise, and Health*.

COACH EDUCATION AND DEVELOPMENT IN SPORT

Instructional Strategies

Edited by Bettina Callary and Brian Gearity

LONDON AND NEW YORK

First published 2020
by Routledge
2 Park Square, Milton Park, Abingdon, Oxon OX14 4RN

and by Routledge
52 Vanderbilt Avenue, New York, NY 10017

Routledge is an imprint of the Taylor & Francis Group, an informa business

© 2020 selection and editorial matter, Bettina Callary and Brian Gearity; individual chapters, the contributors

The right of Bettina Callary and Brian Gearity to be identified as the authors of the editorial material, and of the authors for their individual chapters, has been asserted in accordance with sections 77 and 78 of the Copyright, Designs and Patents Act 1988.

All rights reserved. No part of this book may be reprinted or reproduced or utilised in any form or by any electronic, mechanical, or other means, now known or hereafter invented, including photocopying and recording, or in any information storage or retrieval system, without permission in writing from the publishers.

Trademark notice: Product or corporate names may be trademarks or registered trademarks, and are used only for identification and explanation without intent to infringe.

British Library Cataloguing-in-Publication Data
A catalogue record for this book is available from the British Library

Library of Congress Cataloging-in-Publication Data
A catalog record for this book has been requested

ISBN: 978-0-367-36732-9 (hbk)
ISBN: 978-0-367-36734-3 (pbk)
ISBN: 978-0-429-35103-7 (ebk)

Typeset in Bembo
by Apex CoVantage, LLC

 Printed in the United Kingdom by Henry Ling Limited

We dedicate this book to the educators who have inspired our journeys in coach education, leading us down the path to better understandings of excellence in coach development. We also dedicate this book to our families, who have patiently supported us throughout this process.

CONTENTS

List of tables and figure	*x*
List of contributors	*xi*
Foreword	*xvii*
John D. Bales, Penny M. Crisfield, Masamitsu Ito,	
and John P. Alder	
Acknowledgments	*xx*
Introduction	1
Bettina Callary and Brian Gearity	

SECTION 1
Coach development strategies in higher education   **5**

1 Making direct teaching more learner-centered
in university-based coach education courses   7
Michel Milistetd, William das Neves Salles, Pierre Trudel,
and Kyle Paquette

2 Experiential learning for undergraduate student-coaches   20
Andrea Woodburn

3 Team-Based Learning as an instructional strategy
for undergraduate coach education   33
Melissa Thompson and Erica Pasquini

viii Contents

4 Critically understanding and engaging with the (micro)political dimensions of coaches' work in an advanced undergraduate coaching course 45
Paul Potrac, Adam J. Nichol, and Edward T. Hall

5 Using Project-Based Learning for the graduate student-coach learning strength and conditioning 58
Brian Gearity and Bettina Callary

6 Reflective practice to enhance coach development and practice 74
Clayton R. Kuklick and Michael Kasales

7 Warming up to race: a case study approach to develop engaged athletes 89
Jim Denison and Nathan Kindrachuk

8 Teaching within a social constructionist and critical framework: developing student-coaches in a graduate university program 99
Chris Cushion

SECTION 2
Coach development strategies in organizations 113

9 Social learning in communities and networks as a strategy for ongoing coach development 115
Diane Culver, Erin Kraft, and Tiago Duarte

10 Travel-based learning: Study Tours for high-performance coaches 129
Diane Culver, Darren Holder, and Steven B. Rynne

11 A "personal learning coach" for high-performance coaches: a companion to reflect and learn from one's own coaching practice 141
François Rodrigue and Pierre Trudel

12 A competency-based approach to coach learning: the Sport New Zealand Coach Developer Program 154
Simon Walters, Andy Rogers, and Anthony R.H. Oldham

Contents **ix**

13 Self-paced online learning to develop novice, entry-level,
and volunteer coaches 166
Andrew P. Driska and Jennifer Nalepa

14 Authentic e-learning: using an educational design research
approach to develop a hybrid coach education program 178
Bob Crudgington

15 Differentiated instruction through engaged lecturing
for coach development 190
Kathryn L. Russell

SECTION 3
Inclusive coach development strategies 201

16 Sport coach development: education and mentorship
for women 203
Nicole M. LaVoi

17 What's good for the goose is good for the gander: using
adult learning principles to synergize coach education
and coaching practices in Masters sport 215
Bettina Callary and Bradley W. Young

18 Better coaching, better athletes: developing quality coaches
of athletes with impairments 226
Scott Douglas

19 Stronger together: coach education and coaching practices
for athletes with intellectual disabilities 237
Scott Weaver and Annette K. Lynch

20 Understanding and acting upon White privilege
in coaching and coach education 248
*Brian Gearity, Lynett Henderson Metzger, Derrick S. Wong,
and Ted Butryn*

21 Becoming an agent of change: key strategies for the
development of coaches in Indigenous Sport
for Development contexts 260
Steven B. Rynne, Tony Rossi, Audrey R. Giles, and Carl Currey

Index *271*

TABLES AND FIGURE

Tables

1.1	Comparing instructor-centered teaching and learner-centered teaching along five dimensions	10
1.2	Example of LCT rubrics and rating levels	11
2.1	Considerations for experiential learning activities in three settings	24
3.1	Strategies for increasing impact of individual points	41
3.2	Impact of peer evaluation on final grade	42
5.1	Strength and conditioning program manual rubric	69
5.2	Clinic presentation rubric	70
6.1	Reflective storytelling assignment examples	83
8.1	Task linking to coach learning	106
8.2	Task linking to conceptualizing the coaching process	107
8.3	Task relating to understanding conceptions of coaching practice	107
9.1	Overview of the communities nurtured and/or assessed	120
10.1	Sample value created for the different cycles	132
11.1	Activities performed and coaching topics discussed during each phase of the coaches' learning journey	146
13.1	Guidelines for shaping attitudes with instructional technology in coach development settings	174
14.1	Design matrix for course structure	184
14.2	Design matrix for learning activity, "evaluating team performance" using authentic e-learning framework	185
16.1	Evidence-based support for importance of female same-sex role models and mentors	205

Figure

6.1	DECMAT	79

CONTRIBUTORS

John P. Alder is Head of Performance Pathways at UK Sport/English Institute of Sport (EIS), leading a team of talented practitioners tasked with supporting the development of people, pathways, and systems to enhance the transition of athletes from talented juniors to world class international performers. John is also a consultant trainer to the ICCE and founding member of the NSSU Coach Developer Academy in Tokyo, Japan (NCDA).

John D. Bales is President of ICCE, the not-for-profit, international organization with the mission of promoting coaching as a profession and enhancing the quality of coaching at every level of sport. John serves as Deputy Director of the Nippon Sport Science University Coach Developer Academy and is a former national and Olympic coach in sprint canoeing. He was also Chief Executive Officer of the Coaching Association of Canada (CAC) from 1996–2013.

Ted Butryn is Professor of Sport Sociology and Sport Psychology in the Department of Kinesiology at San Jose State University, USA. His research involves the sport psychology-sport sociology nexus, Whiteness, athlete activism, and mental health.

Penny M. Crisfield has had her own coach education consultancy for 20 years, and works with a range of sports organizations in the UK and internationally. She was a former international lacrosse player and national coach. She helped establish the NSSU Coach Developer Academy in Tokyo, Japan (NCDA), and is currently a master trainer for ICCE and chairs its education and training working group.

Bob Crudgington is Associate Lecturer in Sports Coaching in the School of Human Movement and Nutrition Sciences at the University of Queensland,

xii Contributors

Australia. He is an ICCE accredited coach developer and is currently engaged in doctoral research investigating the structure and design of digital learning landscapes and their impact on coach learning.

Diane Culver is Associate Professor in the School of Human Kinetics, University of Ottawa in Canada. Her research interests include coach development and qualitative research. She is particularly interested in social learning theory and building social learning capability in sport. Diane is also an Alpine ski coach who has worked with all levels of skiers from youth to Olympic levels.

Carl Currey (deceased) was a proud Barkindji man with cultural roots in Western New South Wales, Australia. Carl had personal and professional experience working with Indigenous Australians and assisted with the development and implementation of key strategic and service delivery partnerships with a variety of state and federal departments and non-governmental organizations, and throughout the mainstream sports industry.

Chris Cushion is Professor of Coaching and Pedagogy, and Director of Sport Integration at Loughborough University, UK. He has worked on a number of projects with sport governing bodies, in professional sport and non-sporting contexts such as the police, security, and military. He has over 30 years of hands-on coaching experience in the UK and overseas in professional and collegiate sport.

William das Neves Salles works as an elementary school physical education teacher with experience in the areas of learner-centered teaching and sport pedagogy.

Jim Denison is Professor in the Faculty of Kinesiology, Sport, and Recreation at the University of Alberta, Canada. A sport sociologist and coach educator, his research examines the formation of coaches' practices through a post-structuralist lens.

Scott Douglas is Program Coordinator of the Sport Coaching program in the Department of Sport and Exercise Science at the University of Northern Colorado, USA. He is a member of the Board of Directors for the United States Center for Coaching Excellence (USCCE) and a teacher-scholar in the areas of coaching expertise, coach development in parasport, and perceptions of disability.

Andrew P. Driska is Assistant Professor and coordinates the masters degree program in Sport Coaching and Leadership in the Department of Kinesiology at Michigan State University, USA. He teaches courses in sport psychology, skill development, and coaching science, and through his work with the Institute for the Study of Youth Sports, his scholarship explores the design, implementation, and evaluation of coach learning programs and their intersection with information technology.

Contributors **xiii**

T ago Duarte is a Ph.D. candidate at the University of Ottawa, Canada and has dedicated the last 15 years to working and researching sport psychology and coaching. He was honored to receive funding from some of the most prestigious Canadian organizations to support his research with parasport coaches.

Audrey R. Giles is Professor in the School of Human Kinetics, University of Ottawa, Canada. She conducts the majority of her research, which focuses on injury prevention and health promotion with Indigenous communities in northern Canada.

Edward T. Hall is Senior Lecturer in Sport Coaching at Northumbria University, UK. His research explores how networks of social relations influence the thoughts, feelings and (inter)actions of sport professionals, and how sense is made of experiences, relationships, and the self.

Lynett Henderson Metzger is Clinical Associate Professor and Assistant Director of the Master's in Forensic Psychology Program at the University of Denver's Graduate School of Professional Psychology, USA. Her research is in the areas of clinical training, diversity, and inclusion.

Darren Holder is Elite Coaching Manager for Cricket Australia, where he leads the growth of practice and performance across Australian cricket's elite coach community. Darren is an innovative thinker prepared to challenge traditional models to support and facilitate enhanced coach learning.

Masamitsu Ito is Professor of sport coaching at Nippon Sport Science University (NSSU) in Tokyo, Japan, and Deputy Director of the NSSU Coach Developer Academy. He leads the masters degree program in coaching at NSSU, which integrates academic research and practical coaching. In addition, he helps many coaches and athletes in athletic programs, is a reviewer for the *International Sport Coaching Journal*, and is a member of the ICCE Research Committee.

Michael Kasales is a leadership development consultant, and former Division I and III athletic performance coach. Kasales is a retired US Army colonel and former brigade combat team commander.

Nathan Kindrachuk is Manager of Safe Sport for the Alberta Gymnastics Federation and has coached swimming for ten years. Through the completion of a Master of Arts degree at the University of Alberta, Canada, he studied power relationships in coach development in the context of swimming.

Erin Kraft is a third-year doctoral candidate in the School of Human Kinetics at the University of Ottawa, Canada. Her current research uses a social learning

xiv Contributors

approach to promote coach development in the parasport community and support gender equity and leadership diversity across sport organizations.

Clayton R. Kuklick is Clinical Assistant Professor in the Master of Arts in Sport Coaching program at the University of Denver, USA, where he teaches a variety of courses spanning motor learning and pedagogy, biomechanics, sports technology, exercise physiology, and kinesiology. His research interests center on coach learning and the sociological implications of coaching practices.

Nicole M. LaVoi is Senior Lecturer in the School of Kinesiology and Director of the Tucker Center for Girls & Women at the University of Minnesota, USA. Her research pertains to gender and coaching, and media portrayals of women in sport.

Annette K. Lynch uses her many years of experience and expertise to help others inside and outside Special Olympics through her company AKL Connection, LLC. She worked with the Special Olympics North America (SONA). Her major focus and passion have been coaching excellence and sport education with oversight of coach development, the train-the-trainer program, Athlete Leadership, Unified Sports®, and relationships with national governing bodies and sport organizations (USOC, NBA, NCAA, ASEP, NFHS, NCACE, SHAPE).

Michel Milistetd is with the Department of Physical Education at the Federal University of Santa Catarina (UFSC), Brazil. Certified as Coach Developer at the NSSU/ICCE program, he is working as a consultant in sports federations and sports associations across Brazil.

Jennifer Nalepa is Assistant Professor at Michigan State University, USA, in the department of Kinesiology. She teaches in the Sport Coaching and Leadership Graduate Online Programs and conducts research examining modified sport, coach education, and sport engagement. She also works with the United States Tennis Association on coach mentoring programs and other projects aligned with Net Generation tennis.

Adam J. Nichol is Ph.D. Researcher and Associate Lecturer in the Department of Sport, Exercise and Rehabilitation at Northumbria University, UK. His research is centered on how, when, why, and under which circumstances coaches influence (or do not influence) others.

Anthony R.H. Oldham is Senior Lecturer in Sport Coaching at Auckland University of Technology, New Zealand. His specialisms are in sport psychology, skill acquisition, and mixed-methods research.

Kyle Paquette is with the School of Human Kinetics, University of Ottawa, Canada. He works as the Mental Performance Consultant for both Curling Canada and Volleyball Canada's national team programs.

Erica Pasquini is Assistant Professor in the Department of Kinesiology at Sam Houston State University, USA. Her research focuses on coach-athlete relationships and the coach expectancy cycle, highlighting the impact of expectancy on coach behavior.

Paul Potrac is Professor of Sport Coaching at Northumbria University, UK. His research focuses on the social, emotional, and political dimensions of coaching work.

François Rodrigue is currently examining high-performance coach learning, teaching university courses, and consulting for sport federations. During his masters in Sport Management, he co-founded a high-performance training center. In 2016, he acted as a university football coach after three seasons as the assistant head coach of a junior college football team.

Andy Rogers is a National Coaching Consultant for Sport New Zealand (Sport NZ), which includes oversight of the New Zealand Coach Developer Training Program. Andy is also a regular Trainer for the ICCE/NCDA Coach Developer Academy in Tokyo, Japan.

Tony Rossi is Director of Health and Physical Education in the School of Health Sciences at Western Sydney University, Australia. His research interests are varied and include school teachers' work in health, learning cultures in health-related work environments, and community sport for health and development outcomes.

Kathryn L. Russell is the Education Manager in the USA for the National Strength and Conditioning Association and a current doctoral candidate in Human and Sport Performance. Kathryn's interests include the advancement of strength and conditioning programs in the high school setting, an improved understanding of adaptations made by female athletes to strength and conditioning, and the education of future strength and conditioning professionals through clear identification of evidence-based research.

Steven B. Rynne is Senior Lecturer and Program Convenor for Sports Coaching with the School of Human Movement and Nutrition Sciences and is an affiliate appointment with the Poche Centre for Indigenous Health at The University of Queensland, Australia. Steven has worked and conducted research with a variety of peak domestic and international sporting bodies in the areas of coach learning and Indigenous sport.

xvi Contributors

Melissa Thompson is Associate Professor in the School of Kinesiology and Nutrition at the University of Southern Mississippi, USA. She is recognized as a National Trainer with ICCE and is a Certified Mental Performance Consultant through the Association of Applied Sport Psychology. Her primary area of research interest is coach development, with specific focus on coaching ethics and the internship process.

Pierre Trudel is an Emeritus Professor in the School of Human Kinetics at the University of Ottawa in Canada. He has been a consultant for many sport organizations, developing programs and acting as a personal learning coach for high-performance coaches. During the 2016 Olympic Games in Rio de Janeiro, he conducted a research project for the Canadian Olympic Committee called "Rio As a Learning Environment".

Simon Walters is Head of Coaching, Health and Physical Education at Auckland University of Technology, New Zealand. His research has focused largely on working with children, coaches, parents, and sport organizations to enhance young people's experiences of organized sport. His teaching areas are sociology of sport, coaching and coach development, and qualitative research methods.

Scott Weaver is Senior Manager of Unified Sports and Sports Education for Special Olympics North America. His role is to support further development of Unified Sports and coach education. In 1983, he was involved in the launch of Unified Sports as a player on the North Shore Arc Unified softball team. His career with Special Olympics has also provided him the opportunity to implement coach education programs and develop innovative community-based sports programs.

Derrick S. Wong is a doctoral student at George Mason University, USA, in the Exercise, Fitness, and Health Promotion program in the Kinesiology department at the College of Education and Human Development. His research centers on athlete performance, load monitoring, and analytics.

Andrea Woodburn is Associate Professor in the Department of Physical Education at Université Laval in Canada.

Bradley W. Young is Full Professor in the School of Human Kinetics at the University of Ottawa, Canada. His research relates to the psychosocial aspects of lifelong sport participation, the effective programming of adult sport, and messaging to promote adult sport. His research focuses on how and why older sportspersons commit to sport, barriers to participation, the influence of age-related perceptions, and instructional approaches with older sportspersons.

FOREWORD

John D. Bales, Penny M. Crisfield,
Masamitsu Ito, and John P. Alder

Two key events helped firmly establish the coach developer role in the sport coaching landscape and accelerate its global expansion: The publication of the ICCE International Coach Developer Framework (ICDF) in 2014 and the launch of the Nippon Sport Science University Coach Developer Academy (NCDA) in 2015.

Previously, most formal coach education programs drew heavily on experienced technical coaches or subject matter experts to pass on their knowledge, often with insufficient consideration to both the application of the learning and the effectiveness of the coach or their practice.

The publication of the ICDF shifted the emphasis to the comprehensive preparation of the coach in formal, informal, and non-formal settings, and recognized the importance of going beyond coaching courses to support coaches in their working environment. The framework offered a common language, ideas and concepts to better understand the role, preparation, and deployment of the coach developer.

Stimulated by the ICDF, and with the support of the Japanese government "Sport for Tomorrow" Olympic legacy program, the NCDA has trained a strong leadership group of over 80 coach developers who are now designing, delivering and leading programs in a variety of sport coaching contexts, across five continents and in over 30 countries. The NCDA emphasizes an athlete-centered approach to coaching, and delivers a learner-centered curriculum that promotes and models these aspirational philosophies and practices for sport coaching and coach development: The context and the needs of the learner are essential for an effective learning and development experience.

Into this landscape, we welcome the publication of *Coach Education and Development in Sport: Instructional Strategies*. The chapter authors are outstanding leaders in coach development research and practice, and are major

xviii Foreword

contributors to the global effort to enhance the practice of sport coaching. As our understanding of learning and professional development in sports coaching continues to grow, and new research paves the way to more effective approaches to engage coaches, improve their learning experiences, and advance their practice, this book provides concrete examples of how to apply the latest ideas into your coach developer programs.

Each of the chapters in this book has important messages and ideas for those in coach development, and we challenge you, as the reader, to reflect on and identify ideas and actions you can take to experiment with and advance your work in coaching development. To stimulate your thinking as you read the book, outlined below is a description of the evolving role of the coach developer as formulated by ICCE. We hope this will help you get maximum benefit from your study of this outstanding contribution to the coach education literature.

The evolving role of the coach developer

Over the last 25 years, the way coaches have been educated has undergone significant change. Initially, the emphasis was on *"knowledge transfer"*, and typically, more experienced coaches would share their knowledge and experience with other coaches. They adopted a presentational, often lecture-based, approach and were seen as "course leaders, presenters or conductors".

As the research uncovered, new insight on how people, particularly coaches, learn, there was a shift away from the reliance on knowledge transfer toward *"learning facilitation"*. "Tutors, coach educators and course facilitators" were trained to deliver more engaging and learner-centered formal workshops where coaches were more actively involved in their own learning and helped to develop pedagogical coaching skills and apply new knowledge to their own coaching contexts.

More recently, and as a result of both further research evidence and increased experience of working across a range of different cultures and coaching systems, there has been increased awareness of the need to focus on longer-term *"behavioral change"* in coaches. The recognition that learning new skills takes time and that application needs to be appropriate to the coaching culture as well as the specific coaching context has led to the need to support coaches in the field in a variety of ways. While formal coach education programs and workshops play an important role in many coaching systems, the evidence of strong transfer to coaching practice has been difficult to substantiate despite significant empirical reports. The leadership research does however support the impact of post-workshop interventions in increasing the transfer effect and the impact in longer-term behavioral change.

As a result of these changes, the ICCE uses the term "coach developer" to describe the broader roles and responsibilities of those engaged in coach education and development. More specifically, the role of the coach developer is now described as *"to engage, facilitate, educate and support coaches' learning and behavioural change through a range of opportunities, and may include leading organisational change in coach education programmes and coaching systems"* (ICCE Professional Coach Developer Standards – in development). Depending on the coaching system and culture in which he or she works, the role of a coach developer may include learning facilitation in more formal programs; coach observation review or assessment in the field; field-based, "in practice" or in situ coach support and mentoring; program design, monitoring and evaluation; or contributing directly or more tangentially to the leadership and evolvement of their sport or organization's coaching system.

ACKNOWLEDGMENTS

We offer our sincere thanks and appreciation to all the contributors for sharing their wisdom. We appreciate Cape Breton University and the University of Denver for providing the time and resources to facilitate the completion of this important work. Also, a very special thank you to Christina Aaron, an alumna and former graduate assistant of the Master of Arts in Sport Coaching program at the University of Denver, for her editorial diligence.

INTRODUCTION

Bettina Callary and Brian Gearity

Writing about coach education in our current time is exciting. The economic, cultural, and social capital of sport and sport coaches around the world has never been higher. Sport coaches directly influence millions of lives from participatory to competitive youth and adult leagues, clubs, and school sports, to collegiate, professional, and national teams. And yet, is it not shocking that much sport coach education is unregulated, haphazard, and informal? Unlike many established professions, the pathway into coaching often omits extensive, rigorous formal education, and coaching science researchers have even shown that some coaches criticize the formal coach education programs they do attend for lacking relevance. Furthermore, many sport coaches state that they prefer to learn from their peers and mentors within their specific sport context. An immediate reaction is to question: "How can we provide meaningful instruction and content knowledge to coaches that is relevant?" With more time to reflect, we philosophically wonder if all of education should be a quick and easy tool, method, or drill to be simplistically implemented. Perhaps we are caught in a sort of catch-22. We need to educate today's sport coaches for their current social realities, where skills are needed to just "go coach", and in today's times, we're also in need of imagining and creating new educational structures, systems, and regulations to provide coaches with a well-rounded, holistic, individualized, and comprehensive education. Today's coaches over-rely on previous athletic experiences, available role models, and apprenticeships to prepare them, which leaves them as unprepared technicians needing more, better and deeper answers, wisdom, and skills. Educating coaches for today, while imagining a better tomorrow, inspired our book and its organization.

The purpose of this book is to provide an exploration, analysis, and understanding of tried-and-true and innovative exemplary instructional strategies in and for coach education. Coach education is about how we educate and prepare

2 Callary and Gearity

the thousands of coaches around the world to hone their craft, and to become effective and ethical at achieving desirable ideals. This book is meant as a resource to sport organizations, coach developers, and sport coaches who educate and prepare coaches across all settings. In line with the International Council for Coaching Excellence (ICCE), a non-profit international organization devoted to leading and supporting the development of sport coaching globally, we use the term "coach developer" throughout this book as the "umbrella term to embrace the varied roles played by personnel engaged in the process of developing coaches" (ICCE 2014: 8).

The book is meant to be both practical and theoretical. It is practical in the sense that coach developers will benefit from a deep understanding of how to best select, adapt, and implement an instructional strategy that fits their setting. In other words, this book provides many different concrete instructional examples for coach developers teaching sport coaches. It is theoretical in the sense that chapter authors justify their strategy by connecting it to research and answering questions related to why, when, how, and under what conditions they use a particular strategy. Practical knowledge is supported and extended with theoretical knowledge. We need coach developers and sport coaches to understand what and why they do what they do, and the resulting intended and unintended effects. Like sport coaching, coach education is complex and embedded within powerful psychological, social, cultural, and political forces. And yet, we know that when done well, education can be inspirational and empowering, and create new ways of thinking and practicing solving problems and social issues. Quality coach education enables coaches to be critical of past and current practices, and provides personalized approaches to becoming a master at the craft of coaching.

The field of coach education is flourishing, as evidenced by high-quality academic journals, including the *International Sport Coaching Journal*, *Sports Coaching Review*, and the *International Journal for Sport Science and Coaching*, publishing original research, best practices, and insight papers. Similar to these scholarly outlets, through the chapters in this book, authors show how learning theories underpin instructional strategies in practice, but herein we take a heavier focus on the effective design, implementation, and assessment of these strategies. This reflects the holistic concerns of a coach developer who, as a master of their craft, draws upon a variety of sources to construct an engaging learning activity or assignment to enhance coach thinking, learning, and practice. As a result, this text is highly practical, while maintaining integrity and trustworthiness to diverse theoretical frameworks and research. Still, to advance the professionalization of coaching, the body of literature and research evidence on coach developers' instruction and the learning of coaches in varying settings needs more and varying perspectives and evidence. While ICCE and other groups (e.g. Canada's National Coaching Certification Program, the United States Center for Coaching Excellence, the Australian Sports Commission) have developed and continue to refine standards for sport coaching practice and accreditation of education programs, we do not have a large or longitudinal body of evidence on how to optimize coach preparation. The field will advance when researchers and coach developers substantiate coach education, organize it coherently, and present it for the public good.

This book will benefit all sizes of organizations that employ a few to hundreds of coaches, or coaching staffs on which a de facto sport coach turned coach developer is tasked with the responsibility of developing coaches, such as novices or newcomers, in the organization or on their team. This book will also benefit the seasoned veteran coach looking for novel education or ways to become a better mentor. For example, the novice coach might be well served by a coach developer delivering differentiated instruction through engaged lecturing (see Chapter 15) because this approach fits well to serve the basic educational needs of diverse learners in the same space. Whereas the veteran coach, with greater knowledge, experience, and resources, is likely to find utility in collaborating with a personal learning coach (see Chapter 11) who uses a narrative-collaborative coaching approach to tailor education for an individual coach. Put plainly, an experienced coach won't benefit much, if at all, from listening to a basic lecture with content designed for newcomers. On the other hand, a novice coach might do well in this learning space or from gaining experience within a community of practitioners to subsequently reflect on that practice. Thus, by design, this book balances breadth and depth in an original way for the field, so coach developers across all sports and contexts can broaden and deepen their understanding of instructional strategies. By enhancing their own preparation as a coach developer, they in turn will help their organization to achieve its mission.

The book is organized broadly into three sections that detail exemplary instructional strategies used in different educational contexts. We invite anybody interested in coach development to read through the whole book, extend current understandings, challenge existing beliefs, and pick up new ideas. While each chapter author speaks from personal experience and maps out a plan of action, they also encourage readers to think critically about making changes to optimize coach development in their own setting. The sections reflect the common places where coach developers work, and the instructional strategies vary to provide coach developers a guide toward design and implementation. The sections are not meant to convey that only coach developers in that context would be interested in that content or strategy, nor that these chapters represent all the best strategies that exist in coach development. Rather, freedom was provided for innovative coach developers to write about their meaningful practices, and as such, the chapters within each section provide applied, richly described, and novel examples of a well-fitting instructional strategy used within that context. This scoping foundational text provides numerous instructional strategies – but it is just the start, with more strategies yet to be shared.

In Section 1, the focus is on coach development in higher education. The chapter authors explain instructional strategies they used in undergraduate and graduate coaching programs for "student-coaches". Section 2 delves into coach education delivered by coach developers as employees or consultants of national sport governing bodies. This includes both "large-scale" programming (e.g. weekend workshops, conferences, and courses) and "small-scale" programming (e.g. with fewer coaches, often high-performance or an exclusive group of coaches). Finally, in Section 3, the chapter authors explore instructional strategies that are especially effective for unique populations of coaches, which often rely upon informal learning activities. This section, however, is for all coach developers, precisely because it addresses critical social issues in coach education and broader society that has marginalized or excluded groups of people, which is our shared responsibility.

Each chapter begins with a brief overview and then flows through the essential components of an instructional strategy and how the coach developer designed and implemented that strategy in real life. In keeping with the theme of preparing for our current reality while imagining a better tomorrow, full of possibilities, chapter authors also provide candid personal reflections and wishful thinking. Finally, each chapter ends with suggested activities for coach education and additional resources. Contributors were selected based on their experience and expertise as coach developers. Contributors graciously shared their instructional planning tools and assessment methods. We are thankful to all the contributors, who seamlessly integrated relevant theory, research, and practice. As such, we believe readers will benefit greatly from this text, which is the first to offer numerous high-quality examples of instructional strategies specific to coach education. Thank you for allowing us to support your journey in sport and coach education, and we look forward to hearing from you.

Bibliography

ICCE. (2014) *International coach developer framework: Version 1.1.* Online. Available HTTP: <www.icce.ws/_assets/files/documents/PC_ICDF_Booklet_Amended%20Sept%2014. pdf> (accessed 26 September 2019).

SECTION 1

Coach development strategies in higher education

1

MAKING DIRECT TEACHING MORE LEARNER-CENTERED IN UNIVERSITY-BASED COACH EDUCATION COURSES

Michel Milistetd, William das Neves Salles, Pierre Trudel, and Kyle Paquette

Chapter objectives

By the end of this chapter, the reader should be able to:

1. Recognize the limits of the direct teaching approach in Higher Education.
2. Identify the five key dimensions that characterize a learner-centered teaching approach.
3. Design an action plan for implementing the learner-centered teaching approach in a university-based coach education course.

Brief chapter overview

In this chapter, we start by presenting some of the arguments supporting the paradigm shift from the traditional "instructor-centered teaching approach" (ICT; direct teaching) to the "learner-centered teaching approach" (LCT; active learning) that higher education institutions should make. Second, based on the work developed by some key authors of the area (i.e. Blumberg, Cullen, Harris, McCombs, Weimer), we explain what is an LCT approach by contrasting it to the ICT approach using five key dimensions. Third, based on our collective experience of teaching in three different universities, we discuss four key aspects that faculty members should consider to progressively make their course(s) more aligned with LCT to support coaches' preparation. Finally, we present some challenges we have faced in our efforts to adopt LCT.

8 Milistetd, das Neves Salles, Trudel, and Paquette

Why and when I use LCT

For years, knowledge production and dissemination have been the central tenet of educational institutions. In the post-war Western societies, these institutions played a pivotal role in preparing people for the labor market by offering programs to develop technical skills (Quehl, Bergquist & Subbiondo 1999). The university system has perpetuated this model by creating a hierarchical structure composed of faculties, schools, and departments that developed curricula with the objective of awarding a diploma or degree for a specific profession. These curricula are generally composed of a fixed collection of courses that all the students must take and successfully complete to be deemed as having acquired sufficient knowledge (Barr & Tagg 1995). The quality control process requires that: (a) the sequence of courses must follow an order (i.e. prerequisites); (b) the content must be taught as intended; (c) the amount of time allotted must be respected; (d) there is a minimal score to obtain to pass the course; and (e) not all students can get a high grade, and therefore, a grade adjustment is often made to produce a normal distribution (Tagg 2003). In this environment, what dominates is the mandate given to the instructor (expert in his/her research field), that often includes designing (e.g. syllabus), teaching the predetermined content, and assessing the students' retention of the content. When learning is viewed as a product of good teaching, we might have what is called "instructor-centered teaching" (ICT). According to Cullen, Harris and Hill (2012), in the ICT paradigm, the instructor seeks to control the individuals and master all the knowledge because the students are perceived as mere knowledge receivers.

Globalization and advances in technology have strongly marked the first two decades of the 21st century. This rapid access to constantly updated information makes the world more complex and uncertain, and therefore puts pressure on educational institutions to modify not only their functioning but also to question the values of the paradigm in which they operate (Cullen, Harris & Hill 2012). As such, if the goal of higher education institutions has historically been to prepare graduates for a specific profession, their new challenge is to prepare them for an unknown future. Thus, higher education institutions need to do a paradigm shift whereby the learner, instead of the content knowledge, will be central to their educational initiatives. This new paradigm is called "learner-centered teaching" and "represents an important step in the quest to develop creative, autonomous learners who can readily adapt to a rapidly changing society" (Cullen, Harris & Hill 2012: 21).

In a recent study (Milistetd et al. 2018), in which we have analyzed the learner-centeredness of a bachelor program in Physical Education (sport performance concentration) in Brazil, we suggested, based on the literature, the following definition of a learner-centered (LC) institution:

> A flexible learning environment where teaching and learning strategies are used by instructors to support and facilitate the efforts of the students (individually and in groups) to achieve learning outcomes (knowledge base

Making direct teaching more learner-centered **9**

and learning skills) for their growth as creative and independent learners in ways that both satisfy the Department's/School's expectations for graduation, and also prepare students for an unknown future.

(p. 106)

Experts in the education field (e.g. McCombs & Miller 2009; Tagg 2003) have mentioned that this paradigm shift will be difficult to make and will take time because all the stakeholders (i.e. administrators, faculty members, students) must first understand what is a LCT approach and then be proactive and rugged in their pursuit to bring about the required changes. It is possible to start "locally" by supporting instructors/teachers – or coach developers, as they are called in this textbook – in their effort to progressively modify their courses by applying some of the principles of the LCT.

Two main reasons suggest that the timing is perfect to discuss the integration and implementation of LCT in coach education. First, following a theoretical overview of the LCT and coach education literature, Paquette and Trudel (2016: 60) concluded that "the majority of critiques and recommendations targeting coach education are not only closely aligned with the LCT framework, but in many cases would be satisfied with the adoption of one or more recommendations by Weimer to support LCT". Moreover, the two authors later pointed out that "there is a LC undertone that is permeating the literature and the restructuring efforts of many national coach education programs" (Paquette & Trudel 2018). Second, although for years national governing bodies were the exclusive providers of coach education programs, the reality now is that many higher education institutions are offering such programs (McCarthy & Stoszkowski 2018). Consequently, how can we influence the paradigm shift in this new learning context?

The essentials of learner-centered teaching approach

Definitions, essential components, and goals of LCT

LCT is an approach that corresponds to the learning paradigm in which collaboration and cooperation are central on educational process (Barr & Tagg 1995). LCT can potentialize direct teaching, through different strategies to leverage students' motivations and in turn to improve their responsibilities to build their own knowledge. When coach developers possess a strong theoretical and practical understanding of LCT principles, they are equipped to adjust the learning goals and to adapt the teaching and learning methods based on the programs and course characteristics. Recently, a group of scholars (Blumberg 2009; Cullen, Harris & Hill 2012; Harris & Cullen 2010; Weimer 2002, 2013) have focused their work on how to help higher education institutions to make the paradigm shift from ICT to LCT. In Table 1.1, we contrast the two approaches using five dimensions or key changes in practice that occur when instructors move to an LCT approach.

TABLE 1.1 Comparing instructor-centered teaching and learner-centered teaching along five dimensions

Dimensions	Instructor-centered teaching	Learner-centered teaching
Overview	• Post-positivism • Knowledge transfer, isolation • Goal to provide/deliver instruction	• Constructivism • Knowledge creation, collaboration • Goal to produce learning
Function of content	• Content is covered to build knowledge • Students are allowed to memorize content • No clear organizing scheme	• Content has multiple functions (e.g. helps students know why they need to learn content, use discipline-specific inquiry) • Students are encouraged to transform and reflect on content to make meaning of it • Organizing schemes support learning
Role of the instructor	• Lecturer and giver of information • Use passive teaching methods • Use extrinsic motivators (e.g. grades)	• Facilitator of student learning • Use active-learning methods • Create intrinsically motivating learning environments
Responsibility for learning	• Instructor assumes all responsibility • Achievement of course outcomes • Instructor assesses student learning, strengths and weaknesses	• Student mostly assumes responsibility • Achievement of learning objectives and self-directed, lifelong learning skills • Student routinely self-assesses
Purpose and process of assessment	• Strong emphasis on evaluation • Summative evaluations are prioritized • Evaluation occurs following instruction	• Use assessment strategies that lead to deep learning (e.g. authentic assessment, peer- and self-assessments) • Formative assessment drives learning • Carefully integrated into learning process
Balance of power	• Instructor possesses all power • Instructor determines course content, course policies, and deadlines • Student learning is largely influenced by instruction and evaluation process	• Power is shared with students • Students are empowered to express their perspectives and recommendations on content, learning methods, and policies • Open-ended assignments and mastery grading allow alternative learning

Note: Adapted from 'The Learner-Centered Status of a Brazilian University Coach Education Program' (Milistetd et al. 2018: 107).

Making direct teaching more learner-centered **11**

In the foreword of Blumberg's book on LCT (2009), Weimer makes a serious warning:

> I couldn't agree more that all courses can have learner-centered components but being completely learner-centered is not realistic for all courses. It is both sad and unnecessary when faculty dichotomously position learner-centered teaching and lecturing, assuming the use of one rule out inclusion of the other. There are times when students learn best through the teacher's telling.
>
> *(p. 15)*

Blumberg (2009) developed a multi-purpose framework that aims to help administrators determine the LC status of their institutions or educational programs (i.e. through guided systematic assessment), and to help instructors transform their teaching. In this framework, each of the five dimensions is operationally defined by four to seven components for a total of 29 components. Then, for each of these components, different instructor behaviors are described according to four levels: (a) employs ICT approaches; (b) lower level of transitioning (toward LCT); (c) higher level of transitioning (toward LCT); and (d) employs LCT approaches. For example, Table 1.2 presents the four rating levels corresponding to the second component (level to which students engage in content) of the function of content dimension.

When to transition a coach education course toward a LCT approach

Based on the literature and on our personal experience in planning, implementing and evaluating courses based on the LCT approach in university settings, we

TABLE 1.2 Example of LCT rubrics and rating levels

Component	Employs IC approaches	Level of transitioning		Employs LC approaches
		Lower level of transitioning	Higher level of transitioning	
Level to which students engage in content	Instructor allows students to memorize content	Instructor provides content, so students can learn material as it is given to them without transforming or reflecting on it	Instructor assists students to transform and reflect on some of the content to make their own meaning out of some of it	Instructor encourages students to transform and reflect on most of the content to make their own meaning out of most of it.

Note: Table is adapted from Blumberg (2009).

12 Milistetd, das Neves Salles, Trudel, and Paquette

present four key moments when an instructor of a coach education course should reflect and take concrete actions to gradually move their course further toward a LCT approach. In the following section of the chapter, we detail some of the strategies we have been using in our own courses to create, sustain, and to evaluate the implementation of LCT.

Planning the course

The planning period is the most important, as it defines the course's general aim, intended trajectory, as well as the targeted LCT's dimensions and components to be prioritized.

Reflecting on one's own philosophical assumptions and getting to know the essentials of LCT

Before implementing LCT, it is important to note that it means much more than a set of teaching strategies designed to provide student-coaches with easier access to more information. As pointed out earlier, LCT comprises a paradigm shift, and therefore must involve a change of teaching philosophy. In ICT, the instructor assumes either all or a large part of the control over the teaching process because of the prior assumption that the student-coaches do not have maturity or motivation both to assume responsibility and to appropriately participate in the process. In contrast, in LCT, the assumption is that students are potentially motivated and able to engage in the course and to develop their autonomy, so long as we create an effective learning environment with opportunities for being involved.

Some of the questions instructors need to answer are: Why do I want to adopt LCT instead of the traditional ICT approach? What unquestioned beliefs about learning or teaching do I hold that may work against my adoption of LCT? What do I need to learn before implementing LCT? Without an honest reflection on these questions, the danger exists of simply implementing a set of fashionable teaching strategies (e.g. interactive group activities, problem-based learning, blogs, etc.) that will most likely be ineffective if not grounded on sound learner-centered assumptions and examples of best practices.

Starting to plan your coaching course

Given that transitioning to LCT is not an all-or-nothing process (Harris & Cullen 2010), nor is it feasible, recommended, or likely desirable in most cases (Blumberg 2009), instructors should recognize that planning to develop or transform a course to align with LCT requires measured steps. As such, instructors should consider the scope and type of change both that they want and believe is feasible to implement. Some questions to be answered are: What is the nature of the course to be transformed (e.g. theoretical or practical, general or specific, mandatory or optional)? What is the general aim of the course (i.e. which competencies do we intend to develop in the students)? What are the facilities available (e.g. classroom, laboratory, stadium)? How many students will be enrolled? What could be the main characteristics of the students (e.g. previous sporting experiences, level of progression within the undergraduate program)?

By using Blumberg's framework, instructors will be in a better position to decide the most appropriate actions to ensure an efficient and healthy transition for them and their students. For each component, instructors should identify where they want to be on the continuum ICT–LCT using the instructors' behaviors under the four signposts (see Table 1.2).

Writing a first version of the syllabus

It is now time to align all aspects of the course into a document that will be circulated to the students and administrators when needed. In most university programs, instructors must develop a syllabus which contains: (a) the goal of the course and the main objectives; (b) the teaching approach, along with different learning activities; and (c) the assessment methods. When using LCT, instructors must be aware that it will take more time to develop their syllabi – likely a lot more than expected. The practical manifestation of LCT can at first seem arduous depending on the scope and type of change being made to a course. Simply put, LCT involves a collection of articulated learning outcomes that are achieved through the engagement in diverse, multi-modal learning strategies that offer learning activity options and flexibility to students to accommodate their learning preferences and needs. For example, the students either might have to select learning activities among a list or parts of the grades they are ready to work for. Both the percentage of the final mark being attributed to the different learning activities and the dates to submit the academic works are two elements that are easy to discuss for possible changes.

The first encounter of the learning partners: the instructor and the students

The first meeting between the instructor and the students is of great importance; it is when and where the learning partners will introduce themselves and begin to "negotiate" both the content of the syllabus and the content and strategies incorporated into the learning environment.

Getting to know each other

As a result of past experiences with previous groups, instructors may already have an overall idea of the students' profiles even before the first class. However, it is imperative to validate these hypotheses. Taking into consideration the number of students registered, instructors can organize small-group discussions or ask the students to complete a small survey to answer questions, such as: (a) Do you aspire to pursue a career as a sports coach? (b) What is your highest level

14 Milistetd, das Neves Salles, Trudel, and Paquette

of participation as an athlete and in which sport? (c) Do you have experience as a coach, and if yes at what level? and (d) Have you received any type of coaching certification from a sport organization? Then, the instructors should present what they believe is relevant about their respective academic backgrounds, sport experiences, and so on.

Presenting and discussing the course syllabus

In an LCT approach, the syllabus developed earlier is not definitive; it may be modified during the semester. The more a course is developed following LCT, the more the instructor should expect to have to answer questions from the students, considering that for many of them it will be their first experience with this type of teaching approach. Of course, any further modification in the teaching plan should be well discussed with students to prevent some students from feeling wronged by the changes. In addition, it is important that the instructor ensure that the changes do not imply a major change in the general aim of the course. Therefore, negotiating the content of the syllabus does not mean that every component is open for modifications. In fact, the syllabus might already offer many options to the students.

Keeping the momentum throughout the semester

The syllabus is a kind of contract between the learning partners. This contract can be modified during the semester as needed, but after discussion and agreement among all the learning partners. For example, a new learning opportunity might arise from current news events and replace an already planned activity. Moreover, a class might be cancelled and replaced by specific homework. Each time a modification is to be made, the instructor should carefully consider the impact on the effort to move from ICT to LCT and on student experience and learning. More than a bureaucratic task, this exercise will help instructors to reach their goal of transition and will be a valuable document when revisiting the course in preparation for its next iteration. It is also important that instructors help the students to keep the right LCT mindset in terms of autonomy and responsibility. This can be done by suggesting small learning activities (e.g. video on the web, newspaper articles) that will be optional, without points awarded, but discussed in class by the students who have done the activities.

Evaluating the LCT implementation in the coaching course

For a course based on the ICT approach, the evaluation consists mainly of checking to what extent the plan developed at the beginning of the semester has been followed. Considering that a key LCT principle is the flexibility in the plan to adapt to the needs of the learning partners, the evaluation is ongoing. The changes documented by the instructors are part of the evaluation. Instructors

Making direct teaching more learner-centered **15**

could also use a reflective journal to think about aspects of the course and learning, such as: (a) to what extent the student's learning aims were fulfilled; (b) to what extent my personal goal with the class was achieved; (c) to what extent I was able to develop the intended LCT's dimension and component for that class; (d) what strengths came from using this approach; (e) how I dealt with the contingencies; and (f) in which aspects I can improve for the next class. There is also the possibility to get more structured feedback by asking students to fill out short assessment forms or by organizing focus groups.

Personal reflections and wishful thinking

Michel and William's experiences

We (Michel and William) have been working together for three years instructing a mandatory Sports Pedagogy course offered in the first semester of a bachelor's degree in Physical Education. The course is taught once a week (three-hour classes) throughout an 18-week period, resulting in 18 classes (54 hours) over the semester. We usually have 35–40 students enrolled in the course each semester. The learning goal for the course is to prepare students to plan and conduct training sessions in team sports. To achieve this goal, the classes are organized in three teaching units: (a) Fundamentals of Sports; (b) Team Sports Teaching Approaches; and (c) Coaching Behaviors.

Considering that the course is situated at the beginning of the bachelor's program, most of the students are freshmen coming from high school. The high school system in Brazil generally places the students in a passive role in their learning process, whereby the memorization of information is central to prepare students for the higher education acceptance exam called vestibular. Thus, the students come into the university context with this passive learning bias and expectation, which results in them struggling to assume an active role in their learning process. At the end of the semester, students usually begin to resist learning and lack participation in class because they simultaneously attend other courses – which in our university are mostly organized based on the traditional ICT approach. In these courses, the end of the semester is designed for assessments, which means that the students spend a lot of time memorizing content for tests and other evaluations. Because most students at the university are "strategic learners" (i.e. adapt their studying strategies according to the specific characteristics of the courses and the period of the semester), they decrease their efforts in our Sports Pedagogy course, in which evaluation is developed throughout the semester in a formative approach.

Based on our past experiences with previous groups of students at the same course, we decided to gradually implement LCT over the semester so that the students can learn to feel more comfortable in taking more responsibility for their learning. Thus, the first teaching unit is planned to further explore the dimensions of *function of content* and *role of the instructor* in order to create supportive

16 Milistetd, das Neves Salles, Trudel, and Paquette

learning environments through questioning and interactive activities – the purpose of these activities is to articulate the learning material to the students' personal experiences. The second and the third teaching units are designed to create practical learning situations in which students can assume the coach's role by planning training sessions and coaching their colleagues. Likewise, evaluation activities become more practical and reflexive. Thus, the dimensions of *responsibility for learning* and *balance of power* are emphasized, which allow the students to progressively develop greater autonomy and to assume greater responsibility for their own learning process.

Kyle's experience

My (Kyle) first teaching experience was as a part-time instructor during the doctoral research (studying LCT and coach education). I taught seven sessions of the same course during a three-year period. Given my research interest in LCT and guided by practical recommendations found in the literature, I began making incremental changes to the course, session by session, toward adopting additional LCT approaches. Despite leading to overall high levels of student achievement and satisfaction ratings, my LCT efforts were met with considerable resistance. The primary source of resistance came from the chair of the department, who did not agree with the approaches being used and the resulting high success rate of students. Following Blumberg's (2009) recommendations, I created open and ongoing dialogue with the chair, which included submitting my course outlines early to provide her with an opportunity to help shape the approaches. I also documented all changes and outcomes of the LCT approaches as part of my semester review. In spite of these efforts, the chair appeared to be fixed on the high success rate of students, which ironically, she referred to on countless occasions as a "problem". She continued to push for additional "rigor and research-based practices". I worked tirelessly to satisfy her requests; however, the trend of high success rates continued. A follow-up meeting took place, this time with a clear message that if I couldn't find a way to "lower the marks" the department would be forced to "find someone who could".

The LCT approaches integrated into the design, delivery, and evaluation of the course aimed at providing students with many opportunities to deeply engage with the content and, in turn, to critically reflect on how the content related to their current understanding and more broadly to their objectives post-graduation. Each session, I had the students complete a Course Reflection and Review of Learning as their final assignment. It provided me with important insight into the students' perspectives on the LCT approaches. Looking back at the seven sessions worth of reflections, a few themes had emerged: (a) it was more work – the majority of students stated that this course required a workload greater than any other course they had participated in to that point; (b) clarity supported learning – the students noted the benefit of having a clearly articulated grading/evaluation pathway that outlined the specific learning objectives and requirements for achieving

Making direct teaching more learner-centered **17**

a given letter grade for each assignment; and (c) appreciation for relevance and meaningfulness – the students expressed overwhelming appreciation for how personally relevant and meaningful the course/content was in light of their personal and academic circumstances.

I worked very hard to create a community of learners with each sessional group of students I taught, and I was very pleased to see the students' appreciation, as well as their consistent level of engagement and commitment to their achievement of learning outcomes. Unfortunately, the department chair did not share my sentiments. She continued to create resistance and to push for ICT change, so I chose to resign and to look for a better fit within a department at any institution – I'm glad to say that I have found that better fit in an environment that not only supports LCT approaches, but encourages innovations in the area.

Pierre's experience

I (Pierre) have been teaching a masters-level course for several years to a group of 12–16 students. In this course, which runs from September to December (13 weeks), learning activities are offered to students to help them develop their competence to support and guide sport coaches in their coaching. For eight weeks, students come in class for a three-hour block, and for five weeks they work in small groups (three to four students) on a project called "helping a sport coach in his/her development". Over the years, I have gradually modified the course by applying more and more LCT strategies (see Table 1.1). Teaching in a university environment means that we live within a culture specific to our faculty, school, or department. Thus, there are measures to ensure some kind of homogeneity among courses; therefore, instructors are directly or indirectly compared to each other. I would like to share two of my personal feelings, which are very different from most courses that students have followed or are following.

1   *Pierre's course is a "Mickey Mouse" course* (i.e. can get very good grades without studying and effort): This perception might stem from the fact that: (a) there are no mid-term and final exams; (b) after the second class, the students will have selected the grade they hope to obtain at the end of the course based on specific criteria of quantity and quality of learning activities; and (c) students can, as often as they wish, ask for feedback to help them to produce the possible document to present and submit (reflection papers, PowerPoint presentations, etc.). Interestingly, students' comments obtained at the end of the semester will often indicate that they worked harder in my course than others.

2   *Pierre takes his role of instructor very casually*: This perception might stem from the facts that: (a) outside of a few classes where I need to lecture, I intervene very little during the class, and if the students do not want to speak, there will be moments of silence; (b) although I read and comment on all student documents handed in to make sure that the minimum quality is present, I

18 Milistetd, das Neves Salles, Trudel, and Paquette

will give my comments only if they ask for it; and (c) because I want the students in charge of their learning and being more responsible, I will not alert a student who will probably not reach their selected grade because of their current lack of productivity. The final grade is discussed between the students and me at the end of the semester. Ironically, I invest more time in this course than for the other courses I am teaching because: (a) I need to have a specific file for each student to keep track of their progression; (b) if, for a class, we will discuss two compulsory articles and the students will discuss in sub-groups two articles from a list of four optional articles, I have to (re)read the six articles; and (c) the students seem more at ease and wanting to come to me to discuss scholarly issues not related to my course.

Activities for coach education

1 Systematize what you need to learn/teach before implementing the LCT.
2 Identify the amount of change you are wanting to implement in your course.
3 Try to establish a network of contacts with other members of your school or department who are either interested in learning more about LCT or its implementation – seek to organize periodic group meetings to discuss what has been done (pros and cons, difficulties and rewards) and what to do from now on.

Additional resources

1 Faculty Focus Website (www.facultyfocus.com/). You can find some simple reading articles on teaching strategies for college and higher education settings. You can also contribute to the community's growth by publish articles about your own teaching experiences.
2 The Scholarly Teacher Blog (www.scholarlyteacher.com/). The blog promotes informed and practiced approaches for enhancing student learning through systematic improvement of effective teaching, in higher education. You can use the contents both to stimulate your professional reflection about your own teaching and to discuss teaching practices/strategies with other teachers.
3 The Teaching Professor Website (www.teachingprofessor.com/). As a subscriber, you can enjoy articles on topics such as teaching strategies and techniques, classroom climate, and student learning. You can also find interesting resources, such as video-based mentoring programs.
4 YouTube video (www.youtube.com/watch?v=HRL1EDbQ9rk). Explains the general LCT principles and suggests some LCT strategies.

Bibliography

Barr, R.B. and Tagg, J. (1995) 'From teaching to learning: A new paradigm for undergraduate education', *Change Magazine*, 27: 12–25.

Blumberg, P. (2009) *Developing Learner-Centered Teaching: A Practical Guide for Faculty*, San Francisco: Jossey-Bass.

Cullen, R., Harris, M. and Hill, R. (2012) *The Learner-Centered Curriculum: Design and Implementation*, San Francisco: Jossey-Bass.

Harris, M. and Cullen, R. (2010) *Leading the Learner-Centered Campus*, San Francisco: Jossey-Bass.

McCarthy, L. and Stoszkowski, J. (2018) 'A heutagogical approach to coach education: What worked for one particular learner, how and why?', *Journal of Qualitative Research in Sports Studies*, 12: 317–36.

McCombs, B.L. and Miller, L. (2009) *The School Leader's Guide to Learner-Centered Education: From Complexity to Simplicity*, Thousand Oaks, CA: Corwin Press.

Milistetd, M., Trudel, P., Rynne, S., Mesquita, I. and Nascimento, J. (2018) 'The learner-centered status of a Brazilian university coach education program', *International Sport Coaching Journal*, 5: 105–15.

Paquette, K. and Trudel, P. (2016) 'Learner-centered teaching: A consideration for revitalizing coach education', in P. Davis (ed.) *The Psychology of Effective Coaching and Management*, pp. 53–70, New York: Nova Science Publishers.

Paquette, K. and Trudel, P. (2018) 'The evolution and learner-centered status of a coach education program', *International Sport Coaching Journal*, 5: 24–36.

Quehl, G.H., Bergquist, W.H. and Subbiondo, J.L. (1999) *Fifty Years of Innovation in Undergraduate Education: Change and Stasis in the Pursuit of Quality*, Indianapolis: USA Group Foundation.

Tagg, J. (2003) *The Learning Paradigm College*, Bolton: Anker.

Weimer, M. (2002) *Learner-Centered Teaching: Five Key Changes to Practice*, San Francisco: Jossey-Bass.

Weimer, M. (2013) *Learner-Centered Teaching: Five Key Changes to Practice*, 2nd edn, San Francisco: Jossey-Bass.

2

EXPERIENTIAL LEARNING FOR UNDERGRADUATE STUDENT-COACHES

Andrea Woodburn

Chapter objectives

By the end of this chapter, the reader should be able to:

1   Identify key components in the design of an experiential learning-type activity.
2   Situate his/her role as a coach developer in experiential learning activities for coaches.
3   Apply a video analysis-based method for supporting learning from coaching experience.

Brief chapter overview

This chapter integrates Kolb's experiential learning cycle, with some examples from the undergraduate coaching program in which I work, to show how experiential learning can be incorporated throughout an undergraduate curriculum, and not just in its internships. Experiential learning-type activities are possible and worthwhile for coaches in different settings, from the classroom to the laboratory to the field. In presenting these examples, I show how practice can be informed by theory, suggest some aspects of which to be mindful when coach developers design experiential learning-type activities for different settings, and share lessons learned.

Why and when I use experiential learning

The approach taken in this chapter is influenced by my experience as a professor in a three-year, undergraduate coach education program in Quebec, Canada. I have been responsible for the program's internships for the past 15 years, and this work has required me to wrestle on a daily basis with the realities of incorporating experiential learning in tertiary coach education.

This chapter sits in swampy territory, to use Schön's (1983) metaphor, wherein theory meets practice. It does not aim to provide a review of experiential learning theory. Rather, a few key pieces are referenced that can be helpful in providing a framework and several solid jumping-off points for designing experiential learning-type activities in an any setting. In so doing, I hope to show how theory can inform practice.

The essentials of experiential learning

Definitions, essential components, and goals of experiential learning

The simplest explanation of experiential learning is learning through doing. But that can't be the whole story, because we all know coaches who have coached for many years, but do not seem to learn or evolve at all as a product of their experience. So, what has to happen for learning to occur from experience? Kolb's experiential learning cycle (1984), ubiquitous in the teaching and learning literature, can be helpful in pinpointing what those who learn from their experiences do that distinguishes them from those who don't.

In Kolb's model (1984), learning from experience is represented as a cyclical process composed of two structural dimensions, grasping and transforming. Grasping refers how to we come to experience events through both apprehension (the ephemeral, lived experience itself) and comprehension (the conceptualizing or rendering explicit of what is happening, both while the experience is happening and after it has happened). Transforming refers to doing something with the lived experience through reflective observation and active experimentation. In Kolb's words:

> The central idea here is that learning, and therefore knowing, requires both a grasp or figurative representation of experience and some transformation of that representation. Either the figurative grasp or operative transformation alone is not sufficient. The simple perception of experience is not sufficient for learning; something must be done with it. Similarly, transformation alone cannot represent learning, for there must be something to be transformed, some state or experience that is being acted upon.
>
> *(p. 42)*

In this text, we find insight into key components in the design of any experiential learning-type activity, namely:

1   A live experience must happen. The student-coach must have an opportunity or to have had the opportunity at some point to give something a go.
2   A deliberate effort is required to extract meaning from the experience and reflect on it. Either existing mental models are mobilized during the reflective process as frameworks for analyzing practice, and/or new ideas can be introduced either by others or through one's own research/resourcefulness.
3   Actionable solutions are developed that can be tested in subsequent experiences and are key outputs of the reflective process.
4   There are opportunities for active experimentation, or trying again, so that learning can be reinvested and tested in practice.

Central to learning from experience, therefore, is reflective practice, discussed in Chapter 6. Through my own work with student-coaches in undergraduate internships, I have come to think that there is a skill that can be developed and that is necessary for quality reflection and the development of coaching expertise – the skill of noticing. Noticing is what one attends to in the environment and how one attends to it. It provides the fodder for informing one's actions while coaching, and also for analyzing one's coaching following practice; what Schön (1983) labeled reflection-in-action and reflection-on-action, respectively. Van Es and Sherin (2002) discussed this skill in the teacher education literature and considered noticing to be central to "making pedagogical decisions in the midst of instruction" (p. 571), to interpreting and responding to the actions of the learners. An aim for teacher education, according to Van Es and Sherin, is "to support teachers in learning first to notice what is significant in a classroom interaction, then to interpret that event, and then to use those interpretations to inform pedagogical decisions" (p. 575). They suggest three aspects to noticing: (a) identifying what is important or noteworthy about a classroom situation; (b) making connections between the specifics of classroom interactions and the broader principles of teaching and learning they represent; and (c) using what one knows about the context to reason about classroom interactions (p. 573).

Finally, any discussion on experiential learning in undergraduate coaching programs seems incomplete without addressing the finalities of such programs and situating the role of the coach developer within them. As will be evident in the examples provided, I have come to view the goal of an undergraduate coaching program as the development of coaches that are reflective practitioners. The role of the coach developer is neither, therefore, one of an evangelist of a particular pedagogical method nor of a purveyor of coaching recipes. The role of the coach developer is to create opportunities across the curriculum for experiential learning, and to support the development of student-coaches' reflective practice and initiative. In the words of one of the seminal thinkers on experiential learning in education, John Dewey (1974), when referring to teacher education and the role of the teaching supervisor:

> They should not be too closely supervised, nor too minutely and immediately criticized upon either the matter or the method of their teaching. Students should be given to understand that they not only are permitted to act upon their own intellectual initiative, but that they are expected to do so, and that their ability to take hold of situations for themselves would be a more important factor in judging them than following any particular set method or scheme.
>
> *(p. 334)*

Furthermore,

> criticism should be directed to making the professional student thoughtful about his work in the light of principles, rather than to induce in him a recognition that certain special methods are good, and certain other special methods are bad.
>
> *(p. 335)*

Some practice to inform theory

Internships often come to mind when coach developers think about experiential learning opportunities in an undergraduate program. Though internships are arguably the most significant setting for experiential learning, experiential learning-type activities can also take place in the classroom and the laboratory. Activities in a classroom setting or in a coaching laboratory setting can be excellent stepping stones toward preparing a coach for more complex, field-based experiences. In Table 2.1, considerations for the design and implementation of experiential learning activities in these three settings are presented, and I then provide a practical example for each.

In the examples that follow, I make occasional reference to the student-coach's individual digital portfolio. This portfolio is a place wherein student-coaches add many of the artifacts that are generated as part of the experiential learning-type activities across the curriculum, such as videos of their coaching and practice plans. There is video annotation software built into the portfolio, such that student-coaches can analyze their coaching and see both the evolution of their coaching and the progress in their analysis of their coaching over three years of the program.

Experiential learning activities in a classroom setting

A critical factor in incorporating classroom-based experiential learning activities into the curriculum is the engagement of student-coaches in real coaching while

TABLE 2.1 Considerations for experiential learning activities in three settings

	Classroom-based experiential learning activities; *Learning from activities designed to actively engage the coach in a classroom setting*	*Laboratory-based experiential learning activities;* *Learning from coaching in a simulated setting*	*Field-based experiential learning activities;* *Learning from coaching in a real setting*
Examples (described in the next section)	*Presenting your evolving vision for coaching effectiveness*	*Micro-coaching with guest participants/ athletes*	*Video analysis of your coaching*
Nature of the learning environment	Bounded environment (highly controlled)	Semi-bounded environment (moderately controlled)	In the field, open environment (not controlled)
Risk perceived by the coach	Low	Medium	High
Parameters of the learning activity are normally set by the . . .	Coach developer or coach developer and student-coach (shared design)	Coach developer or coach developer and student-coach (shared design); participants have some influence	Coaching environment and participants
Can be particularly useful when . . .	Diving more deeply into understanding and applying theory; often used as a starting point before applying it in a lab and/or real setting or in response to a need that arises in a lab and/or real setting (e.g. an analysis of practice reveals a gap in knowledge) A coaching competence that is cognitive (e.g. planning)	Working with novices who are nervous/unsure in their first coaching experiences Testing approaches that are new to the coach (provides some safety, and can allow for more controlled measurement)	Always useful, provided the experience is appropriate to the coach's needs/current skills and a reflective cycle is built in

Human resource requirements (estimates only)	Low – one coach developer can manage these types of activities with entire classes of student-coaches working individually or in small groups (up to approximately 60 student-coaches, but the sweet spot is probably around 25–30)	Medium – these types of activities generally require a smaller ratio of coach developer to student-coaches in order to manage the exchanges with each student-coach, and the groups of athletes/peers who are also participating (suggested ratio is about 8 student-coaches to 1 instructor, plus the group of athletes/peers that are being coached)	High – accompanying coaches in their real coaching environments requires many one-on-one exchanges between student-coaches and coach developer, both in live settings and in subsequent video analysis
Problems may arise when . . .	The activities are poorly planned (understructured or overstructured) The activities are poorly supported by the coach developer	The activities are poorly planned (understructured or overstructured) The activities are poorly supported by the coach developer	Coaching requirements do not match current skill level of coach (too low or too high) There is no reflection accompanying experience Note: There is not necessarily a need for accompaniment of a coach developer for learning to occur, but it can be helpful for reflection, particularly in developing the skill of noticing

they are enrolled in the program. Having at least some relevant experience upon which to draw, and having the opportunity to actively experiment in practice, is arguably what allows for a classroom-based activity to be considered truly an experiential learning activity. Learning is much richer for student-coaches who are able to implement their classroom-based work in a real setting and revise it through active experimentation.

Example: presenting your evolving vision for coaching effectiveness

To mark their understanding of what is coaching effectiveness, upon arrival in the program, I ask student-coaches to prepare a 15-minute oral presentation on their vision for coaching effectiveness. This presentation is filmed and saved directly into their portfolio. Then, as part of the formative assessments of one of their classes, student-coaches analyze their video through three lenses: (a) the depth of content they presented (what informed their vision); (b) the quality of the visual support; and (c) the quality of their presentation. To support their analysis, they are provided current literature on coaching effectiveness (and must find some for themselves), and resources on creating effective visual supports and presenting well, as well as analysis tools for each of the three components. The principal summative assignment of this class is to repeat their presentation, this time drawing on the relevant literature and what they've learned in the program to that point in order to show how their vision of an effective coach has evolved since arrival in the program. Our future plans include repeating this cycle a third time, as part of the capstone assessments of the program, to have a marker of each student-coach's evolving vision over their three years in the program. Because the portfolio also includes videos of their coaching practice, student-coaches are also able to examine their coaching actions through the lens of their espoused vision for coaching effectiveness (i.e. whether what they actually do aligns with the vision they articulate).

With respect to Kolb's cycle, the grasping dimension is achieved through a lived experience (the initial presentations itself), as well as through watching their presentation. The transformation dimension is achieved through the reflection required in the formative analyses, and the active experimentation is accomplished by repeating the presentation after learning what could be improved.

Critical for a classroom-based learning activity to be an effective experiential learning activity is the opportunity to try, learn something to become better, and then try again; a complete cycle that is not always easily achieved within the confines of a single course. Having the opportunity to try again following either self, peer, or teacher feedback is a critical piece that is most challenging to incorporate into classroom-based activities, mainly due to the time constraints that the semester structure imposes. A suggested strategy, as presented in this example, is to have the experiential learning activity take place at several points across the curriculum, in several classes, providing the

Experiential learning for student-coaches **27**

students time to get better and opportunities to try, and try again. This is particularly important when the scope of the objective is large. As in this example, evolving one's understanding of coaching effectiveness requires new inputs, new experiences, and time.

A second consideration when incorporating experiential learning activities within a classroom setting is the perceived risk of trying, and of trying again. The initial try has to happen in a safe setting (i.e. not graded) so that student-coaches feel free to really give the activity a go. Ideally, the entire cycle(s) would remain formative. However, if summative assessment must take place for grading purposes at some point, it is critical that the criteria and tools used for assessment purposes are available to student-coaches from the moment the activity is introduced. This not only increases student-coaches' perceptions of safety (because there will be no surprises upon assessment), but the tools also serve as learning resources because they articulate ahead of time what excellent work looks like.

Experiential learning activities in a laboratory setting

Coaching is a highly complex endeavor that can feel risky and uncertain for novices. A lot is happening at the same time, constantly modulated by changing conditions and human interactions. Placing novice student-coaches in settings wherein some of the variables can be controlled and/or directed can be of great value to enhance their learning. Also, whether the coach is novice or more experienced, placing coaches in environments wherein constraints can be manipulated to emphasize certain aspects of coaching practice can prove instrumental to learning. Laboratory settings can provide such affordances. They should not be considered poor cousins to coaching in a real setting, but rather an alternative environment that can also provide valuable opportunities for learning, provided the objectives align with what is possible in a laboratory setting.

Example: micro-coaching with guest participants/athletes

In their first year in our program, student-coaches participate in a class on teaching effectiveness, together with their peers from our sister physical education program. In this class, student-coaches are introduced to relevant theory and provided opportunities for teaching experimentation in a safe, lab-like environment. The student-coaches teach primary school-aged children who are bussed to the university as part of their physical education courses. During this experiential learning activity, designed and implemented by two colleagues, the student-coaches are exposed to tools and theoretical frameworks on teaching effectiveness that will be used repeatedly in other classes and in their internships, with increasing nuance in real coaching environments. The tools are oriented on the measurement of active-learning time, the quality of opportunities to practice and evidence of learning, clarity of the explanation and demonstrations, efficacy of active supervision and feedback, and group management.

28 Woodburn

Student-coaches are paired and assigned a small group of five to eight children to lead over a period of several weeks. They are provided an instructional plan (a sequence of what to teach), and alternately teach the children or observe and provide feedback to their peers. Theory on teaching effectiveness is connected with this practice teaching through self-, peer-, and coach developer-led formative analysis of the student-coach's teaching, using the assessment tools provided.

One of the lessons learned in implementing this experiential learning activity is the importance of initially removing the planning component, and allowing student-coaches, most of whom are relative novices, to focus on their teaching. In past years, student-coaches were free to plan the content they would then teach to the children. However, this freedom ended up detracting from the work the coach developers could accomplish with them on their teaching effectiveness because what they planned was often inadequate. Working with plans designed by experts as an initial foray into practice teaching has since proven a successful strategy; it allows student-coaches to focus their attention on how to teach, which is the objective of this learning activity, and not on what to teach. Problems that arise as fodder for learning are no longer due to the content that was planned, but rather due to their teaching practice.

In the activity presented, student-coaches have the opportunity to engage in a full experiential learning cycle; from initially teaching the children (concrete experience), to receiving feedback from peers and staff and being introduced to new theoretical content (new input), to reflecting on what could be improved in light of this new input, and finally to actively experimenting by teaching again. Because this cycle is repeated over several weeks and in similar conditions in a laboratory setting, the opportunities for experiential learning on targeted aspects of coaching effectiveness are rich.

Experiential learning activities in a field setting

In a university environment, experiential learning activities in a field setting are usually in the form of internships that are part of the curriculum. Learning from experience in internships is maximized when they include sufficient structure to engage student-coaches in an experiential learning cycle, and do not simply provide credit for field experience. While the latter does have value, its potential as a catalyst for growth as a coach is arguably less than the former. Simply including practicum-type coaching experience on its own is unlikely to lead to purposeful learning that is informed by the theory on coaching effectiveness. Internship experiences without structure in milieus that are not vetted can even be potentially dangerous in coaching environments, wherein good intentions abound, but teaching practices based on pseudo-science (e.g. visual/auditory/kinesthetic learning styles) seem to have deep roots. Internships can serve to reinforce ineffective or ill-advised practices or, in a worst-case scenario, can introduce a novice student-coach to them. It is critical to recognize this reality and mitigate for this risk.

Internships in real coaching environments are necessarily individualized, and tend to be resource heavy, requiring one-on-one support by a coach developer, because each student-coach is practicing in a different milieu, with roles and responsibilities commensurate with their prior coaching experience. There is little need to motivate student-coaches to engage in their internships – the environment is true, the problems faced are real, and so are the rewards. The central challenge of internships lies not with how to engage the student-coaches, but rather how to ensure that there is learning from their experience, and how to ensure learning is informed by current empirical evidence on coaching effectiveness.

As was the case for Van Es and Sherin (2002), I have found video-based analysis to be a powerful means of supporting student-coach experiential learning in the field. During live coaching, there is so much going on that it is difficult to work with the student-coaches on their coaching. Video analysis provides the opportunity to take a step back from the action, to pause and rewind, and to engage in reflection and discussion on practice. The example that follows is a process that is used multiple times over the course of their internships.

Example: video analysis of your coaching

The following learning activity is the scaffolding of the activity previously described in the laboratory setting to a real setting. During each coaching internship, student-coaches film themselves delivering a full practice session they have planned to the athletes they are coaching. They film from two points of view, from two different types of cameras. The first point of view is from a standard video camera, capturing the action of all athletes involved, as well as that of the student-coach. This wider point of view provides information on group organization and management, use of space, and active-learning time. The second point of view is from an action camera worn on the chest of the student-coach. This camera captures the student-coach's physical point of view at any given moment (what he can or cannot see by virtue of his positioning), as well as all verbal exchanges between coach and athlete, including feedback (possible even in outdoor sport environments), and often also the facial and physical expressions of the athletes while the coach is talking or demonstrating. The student-coaches then transfer their two videos (one from each camera) into their digital portfolios.

The student-coaches then use video analysis software embedded into the portfolio to annotate their videos. Each annotation consists of written notes on the segment, linked to an automatically extracted segment ready for playback when the annotation is opened. The annotation can be tagged to a predetermined category (i.e. a theoretical concept on teaching effectiveness), or the student-coaches can define their own categories. Once all annotations are completed for both videos, the student-coaches prioritize them based on which ones they would like to discuss with a coach developer. They also complete a summary of what they will keep doing and what they will change moving forward, with respect to practice planning and delivery.

This student-coach-driven annotation process has two purposes. First, it provides an artifact of both the student-coach's actual coaching, as well as her analysis of her coaching, so that the evolution of both over the three years of the program can be observed. Second, it provides information on the noticing skills and reflections of the student-coach, without external influence. To what is she attending? What is she not seeing? What is she noticing most often? To what has she attributed the highest or lowest priority for discussion? It also provides clear evidence of what the student-coach has integrated from the curriculum on teaching effectiveness (either accurately, inaccurately, or not at all).

This first step of the activity offers opportunity for learning in itself. However, there is a next step, and it is where we circle back to the theory presented in the first part of this chapter and position the role of the coach developer in the experiential learning cycle of the student-coach. Student-coaches participate in a one-on-one, one-hour discussion with a coach developer once their work is annotated.

By working from the video analysis of real coaching, the coach developer is able to engage with the student-coach in a reflective conversation based on real coaching experience and refer back to actual practice when needed (remember, the annotations have video segments tagged to them). The role of the coach developer during the discussion is two-fold; that of a seeing friend, helping student-coaches develop their noticing skills, and that of a thinking friend, helping them develop their reflection.

One of the key learnings for student-coaches in this activity is achieved through the coach developer's support in drawing out what the student-coach is currently attending to in the environment in order to gather information upon which to adapt her interventions or acting as a seeing friend. When initially examining their teaching effectiveness, novice student-coaches tend to be preoccupied by how they look and by what they say. When they do pay attention to the athletes, the criteria they initially seem to use to judge their teaching effectiveness are what Placek (1984) has described in the physical education literature as children being busy, happy and good, not on whether there was any evidence of learning having taken place. In such a case, the coach developer encourages the student-coach to look for evidence of learning in the athletes and not simply for whether they are busy, happy, and good.

Sometimes the student-coach is looking at the athletes but is not attending to the important information that is in plain sight. For example (this one happens often in their first internship), a student-coach has selected and annotated a video segment, correctly recognizing that something is off in the athletes' responses during an exercise. The annotation refers to deviant behavior on the part of some of the athletes, and the student-coach draws the conclusion that she must not be strict enough while coaching. However, the student-coach missed seeing other information that was clearly visible and that provided valuable information on the likely cause of the athletes' behavior. For example, the organization of the exercise was suck that the athletes were standing in line with lots of wait time, faced no opposition when executing, and were likely bored; a recipe for distracted behavior. The cause was likely in the design of the activity itself, which was lacking in relevance and active engagement time. It was essential to be able to rely on the video segment and look at the situation together with the coach developer in order to have someone else point out what was visible, yet initially not noticed by the coach.

The role of the coach developer is also one of a thinking friend, helping the student-coach develop the habits and skills of a reflective practitioner. To accomplish this, the coach developer must work from the priorities set by the student-coach. The coach developer must also be able to operate at a metacognitive level while engaged in discussion with the student-coach, attending to the broader patterns of the student-coach's analysis, including: On what aspects of practice is attention directed? On what basis is the student-coach selecting moments of her practice that she wants to discuss? What mental models or frameworks is she using on coaching effectiveness to assess her actions? It is by highlighting and discussing these broader questions with the student-coach (as opposed to judging her coaching behaviors) that the coach developer supports the development of the student-coach's habits and skills of reflection.

Personal reflections and wishful thinking

The video analysis example describes my favorite work as a coach developer. At the end of every one-on-one discussion, there is a shared feeling of joy (and fatigue!) at having been engaged in meaningful learning together. I think it comes down to both student-coach and coach developer being in a vulnerable space where we are both exposed; the task requires us both to come into the discussion whole-heartedly. The student-coach can't hide, because we are working from her real coaching and from her own analysis. I (or any coach developer) can't hide, because each discussion is unique, and my own noticing and reflective skills are tested live. This sets the stage for collaborative learning, where the student-coaches realize their expertise and do not rely on the coach developer to give them answers.

My wish is to do more of these types of activities across the curriculum, to build in peer collaboration among student-coaches, and to find ways of making the filming process easier and better (this has been improving as cameras and file management software evolve). I would also like to develop, collaboratively with other coach developers who are doing similar work, some tools and training for being an effective seeing friend and thinking friend when supporting student-coaches' video analysis of their practice.

Activities for coach education

1   Think of meaningful learning activities you have experienced as a coach or as coach developer, times when you felt that your practice changed for the

better as a direct result of having participated in the activity. Were there any common characteristics among them? If so, how do these common characteristics compare with the key components for experiential learning?

2   In small groups of coach developers, discuss some of the challenges you might experience in incorporating experiential learning activities in your milieus, and how you might address them.

3   Individually or in small groups, prepare and share a few reflective prompts that you can use when supporting a student-coach during a video analysis discussion on their coaching practice. Here are a few to get you started:

a   In order to come to that choice, where were you looking and what did you see? (this is a noticing prompt).

b   Tell me more about . . . (this is a reflection prompt).

Additional resources

1   Moon, J. (1999) *Reflection in Learning & Professional Development: Theory & Practice*, London: Routledge Falmer. She provides an overview on reflection and its role in learning in professional practice.

2   Stiggins, R.J. (2005) *Student-Involved Assessment FOR Learning*, Upper Saddle River: Pearson Merrill Prentice Hall. This book was written for school teachers, but is a great overview of assessment for anyone that engages in it.

3   Type "reflective prompts" in any internet search engine for some inspiration (being mindful that all prompts/questions are not of equal quality).

Bibliography

Dewey, J. (1974) 'Relation of theory to practice', in R.D. Archambault (ed.) *John Dewey on Education*, Chicago: Random House.

Kolb, D.A. (1984) *Experiential Learning: Experience as the Source of Learning and Development*, Upper Saddle River: Prentice Hall.

Moon, J. (1999) *Reflection in Learning & Professional Development: Theory & Practice*, London: Routledge Falmer.

Placek, J.H. (1984) 'Conceptions of success in teaching: Busy, happy and good?', in J. Templin and J.K. Olson (eds.) *Teaching in Physical Education*, Champaign: Human Kinetics.

Schön, D.A. (1983) *The Reflective Practitioner: How Professionals Think in Action*, New York: Basic Books Inc.

Stiggins, R.J. (2005) *Student-Involved Assessment FOR Learning*, Upper Saddle River: Pearson Merrill Prentice Hall.

Van Es, E.A. and Sherin, M.G. (2002) 'Learning to notice: Scaffolding new teachers' interpretations of classroom interactions', *Journal of Technology & Teacher Education*, 10: 571–96.

3

TEAM-BASED LEARNING AS AN INSTRUCTIONAL STRATEGY FOR UNDERGRADUATE COACH EDUCATION

Melissa Thompson and Erica Pasquini

Chapter objectives

By the end of this chapter, the reader should be able to:

1 Describe the four primary tenets of Team-Based Learning.
2 Discuss research on Team-Based Learning.
3 Describe how to implement Team-Based Learning into a coach education undergraduate level course.

Brief chapter overview

Team-Based Learning (TBL) is a high-impact, interactive instructional strategy utilizing peer interaction and application-based activities. These classroom-based activities foster motivation and higher-order thinking. To optimize TBL, coach developers must be intentional and consistent in their approach. The purpose of this chapter is to describe the TBL strategy and its systematic implementation in sport coaching courses at the undergraduate level, along with the implications for student-coaches.

Why and when I use Team-Based Learning

We (both authors) are currently faculty at higher education institutions, where student-coaches are studying a wide array of undergraduate curriculum. As previous research indicates (Michaelsen, Davidson & Major 2014), TBL works best in higher-level, application-based courses, such as sport and exercise psychology or foundations of coaching, because it supports learning in courses that involve higher-level thinking and application of materials for the future. Specifically, student–coaches with jobs that involve working in team settings will benefit from the team process. For example, students studying sport coaching might need to remember and understand a significant amount of knowledge related to the skills, tactics, and strategies of a given sport. The creation of a practice plan with appropriate progressions and drills, however, requires not only the basic knowledge of skills and tactics, but also the more advanced understanding of what is developmentally appropriate and how to evaluate the effectiveness of the plan. Thus, Bloom's taxonomy serves as a conceptual framework for many teaching strategies used in higher education, including TBL.

Most student–coaches come to the classroom with previous experiences on teams, supporting the exploration of ideas around how teams function and what makes a good teammate, which may also increase the student–coaches' motivation in TBL. Many student–coaches pursuing a coaching degree are leaders, and TBL requires them to explore how to share leadership, adding another layer of learning. TBL also prepares student–coaches for their future coaching experience. Very rarely does a coach work as a single entity. Rather, coaches work with teams of other coaches, administrators, and as the leader of a team that will have ups and downs and individuals with differing opinions – just as is the case in TBL. Thus, the experience of working with others for the success of the group is an excellent tool for professional preparation. It also offers student–coaches an applied example of how one might facilitate the development of a team over time because most TBL projects include a component of team development. They will leave the classroom with a first-hand account of how important it is for teams to have expectations for performance and behavior, good communication skills, joint goals, and shared accountability for success.

The essentials of Team-Based Learning

Definitions, essential components, and goals of TBL

Research on active-learning classrooms suggests an increase in student–coaches' engagement over more traditional, passive learning environments (Haidet et al. 2004). These findings support the use of strategies like TBL. Clark, Nguyen, Bray and Levine (2008) corroborate these findings in their study comparing nursing classes that used a TBL format to those with traditional lecture format. Students in the TBL classroom reported statistically significantly greater engagement during class than students in the lecture format. More than 20 peer-reviewed papers have been published in the last five years on the effectiveness of TBL. TBL strategy has evolved, but the four primary principles have remained – properly formed teams, student accountability, team assignments, and frequent and timely feedback (Michaelsen & Richards 2005). Collectively, these principles form a highly structured instructional strategy that should be implemented in whole, and consistently, to garner the best results.

Four principles of TBL

Principle one: properly formed teams

The power of the team in the learning process cannot be understated. As noted by Michaelsen, Davidson and Major (2014), teams provide a unique twist on small groups because students have an opportunity to get to know one another and each team member's strengths. Further, because the class activities are designed to be problems that are personally meaningful to the students, their commitment to their team's ability to solve the problem is high. Zingone et al. (2010) found that, when compared to students in courses taught with a variety of active-learning methods, students in the TBL classes earned significantly higher grades (as measured in quality points). One distinction of TBL from other instructional strategies is that groups remain intact for the duration of the semester. Teams stick together to grow and experience the stages of team development. By the end of the semester, teams have created norms, informal and formal roles, and rely on each other's experiences to aid in group success. Therefore, coach developers must consider multiple criteria when forming teams. Teams are most effective when a distribution of ability exists. This requires the coach developer to consider what knowledge and experiences the coaches may have (both in and out of the classroom) that aid in learning and then determine an effective strategy of group assignment. Student-coaches should not select their own groups in a TBL classroom. As many coach developers have likely experienced, students tend to build groups in classroom with friends who have similar personalities and experiences – this tendency innately goes against the idea of developing teams that mimic real-world workplaces and diverse groups. It also limits the amount of team development happening inside the classroom, as friends have already developed group norms and roles. Finally, self-selected groups increase the likelihood of social loafing or segregated responsibilities that might not otherwise occur in groups of mixed experiences and social groups.

Principle two: student accountability

Ensuring that all student-coaches commit to the learning process is a critical component of the TBL strategy. Otherwise, the potential for loafing in the group is high. However, comparing students from a lecture course to students in a TBL course, researchers found that TBL students reported higher levels of accountability (Sharma, Janke, Larson & Peter 2017). Further, Stein, Colyer and Manning (2016) found evidence of increased student accountability though the peer evaluation process. In their examination of more than 200 student-coaches in a TBL classroom, the least involved group member consistently received the lowest peer evaluations. This is evidence of the power of the team process at increasing student-coaches' accountability. In TBL, it is imperative that student-coaches are held accountable for their own learning, as well as their contributions to the team. Therefore, methods of accountability must exist for the pre-learning that happens in the preparation phase. Otherwise, student-coaches might opt to rely heavily on their teammates for most of the coursework. More specific strategies for accountability and avoidance of social loafing will be discussed in the section of this chapter on grading procedures. However, providing student-coaches with choices in how grades are calculated can increase autonomy and accountability.

Principle three: team assignments

Because much of the work done in class is completed as a team, the assignments created by the coach developer are crucial and should always prompt deeper learning of the course material, while simultaneously promoting team development. This poses a challenge for coach developers to not only be thinking about content, but also to consider the phases of team development. This concept fits nicely in a sport coaching program as coach developers can adopt a metacognitive approach that helps student-coaches interpret their experience in the classroom as similar to their experience coaching a sport team. Coach developers can help student-coaches make connections to their experiences as a coach and relate to their athletes' experiences. Creating an explicit parallel to sport experience also helps the student-coaches consider why and how coach developers are structuring activities to develop the teams.

Principle four: frequent and timely feedback

The structure of a TBL classroom requires that student-coaches grasp basic concepts, then apply them in multiple ways. Therefore, immediate and frequent feedback on their performance, both individually and as a group, is critical. Since an important concept of TBL is applied team projects, student-teams need instructor feedback to ensure they are interpreting the material correctly. Information that is unclear or misunderstood could potentially result in a group being unable to complete the applied activities, as these build on the basic course content. One of the most effective ways to provide feedback to students is through learning management systems. Often grading of the team multiple-choice quizzes, like those used in the readiness assurance process, can be set up to take place automatically and be available to the student.

Using the TBL strategy in coach development

Course structure

Using TBL requires a considerable amount of preparation by the coach developer at the beginning of the course. The coach developer should aim to design the entire course structure prior to the start of class. TBL is most often designed and implemented in units that are connected in some way. Depending on the course, the coach developer might design a larger module to include two to four chapters of information per unit. If a coach developer is not using a predetermined textbook, information can be divided into small groupings of like subjects. For example, in sport psychology, one could group sport psychology skill training (imagery, goal setting, arousal management) into one module. Once the content is divided, the coach developer should consider each unit's primary learning objectives. These objectives should be stated in terms of what the students will be able to *do* with the course information in that unit (i.e. develop a sport psychology plan for a coach to implement). Action-oriented learning objectives support the development of high-quality course assignments. Next, the coach developer can determine what information or course content student-coaches need to know to support that *doing*. These secondary learning objectives aid in the readiness assurance process questions, as well as some of the foundational application questions. Once all learning objectives have been identified, the coach developer can begin the design of course materials.

Unit sequence

Preparation

A consistent process is used for each unit in the TBL process. Each unit begins with the student-coaches engaging in individual preparation activities that might include reading assigned course content, watching a video related to the material, or reviewing blogs or web content. This preparation work happens outside of class and is the foundation for the rest of the unit. For example, students in a sport psychology course might be asked to read two chapters in a text about mental skills training and watch a video on implementing mental skills in practice.

Readiness assurance

This phase is initiated during class. It begins with an individual quiz (iRAT (readiness assurance test)) covering the basic content from the independent, out-of-class study in the preparation phase. These quizzes usually consist of 15–20 multiple-choice questions. Each student-coach in the class completes his or her own quiz to provide an assessment of their individual understanding of the content. The individual quiz also provides a level of individual accountability for the group's success. Once all students have completed the individual quiz, teams take the same quiz as a group (tRAT). During the team quiz, teams must work together to come to a consensus about their answers for each question. These peer discussions and debates serve to solidify the important foundational concepts of the unit material. An important element of the tRAT is immediate grading. Teams must get immediate feedback about their performance (because student-coaches already took the same test, they will receive feedback on their individual performance, as well; coach developers should also try to get individual work back to student-coaches as quickly as possible). Currently, the most common approach is the use of IF-AT scratch cards (Epstein Educational Enterprises 2019). Much like the traditional scantron, scratch cards are ordered from developers and the correct response for each question is designated beneath a scratch-off surface. For example, if the team chooses answer A, they would scratch off that section on the card for the corresponding question. If A is the correct answer, a star would be visible. If it is not the correct answer, students would see nothing. Not only does this serve to provide immediate feedback to the student-coaches; it also provides the coach developers immediate feedback about confusing concepts while simultaneously creating a system whereby student-coaches can get partial credit for responses depending on how many scratch attempts are used before they got the right answer. Coach developers can also achieve immediate feedback by asking student-coaches to use a learning management system for the quiz and setting the grading to automatic and immediate.

Once teams have completed the tRAT, an important opportunity for a focused re-study of material is provided during an "appeal process". If a team missed a question on the tRAT, they can use the assigned course materials to work together to create a concise, written justification for the incorrect response to regain credit for the question. The student-coaches might challenge the clarity of a question or justify why the response they selected might also be right. The appeal process is critical because it allows for a review of the course material that may have been most confusing. It is also possible that the group was swayed on the selection of a response based on group discussion. The appeal process provides an opportunity for them to share that logic with the coach developer, while exploring why the correct answer is correct. Coach developers can set parameters around the content of appeals, but a good rule of thumb is that student-coaches should include references to the course preparation materials, as well as some discussion of the "right" answer and justification for their selected answer.

Once the iRAT, tRAT, and appeal process is complete, the last stage of the readiness assurance process is a short clarifying lecture. If the coach developer is attending to the most commonly missed questions on the iRAT and tRAT, they will have an idea of where confusion exists. In a brief lecture, the coach developer can clear up concerns or confusion to ensure that student-coaches are ready to begin the more challenging application activities. Depending on class duration, the readiness assurance process typically lasts an entire class period (45–75 minutes). But, by the end, the coach developer has ensured coverage of all the basic material that may have otherwise taken several class sessions to cover. The remaining class time for the unit (generally one to four hours) is spent on application activities where teams are actively working together during class.

Application activities

The purpose of the application activities in the TBL process is to provide teams an opportunity to wrestle with the application of the course content to a real-world problem or setting. Coach developers should reiterate this to student-coaches at the beginning of this phase of the process to increase motivation and engagement. Creators of the TBL strategy encourage coach developers to use the 4S Framework when designing application activities (Sibley & Spiridonoff 2014). First, coach developers must choose a *significant problem* for student-coaches to explore. It must be a problem important to the field that requires the use of course content to solve. The problem, of course, adds a level of complexity to the thinking that is deeper than the multiple-choice questions in the RAT process, thus requiring a synthesis of information, resulting in deeper learning. Second, coach developers should require all teams to use the *same problem*. This is different than some other approaches to in-class group work. If, however, all groups are working on the same problem, the opportunity arises to have groups share their approach to the problem, their logic, and a defense for their process, thus increasing student-coaches' engagement and interest in both their team discussion, and the decisions of the other teams. Third, coach developers should provide a short list of *specific choices* for the application exercises. Adding the constraint of a limited set of options allows the coach developer to control some of the direction of the discussion, while simultaneously allowing student-coaches to compare their team's decision and logic to that of the other teams. A key role for the coach developer is the facilitation of the discussion around the choices to ensure student-coaches remain engaged in the sharing of ideas. Fourth, coach developers should allow groups to *simultaneously report* their choice to the whole group. To do this, more technologically advanced classrooms might use an app like PollEverywhere (www.polleverywhere.com), while others might choose colored or numbered cards that correspond to specific answers that can be lifted when prompted. By using this method, teams instinctively begin to defend their response and think more critically about how to justify their selection, especially when other groups have made a different choice. The coach developer can then facilitate a discussion about the logic used to arrive at a choice, providing student-coaches with deeper thinking about the question and content. Simultaneous report also helps avoid the all-too-common situation in the classroom when a coach developer poses a question and most of the group isn't thinking about a response. The team format and simultaneous report allows for team discussion and decision-making, and then report and discussion. Using a unit on motivational climate as an example of this process, student-coaches could be presented with eight statements describing coaching behaviors. Their team must decide if each behavior represents an ego or task-involving climate. Then, as groups respond to each, a discussion of what makes it ego or task evolves. By the end, the student-coaches have a good understanding of the two types of coach-created motivational climates and what those look like in actual coaching behaviors.

Projects

Projects are a unique type of application activity that are often used in TBL to conclude a unit (or sometimes two units) of information. For example, in a sport psychology course, student-coaches might be asked to create a Psychological Skills Training Plan for an athlete. This project would require synthesis of information from several chapters on how to assess skills, how to teach new skills, stages of skill acquisition, major components of different psychological skills and their effectiveness, etc. As with all application activities, projects are completed in class, as a team, and for the coach developer to be available to respond to questions or ideas.

Evaluation

Because a significant portion of the work in a TBL classroom is done in the team, this teaching strategy poses some unique challenges for evaluation. However, if the coach developer designs an evaluation system that ensures both individual and group accountability, many of the initial evaluation concerns associated with group work are alleviated. Therefore, it is critical that student-coaches believe that both the individual and team assessments will impact their final evaluation in a reasonable way.

Individual assessments

To increase accountability for the out-of-class preparation, the impact of the individual assessments (e.g. iRAT) must be significant. Otherwise, some student-coaches will slide by, allowing their team members to do the bulk of the work. Table 3.1 provides some suggestions for making individual assessments impactful. The coach developer should spend time explaining the importance of the initial preparation to the rest of the course activities to help student-coaches see the value in the out-of-class preparation.

Team assessments

Because team application activities and projects provide a rich learning opportunity, engagement, and effort, these assessments should also be impactful to the final evaluation. The coach developer should demonstrate the importance and value of everyone's contribution to the team assessments. Typically, coach developers will show data of individual vs. team RAT scores to demonstrate that the performance of the collective is higher than that of the individual. To further increase team motivation, coach developers might also make visible the tRAT scores for each group so every team knows how it is performing compared to the rest of the teams.

Team member evaluations

The final piece of evaluation is how the performance of each a member of the team is assessed. Student-coaches should be made aware at the beginning of

Team-Based Learning for undergraduate coach education **41**

TABLE 3.1 Strategies for increasing impact of individual points

Strategy	Justification
Increase possible points on iRAT	Making the iRAT worth a significant portion of the grade increases accountability for individual preparation
Display individual points using team ranges, etc.	Providing evidence of how the individual performed in reference to the rest of the group increases the personal sense of responsibility for group success
Incorporate other individual assignments	Case analyses or other out of class preparation items increase the impact of individual points while increasing preparation and work with the course content
Set standards for performance on individual points	Requiring a minimum performance by the individual eliminates the potential for social loafing (e.g. you must score an average of 70% or better on individual points to earn group points) and also serves as a minimum indicator of individual knowledge
Increase weight of individual points	Makes the impact of individual points greater, increasing accountability for preparation and individual work

the course (and throughout) of the criteria on which their teammates will be evaluating them. Michaelsen, Knight and Fink (2004) provide several suggestions for evaluation forms, but the coach developer can select any characteristics. For example, a typical TBL evaluation form asks group members to evaluate the rest of their group members on: (a) preparation; (b) contribution; (c) respect for other's ideas; and (d) flexibility. This prompt, along with the required written comments, requires group members to reflect on these aspects rather than general interpersonal perceptions. There are several options for structuring peer evaluations, but in general, TBL evaluations ask team members to evaluate all members of the group, excluding oneself and to incorporate some variability in ratings. For example, coach developers might ask team members to numerically evaluate the rest of the group by distributing 100 points without giving any group members the same number. This requires a critical evaluation of team member performance rather than a passive, even distribution. Coach developers can then either use the 100 points as an addition the individuals' total scores or as a percentage multiplier of student-coaches' team points. As seen in Table 3.2, this can significantly change a student-coach's final grade.

Autonomy in the assessment scheme

One option for increasing student-coaches' motivation and effort is to build in autonomy in the selection of the grading scheme. Coach developers might allow

42 Thompson and Pasquini

TABLE 3.2 Impact of peer evaluation on final grade

	Evaluation as Separate Component (e.g. 100 points possible added)	Evaluation as Percentage Multiplier (e.g. eval % multiplied by team points)
High Peer **Evaluation** (e.g. 100/100)	265/300 individual points 280/300 team points 100/100 evaluation points Total = 645/700 = ~92%	265/300 individual points 280/300 team points × 1.0 = 280 pts. Total = 545/600 = ~91%
Low Peer **Evaluation** (e.g. 85/100)	265/300 individual points 280/300 team points 85/100 evaluation points Total = 630/700 = ~90%	265/300 individual points 280/300 team points × .85 = 238 pts. Total = 503/600 = ~84%

Note: This example is based on a scenario with 300 individual points possible and 300 team points possible, and the individual has earned 265 individual points and the team has earned 280 points.

student-coaches some choice in grading at the class or team level. For example, the coach developer might allow each individual team to work together to decide what percentage of their final evaluation would be weighted, based on individual assessments and what percentage would be based on team assessments. This activity right at the beginning can aid a team in discussing their commitment to one another for the success of the group and may even help them set parameters for group functioning. Regardless, allowing student-coaches to provide input in the grading system can increase their motivation to perform well in the class and can serve as a great first team-building exercise.

Personal reflections and wishful thinking

Incorporating TBL into our setting has provided many learning opportunities for us as coach developers. First, student-coaches are deeply engaged in the material in our TBL courses and provide much deeper and more significant questions and discussions throughout the course. Having the opportunity to guide rich discussions, as opposed to direct a lecture, allows us to see where the student-coaches are most interested. As mentioned, we use this primarily with sport and exercise psychology or foundations of coaching courses, and most student-coaches can personally relate to the material in some way, which makes the projects and case studies very interesting. Student-coaches tend to come to the classroom with experience in team cohesion, whether negative or positive, and the applied material provides them with an outlet to construct meaning around these experiences. Through teamwork, students get to actively discuss their different outlooks on course content and its implication to practice.

At first, when the coach developer moves away from lecturing, they may feel less engaged in coach learning. However, in our experience, the level of feedback and idea-sharing in our TBL courses is significantly greater than in lecture-based courses. In fact, in a TBL course, we have an opportunity to have meaningful discussions with student-coaches because they have covered the basic material in the preparation tasks. Further, taking a more active role in a less formal way mimics what student-coaches can expect in a real-world setting. As a coach, individuals have mentors, but rarely someone standing in front of them every day giving them a play-by-play of what to do. The TBL classroom gives the coach developer an opportunity to act as said mentor to teams while they work through application of materials. Further, the coach developers lean on one another for insight, deeper thinking, and problem solving in a safe, low-stakes environment. Overall, adopting a TBL approach to course delivery has resulted in a much more engaging and meaningful learning experience for our student-coaches, as well as ourselves.

We would be interested in seeing models of coach development emerge in higher education and in governing agencies that are not assessment- or credential-based, but that still maintain a high level of commitment and engagement from participants. For example, the implementation of TBL in a non-graded setting that is a combination of TBL and communities of practice (CoPs). This might serve to increase the engagement (an essential component of CoPs) in the group and maximize the depth of learning that might occur because of the more structured, problem-based activities (inherent to TBL), along with a coach developer to serve as a group facilitator.

We would also be interested in research on the implementation of TBL in coach development settings; particularly aimed at the application-based activities that garner the most discussion and engagement from student-coaches. This would provide coach developers with evidence on the most pressing issues for developing coaches throughout their coaching career.

Activities for coach education

1   An often-used activity within TBL, which requires significant higher-order thinking, is to ask coaches to redesign the system for a sport from grassroots to high performance. This requires and understanding of developmental abilities of athletes at all phases of the system, and requires coaches to consider myriad factors that impact the system.
2   At the end of a TBL course, coach developers could ask coaches to complete an experience-based analysis paper on team dynamics. This would require coaches to understand their experience of working on a team and the impact of experiences or challenges on their group's dynamics. Coaches could also analyze these experiences with theory (or theories) of team cohesion or team development.
3   Participating in a TBL course may raise awareness of some interpersonal skills that inhibit a coach's success. Coach developers might conclude the TBL course or program with an assignment that requires coaches to identify two or three interpersonal strengths, as well as two or three areas to improve. Then, coaches can generate a personal plan to develop those skills.

Additional resources

1   TBL website: www.teambasedlearning.org
2   Clark, M., Merrick, L., Styron, J., Dolowitz, A. and Dorius, C. (2018) *Off to on: Best Practices for Online Team-Based Learning*™, Ames: Center for Excellence in Learning and Teaching Publications. Online. Available HTTP: <www.teambased learning.org/wp-content/uploads/2018/08/Off-to-On_OnlineTBL_White Paper_ClarkEtal2018_V3.pdf>.
3   Sweet, M. and Michaelsen, L.K. (2012) *Team-Based Learning in the Social Sciences and Humanities: Group Work that Works to Generate Critical Thinking and Engagement*, Sterling: Stylus Publishing.

Bibliography

Clark, M.C., Nguyen, H.T., Bray, C. and Levine, R.E. (2008) 'Team-Based Learning in an undergraduate nursing course', *Journal of Nursing Education*, 47: 111–17.

Epstein Educational Enterprises. (2019) *What is the IF-AT?* Online. Available HTTP: <www.epsteineducation.com/home/about/> (accessed 13 February 2018).

Haidet, P., Morgan, R.O., O'Malley, K., Moran, B.J. and Richards, B.F. (2004) 'A controlled trial of active versus passive learning strategies in a large group setting', *Advances in Health Sciences Education*, 9: 15–27.

Michaelsen, L.K., Davidson, N. and Major, C.H. (2014) 'Team-Based Learning practices and principles in comparison with cooperative learning and problem-based learning', *Journal of Excellence in College Teaching*, 25: 57–84.

Michaelsen, L.K., Knight, A.B. and Fink, L.D. (2004) *Team-Based Learning: A Transformative Use of Small Groups in College Teaching*, Sterling: Stylus Publishing.

Michaelsen, L.K. and Richards, B. (2005) 'Drawing conclusions from the team-learning literature in health-sciences education: A commentary', *Teaching and Learning in Medicine*, 17: 85–8.

Sharma, A., Janke, K.K., Larson, A. and Peter, W.S. (2017) 'Understanding the early effects of Team-Based Learning on student accountability and engagement using a three session TBL pilot', *Curriculum in Pharmacy Teaching and Learning*, 9: 802–7.

Sibley, J. and Spiridonoff, S. (2014) *Introduction to Team-Based Learning*, Vancouver: Centre of Instructional Support. Online. Available HTTP: <https://cdn.ymaws.com/teambased learning.site-ym.com/resource/resmgr/Docs/TBL-handout_February_2014_le.pdf> (accessed 16 January 2018).

Stein, R.E., Colyer, C.J. and Manning, J. (2016) 'Student accountability in Team-Based Learning classes', *Teaching Sociology*, 44: 28–8.

Zingone, M.M., Franks, A.S., Guirguis, A.B., George, C.M., Howard-Thompson, A. and Heidel, R.E. (2010) 'Comparing team-based and mixed active-learning methods in an ambulatory care elective course', *American Journal of Pharmacy Education*, 74: 1–7.

4

CRITICALLY UNDERSTANDING AND ENGAGING WITH THE (MICRO)POLITICAL DIMENSIONS OF COACHES' WORK IN AN ADVANCED UNDERGRADUATE COACHING COURSE

Paul Potrac, Adam J. Nichol, and Edward T. Hall

Chapter objectives

By the end of this chapter, the reader should be able to:

1. Articulate the need for coach education provision to move beyond rationalistic and unproblematic representations of coaches' working relationships with various contextual stakeholders (e.g. athletes, administrators, other coaches, and parents, among others).
2. Illustrate how features of Project-Based Learning (PBL) and Social Inquiry (SI) can be integrated to help student coaches critically understand and engage with the (micro)political features of everyday organizational life.
3. Develop an educational strategy that engages with the (micro)political dimensions of coaches' work.

Brief chapter overview

In this chapter, we provide an overview of "why" and "how" we have chosen to integrate elements of Social Inquiry (SI) and Project-Based Learning (PBL) to facilitate university student-coaches' active engagement with the (micro) political dimensions of coaching. We begin by briefly defining the concept of (micro)politics and outline why we believe this topic should occupy a more prominent place in coach education curricula than it has to date. We

46 Potrac, Nichol, and Hall

> then introduce a hybrid approach joining PBL and SI, and describe how their combination has utility for enhancing the critical thinking and professional judgment of student-coaches. Following this, we describe how we have utilized this approach with student-coaches in a final-year undergraduate coaching module. While we believe this hybrid approach has many merits, we acknowledge that it is just one way, among many, to facilitate learning.

Why and when I use the (micro)political dimensions of coaching

According to Leftwhich (2005: 107), (micro)politics is an "absolutely intrinsic, necessary and functional feature of our social existence". It is comprised of all the acts of interpersonal negotiation, conflict, and collaboration that occur whenever two or more people engage in any form collective activity. He suggested that (micro)politics consists of three key ingredients including: (a) people (who often have differing views, preferences and interests); (b) resources (which are predominantly scarce and may be material or non-material in nature); and (c) power (which is the potential for an individual or group to achieve a desired outcome). Unfortunately, much coach education has traditionally ignored, and failed to prepare coaches for, how the coaching role entails developing relationships with a "diverse range of individuals (such as athletes, assistant coaches, parents, and administrators), who may not only bring different traditions and goals to the workplace, but who would also not hesitate to act on their beliefs if the opportunity arose to do so" (Potrac & Jones 2009: 566). For us, facilitating critical thought about how relationships with various situational stakeholders may influence the time, space, and resources afforded to a coach – and, indeed, the climate in which a coach operates – is crucial if we are to help coaches understand, and engage with, the communal and emotionally laden nature of their work (Potrac, Mallett, Greenough & Nelson 2017; Potrac, Jones & Nelson 2014).

To facilitate the micropolitical competencies of our student–coaches, we ask them to engage in several interrelated and inquiry driven activities including:

1 Generating data (observations and interviews) through field work with other coaches, athletes, parents, and club administrators in their chosen sport.
2 Interpreting their data using social theory and research.
3 Critically considering the practical implications of this field work for their personal coaching practice and coach education in general in their chosen sport.

Our subscription to this way of teaching and learning has been influenced by several factors. These not only include our shared personal beliefs about actively engaging student-coaches in the learning process and the value we attach to using social theory and research to interpret and inform coaching practice, but also the feedback we have received from student-coaches regarding their desire to engage with practicing coaches and "real-world" coaching issues. Our decision

(Micro)political dimensions of coaching **47**

to employ this pedagogical approach was also informed by the strategic vision of our University, which prioritizes the provision of research-rich learning and the development of professional praxis.

The essentials of (mirco)political dimensions of coaching

Definitions, essential components, and goals of MPDC

Like others in this book, we have increasingly recognized the value of utilizing PBL in our work with student-coaches. For us, PBL's main strength is its focus on asking learners to individually and collectively engage with disciplinary knowledge and ideas and then apply them to "real-world" issues (Richards & Ressler 2016; Thomas 2000). For further detail on using PBL with student-coaches, we encourage you to engage with Chapter 5 in this book, as well as the insightful work of Richards and Ressler (2016).

We have also increasingly explored the utility of SI in our courses. SI is primarily concerned with the exploration of the essential social, cultural, and interpersonal dimensions of human life (Hill 1994; Keown 1998). This includes, for example, issues pertaining to human behavior, social arrangements, and different modes of political, social, and economic organization (Wood 2013). At the heart of SI is the desire to help learners understand human behavior and exercise responsible citizenship through the in-depth study of various behaviors, relationships, and social issues; inclusive of the ways in which these may vary across time, space, and individual circumstance (Stanford University 2019). As part of the SI approach, learners are encouraged to engage in many activities. These include:

1 Asking questions and examining relevant issues through the gathering of various forms of qualitative and quantitative data.
2 Exploring people's perspectives, actions, and values.
3 Reflecting on and evaluating why people think, feel, and act as they do.
4 Developing ideas, suggestions, and responses to any identified issues.

In terms of its potential benefits, SI provides a vehicle for integrating learning, inquiry, conceptual understanding, and critical thinking, and provides a platform for supporting lifelong learning. Indeed, for us, at least, it is essential that student-coaches continue to critically reflect upon, refine, and develop several social competencies. These include their personal and interpersonal skills, the ability to read people and situations, and, relatedly, being able to build alignment and alliances with others in the coaching environment (Hartley 2017; Potrac 2019).

While SI can be undertaken in many ways, we have found the following chain of logic to be useful with our student-coaches (Ministry of Education 2008):

1 Focus of learning: This initial phase entails identifying the questions or issues that we can ask about the topic at hand (e.g. the [micro]political dimensions of coaches' work).

2   Concepts and conceptual understanding: This phase is primarily concerned with reviewing pertinent literature, identifying key theoretical ideas and concepts, and, importantly, understanding them.
3   Generating data: Here, the focus is on considering what type of data needs to be generated from whom, and how this could be achieved. This includes mapping the network of social relationships within a selected sport club or organization and undertaking any necessary pilot work (e.g. interviews, focus groups, and observations, among others).
4   Exploring values and perspectives: The focus of this phase of data gathering and analysis is on exploring the values and perspectives of various relevant people identified in the previous mapping exercise (e.g. coaches, athletes, parents, club administrators). Specifically, the emphasis is on examining "what matters" to these individuals and groups, and "why", as well as "how", they have come to think and feel in particular ways.
5   Considering responses and decisions: This phase of data generation and analysis is concerned with exploring the decisions, actions, and feelings of the participants and the various consequences of their choices and ways of behaving.
6   Reflecting and evaluating: This activity occurs throughout the process of inquiry and is concerned with enriching the quality of the knowledge and understandings developed through the process of SI, inclusive of the depth of data obtained and critical thinking about the topic in question.
7   So what? Here, the emphasis is on identifying what has been learned in and through the process of SI (e.g. the key findings, theoretical interpretations and insights, and the personal development of student-coaches) and their application to the student-coaches' coaching practice and ongoing learning.
8   Now what? This final sequence is concerned with thinking about what they might do next. For us, this often entails asking student-coaches to develop a coach education resource that is based on the findings and analysis of their project. It may also include identifying topics and questions that they would like to explore in the future, either formally (i.e. further study/higher degree) or informally.

There are many synergies between PBL and SI, and as a consequence, we believe their integration has much to offer in terms of providing a rich and creative platform for actively engaging student-coaches in the process of learning that is both inquiry driven and clearly connected to relevant real-world issues and topics. In the next section, we enact these core elements in a variety of ways. First, the module content, which focuses on the (micro)political and emotionally laden nature of coaching work, is directly tied to the project work that the student-coaches are asked to undertake (Potrac, Smith & Nelson 2017). Indeed, the assessment requires student-coaches to explore these issues through an in-depth study of the experience of coaches, parents, athletes and club administrators in a sporting context of their choice (e.g. community, development, and/or performance setting).

(Micro)political dimensions of coaching **49**

Second, during the various taught sessions (e.g. lectures, seminars, practical sessions, and tutorials) that comprise the module, student-coaches engage with the key theoretical concepts related to:

1 The (micro)political nature of organizational life.
2 Individual and collective impression management strategies.
3 Interpersonal (dis)trust.
4 Emotions and emotion management.

While the concept of (micro)politics was introduced at the beginning of this chapter, it is useful to introduce the other key concepts in the preceding list. Individual and collective impression management refers to how individuals or groups seek to present themselves to others (Goffman 1959). This includes, for example, considering how coaches may attempt to purposefully control the impression they give off to others and, relatedly, the kinds of actions that they may or may not engage in to protect and advance the version of the self-exhibited to these others (see Cassidy, Jones & Potrac 2015). Trust is the glue "upon which all social relationships [and shared endeavors] ultimately depend" (Ronglan 2011: 155), and is concerned with an individual believing (or not) that another individual will take his or her interests into account when making a decision or will not intentionally harm their interests. In our module, the coverage of interpersonal trust focuses on the ways in which a coach may demonstrate their trustworthiness to others, as well as considering what might cause others to distrust a coach (and vice-versa) inclusive of the associated consequences (Gale, Ives, Nelson & Potrac 2019; Ward 2019). Finally, we draw on literature addressing the emotional dimensions of coaching work. This includes considering the emotions that may be experienced (e.g. joy, pride, anger, guilt, and shame, among others) by a coach and how these emotions are generated in and through a coach's relationships with others, as well as when, how, and why a coach may choose or feel obliged to variously show, hide or manufacture emotions for their own or others' benefit (Hochschild 2000; Nelson et al. 2013; Potrac & Marshall 2011). Importantly, these concepts provide the theoretical underpinnings for the student-coaches' project work. As a teaching team, we provide an overview of this material. However, student-coaches are not only required to explore these topics in their chosen context; they also should undertake further literature searches to inform their work.

Third, although we provide a broad overview of the assessment requirements and the specific criteria that will be used to evaluate their submissions, student-coaches are encouraged to define the specific focus or foci of their projects and are also responsible for contacting and communicating with the "gatekeepers" to their chosen coaching context and those who wish to participate in the project (i.e. coaches, athletes, parents, club administrators). Finally, to increase the authenticity of the project, student-coaches are challenged to:

1 Describe the issues and dilemmas they identified in their chosen coaching context and, relatedly, outline the advice they would subsequently give to coaches.

50 Potrac, Nichol, and Hall

2 Critically review the place of knowledge regarding (micro)politics, (dis) trust, impression management and emotion management in the formal coach education provision offered by the national governing body (NGB) of their chosen sport.
3 Suggest when, where and how these topics could be productively explored as part of formal coach education programs in their chosen sport.

Using elements of PBL and SI to develop (micro)political literacy in a final year undergraduate coaching module

In this section, we describe our approach to using critical PBL and SI in terms of our module's aims and assessment requirements. Specifically, we elucidate the roles and responsibilities for us as tutors and the student-coaches, the delivery of key taught content, and how student-coaches typically undertake the assessed project work.

Aim of the module

The undergraduate module is delivered in a traditional format (e.g. face-to-face lectures, seminars, tutorials, and practical sessions) across the whole of the student-coaches' final year of study. Our overarching aim, which is set out in a module outline document, is to support the development of critical skills related to (micro)political literacy and (micro)political action (e.g. the ability to establish, safeguard, advance, or restore desired working conditions within the coaching context). We seek to stimulate student-coaches' sociological imaginations to become critically aware of the interconnectedness of their own professional interests and experiences, and the wider networks of social relations, organizations, and institutions of which they are part. For instance, attention is drawn to examples of coaches being competitive, calculating, and uncaring toward each other as they act in accordance with their own motivations and ambitions, such as to achieve job security (e.g. Potrac, Jones, Gilbourne & Nelson 2013). Indeed, we expect that through learning during the module, the student-coach will come to recognize how workplace opportunities and career trajectories may be vulnerable to the competing ideologies, goals, and interests of other contextual stakeholders (e.g. athletes, administrators, other coaches, parents, etc.). Similarly, we challenge the student-coaches to critically consider how they might seek to obtain the trust and "buy-in" of various others that comprise their chosen coaching settings.

The driving questions arising from these aims and intended to promote curiosity, inquiry and engagement are:

1 How do the interests of different stakeholders influence the support and resources the coach is afforded to undertake their work and the climate they work in?
2 How can the coach manage others' impressions of themselves to generate the working conditions necessary and desirable to perform their work productively and in a positive atmosphere?

Module assessment

Student-coaches are assessed via a project comprising three related components: An essay (worth 40 percent of the overall grade), a presentation (worth 30 percent), and a viva (an oral examination; worth 30 percent). Although these are submitted separately, they are interlinked, with each successive component intended to inform subsequent thinking and content.

Component One, the essay, requires each student-coach to undertake inquiry in a coaching context of their choosing, responding to the driving questions identified in the preceding list. Data gathering takes place in the field, through observations and interviews, in order to establish key stakeholders (e.g. athletes, administrators, other coaches, and parents), map their relationships, and understand the choices, values, interests, and motives that these stakeholders bring to the coaching context. At this stage of the assessment, the purpose is to develop a (micro)political picture of the unique working environment, incorporating the networks of social actors, their circumstances, and their (micro)political interactions. Each essay must include analysis and interpretation of the gathered data, judiciously deploying the concepts and theory of (micro)politics to develop a "reality-grounded", critical discussion of the sociocultural environment under investigation. This requires student-coaches to comprehend the implications of stakeholders' interests for the working climate and for the coach's ability to properly perform their work. Thus, through their own exploration and inquiry, student-coaches are challenged to recognize the contested, negotiated character of coaching, and to be sensitive to how the above relates to tensions, conflict, struggles, or rivalries, and to collaboration, cooperation and coalition within the working environment. Importantly, aside from having the topic to be studied defined by tutors, in line with the combined elements of PBL and SI informing our work on this module, each student-coach is expected to take responsibility for all parts of the process including organizing their access to an appropriate coaching context, generating data to respond to the driving questions of the module, and analyzing these data in response to the assessment brief and marking scheme.

Component Two, the presentation, further develops the initial analysis of the (micro)political landscape of the coaching context from Component One by turning attention to the problems and tensions evident in how the coach could manage their micro-relations with other stakeholders. Here, each student-coach needs to draw upon research, concepts, and theory in order to address and iteratively interpret their findings from Component One. Specifically, they must propose, explain, and justify recommendations for the coach's (micro) political action; actions which respond to interpretations of the challenges and opportunities identified in their prior essay. The purpose of these proposals is to consider how the coach could generate more desirable working conditions and advance the necessary professional support, space, time, and resources to carry out their work. Specific strategies for interacting with different groups of stakeholders need to be identified, and the interconnections of these varied networks of stakeholders and their implications for the coach's working climate should be critically considered. Each student-coach's discussion of these recommendations should include consideration of the potential consequences (intended and unintended) of the coach's (inter)actions, and how these may contribute to the emergent constraints and opportunities of their ongoing (inter)actions.

Component Three, the viva, is concerned with the virtues of (micro)political knowledge for informing coach education and professional development provision. Student-coaches are required to present a critical review of a national governing body coach education qualification, which is linked to the coaching context studied in Components One and Two. Using documentary analysis, and, perhaps, drawing upon their own experiences as a participant on the coaching qualification, the critique should concern how (micro)political issues and knowledge are currently presented (or omitted) within mainstream coach education. In response to their critique, each student-coach is required to outline how (micro) political literacy (knowledge and action) could be more usefully situated within the coach education program, including proposing their own ideas for activities, resources, and/or questions that could be incorporated to enhance the emotional and political dimensions of coaches' professional preparation and development. Additionally, based upon their learning in the module, student-coaches are asked to identify (micro)political topics and dilemmas of personal interest that they would like to explore through further study and/or in their own practice, and to discuss how these may be beneficial to their continuing development, workplace opportunities, and career trajectories as coaches.

The assessed project is introduced and explained in detail during the first week of the module, and student-coaches are encouraged to begin their fieldwork as soon as possible. We have found this has many benefits, including:

1   Ensuring each student-coach is sufficiently familiar with their coaching context.
2   Giving them time to explore every aspect of the module's content and assessment components in depth.
3   Increasing opportunities for tutors to facilitate peer-to-peer student-coach reflections about emergent concerns and interests.
4   Promoting iterative and increasingly critical sensemaking, whereby student-coaches revisit the focus of learning with more developed and alternative conceptual frameworks to support interpretation and understanding.

Supporting student-coach learning

Our shared constructivist assumptions about learning inform a pedagogical approach in which knowledge is produced through active interpretive processes as people make sense of their experiences in the social world (Stewart 2013). Reflecting the focus of the module, our faciliatory approach recognizes that student-coaches' engagement and learning are mediated by their emotional and

(Micro)political dimensions of coaching **53**

personal connections to others (e.g. peers, tutors, and coaches, among others). Consequently, our teaching practices emphasize peer interaction and collaboration by encouraging student-coaches to relate their learning with us to their experiences as coaches and athletes outside of university. The planning of lectures, for instance, includes identifying material to actively promote involvement, as well as ensuring there is sufficient time for previous experiences and knowledge to be shared, and for these to be discussed and reflected upon by student-coaches. For example, we have shown clips from *Remember the Titans*, a biographical sport drama, set in the Southeastern United States during the 1970s. The movie focuses on the experiences and interactions of an African-American head football coach working with a mixed-race high school team in the first playing season following racial integration. In small groups, the student-coaches are then asked to discuss examples from the film, as well as from their own experiences, and make links to the theoretical concepts we have introduced. Here, the focus is on the choices, values, interests, and motives of the stakeholders (e.g. the school board, White and Black players, parents, and coaches, among others), and, importantly, how these impinge upon the work and experiences of the coach. As tutors, we can then responsively elaborate explanations of the concepts we introduce in lectures, drawing upon the student-coaches' own examples and experiences, as well as those identified in the film.

Seminars emphasize student-coach group discussion, as well as the application and analysis of skills and knowledge introduced in lectures and generated through related practical sessions, independent study, and personal experience. The focus is very much on encouraging the sharing of ideas, consideration of alternatives, development of planning and reflecting skills, and understanding relationships between theory and practice. These regularly include preparatory or follow-up tasks to support engagement with the learning process. For instance, we often ask student-coaches to have reviewed and made notes on two or three identified source materials (e.g. journal articles, book chapters, videos) in preparation for seminar tasks. These tasks vary, but examples include: (a) comparing their notes on research findings in small groups in response to prompts (e.g. 'Before reading this I'd not thought of . . .', 'These findings are similar to/different than . . .', 'I think future research needs to look more closely at . . .', etc.); (b) presenting reports on different case studies of coaching practice; (c) identifying quotes or sections from a video that best connect with their own experiences of the topic; (d) developing and then sharing their own short, evocative narratives about personal coaching experiences stimulated by exemplar texts (e.g. Potrac, Jones, Gilbourne & Nelson 2013; Jones 2006; Hall & Gray 2016); and (e) identifying concepts or terminology encountered in the source material that need further clarification, and then researching working definitions of these things. A popular activity among student-coaches is to debate alternative courses of action that could have been taken by the coach of an amateur women's soccer team featured in Potrac, Mallett, Greenough and Nelson's (2017) in response to the unfolding (micro)political dilemmas and challenges he encountered. This debate links well

54 Potrac, Nichol, and Hall

to a follow-up task (itself closely related to the assessment task) whereby student-coaches are asked to collate evidence of the potential practical implications of the debated (micro)political action for the coach's working climate.

Practical sessions enable student-coaches to experience different roles connected to the planning, enactment, and review of coaching practice. This form of taught activity spread throughout the year-long module, along with the others discussed here, also allows us as tutors to judge what the student-coaches have progressively learned, and how capably they can discuss, write about, and embody this knowledge in their practice. Importantly, in this module, the definitional boundaries of coaching encompass more than that which happens on the court or pitch, by the pool or track, or in the gym. Consequently, we use role playing tasks to draw attention to themes including (micro)political literacy, (micro)political action, and impression management in different situations and with different stakeholders. Example scenarios we ask student-coaches to act out include: (a) imagine you are a newly appointed director of coaching in a professional youth academy environment – deliver a briefing to parents and field questions from the audience about your vision and ethos for the organization; (b) your team has just been relegated from its league – as a coaching staff member, present your review to the board of directors; and (c) as head coach you want to add a new assistant coach to your established staff – hold a meeting with your current assistants to discuss the issue. Other roles (e.g. parents, assistant coaches, etc.) in the scenarios are also fulfilled by student-coaches, who are encouraged to consider how and why different stakeholders might think, feel, and act as the scenarios unfold. Finally, a further group of student-coaches act as coach mentors. Their role is to offer theoretical interpretations and insights into the observed action, and to suggest alternative choices and ways of behaving that could generate different consequences for the coach.

Tutorials are small-group or individual meetings with a tutor. These are intended as a relaxed forum in which student-coaches can develop confidence in exploring different ways to approach material, generating evidence for their ideas, and sustaining their arguments. Tutorials provide a valuable opportunity for us as tutors to offer feedback to student-coaches on prepared work and their developing understanding of topics, as well as to share personal, research, and real-world examples that help them to understand the practical application of concepts and theory. Although tutorials are typically less structured than other taught activities and more responsive to individual student-coach needs, a valued small-group tutorial activity is reviewing video footage together that student-coaches capture in their fieldwork for Component One of the assessment portfolio. Student-coaches present their initial interpretations of the footage in the light of relevant theory, which tutors then probe and challenge. Through activities such as this, we believe student-coaches learn to evaluate evidence independently, to question existing knowledge and beliefs, and to identify where their reading, learning, and research might go next.

Each of these example means of supporting student-coach learning are intended to be underpinned and enhanced by extensive independent study. This includes tutor-suggested reading, research, and information gathering (e.g. via the module's reading list), as well as student-coaches' self-directed learning in relation to the topics of the module and assessment requirements.

Personal reflections and wishful thinking

Our work on this module is hugely rewarding. This is especially so when we witness the "lightbulb moment" of student-coaches recognizing the value that social theory can have for them as coaches. That said, we feel it is important to acknowledge that not all student-coaches welcome the view that coaching can be a problematic, contested, and emotionally demanding activity, or the suggestion that there are no absolute guaranteed solutions to the (micro)political dilemmas that they may encounter in practice. In exploring these issues with student-coaches (often for the first time), we frequently find that they have been exposed to various (and contradictory) ontological assumptions about, and representations of, coaching inside and outside of the university setting. We have been fortunate by being able to include guest talks from some practicing coaches in our module that focus on the political challenges of their work and the strategies that they utilize to achieve desired ends. For some student-coaches (but not all), such interventions have led them to critically question their subscription to an overly straightforward and functional view of coaching practice. However, it is not a panacea.

We believe that more can and ought to be done. Indeed, our wish is that academics in the social science and bioscience disciplines, and coach educators, can find some common ground regarding the essential nature of coaching. For us, at least, this is that coaching is an inherently communal, political, and interactive activity in which both the biosciences and the social sciences have important roles to play in terms of enhancing coaching practice. In the university setting, for example, there is perhaps much to gain from structuring courses so that the forms of knowledge that student-coaches need to draw upon are not taught in isolation from each other (e.g. physiology, motor learning, sociology, and psychology, among others). Instead, we need to find ways of integrating these forms of knowledge so that student-coaches better understand how they are inextricably entwined in their efforts to positively influence the learning, performance, and experiences of athletes, as well as develop, sustain, and advance their relationships with a variety of other situational stakeholders (e.g. parents, administrators, other coaches). Similarly, it would also be helpful if the notion of politics was constructively engaged with in coach education provision more generally. For us, (micro)politics is often viewed or presented in a negative or pathological way – that is, it is something that ought to be avoided or is practiced only by egotistical and Machiavellian individuals (Potrac, Jones, Gilbourne & Nelson 2013). Instead, coach education could learn much from recent work and initiatives in the disciplines of leadership, management and education, which has increasingly advocated for – and considered how – the political astuteness of

56 Potrac, Nichol, and Hall

teachers, managers, and senior leaders could be developed and ethically utilized in everyday practice (Close 2013; Hartley 2017).

Activities for coach education

1   Critically review the content of your own coach education curricula. To what extent does it consider and prepare coaches for the (micro)political and emotional challenges that they may encounter as an everyday part of their work? What changes could you make to facilitate micropolitical and emotional challenges, and why?
2   Consider the coaches that you are working with. What are the likely or possible dilemmas and challenges that they may encounter in their working relationships with others (e.g. athletes, parents, club administrators) and you as a coach educator? Can you identify a topic or issue whereby PBL and/or SI could be deployed to develop the (micro)political literacy and interactional strategies of these coaches? What topic, issue, or relationship(s) would you address? How might you structure the learning of the coaches?

Additional resources

The following chapters and articles provide some insight into the (micro)political and emotional dimensions of coaching:

1   Jones, R., Armour, K. and Potrac, P. (2004) *Sports Coaching Cultures: From Practice to Theory*, London: Routledge.
2   Magill, S., Nelson, L., Jones, R. and Potrac, P. (2017) 'Emotions, identity, and power in video-based feedback sessions: Tales from women's professional football', *Sports Coaching Review*, 6: 216–32.

Bibliography

Cassidy, T., Jones, R. and Potrac, P. (2015) *Understanding Sports Coaching: The Social, Cultural and Pedagogical Foundations of Coaching Practice*, 3rd edn, London: Routledge.
Close, P. (2013) 'Developing political astuteness: A leadership coaching journey', *School Leadership & Management*, 33: 178–96.
Gale, L., Ives, B., Nelson, L. and Potrac, P. (2019) 'Trust in community sports work: Tales from the "Shop Floor"', *Sociology of Sport Journal*, 36: 244–53.
Goffman, E. (1959) *The Presentation of the Self in Everyday Life*, London: Penguin.
Hall, E.T. and Gray, S. (2016) 'Reflecting on reflective practice: A coach's action research narratives', *Qualitative Research in Sport, Exercise and Health*, 8: 365–79.
Hartley, J. (2017) 'Politics and political astuteness in leadership', in J. Storey, P. Hart and D. Ulrich (eds.) *The Routledge Companion to Leadership*, pp. 197–208, London: Routledge.
Hill, B. (1994) *Teaching Social Studies in a Multicultural Society*, Melbourne: Longman Cheshire.
Hochschild, A. (2000) *The Managed Heart: Commercialisation of Human Feeling*, Berkeley: University of California Press.
Jones, R. (2006) 'Dilemmas, maintaining "face," and paranoia: An average coaching life', *Qualitative Inquiry*, 12: 1012–21.

Kelchtermans, G. and Ballett, K. (2002) 'Micropolitical literacy: Reconstructing a neglected dimension in teacher development', *International Journal of Educational Research*, 37: 755–67.

Keown, P. (1998) 'Values and social action: Doing the hard bits', in P. Benson and R. Openshaw (eds.) *New Horizons for New Zealand Social Studies*, pp. 137–59, Palmerston North: ERDC Press.

Leftwhich, A. (2005) 'The political approach to human behaviour: People, resources and power', in A. Leftwhich (ed.) *What Is Politics*, pp. 100–18, Cambridge: Polity Press.

Ministry of Education. (2008) *Approaches to Social Inquiry*, Wellington: Learning Media Limited.

Nelson, L., Potrac, P., Gilbourne, D., Allanson, A., Gale, L. and Marshall, P. (2013) 'Thinking, feeling, acting: The case of a semi-professional soccer coach', *Sociology of Sport Journal*, 30: 467–86.

Potrac, P. (2019) 'Exploring politics and political astuteness in coaching: Some critical reflections', in C. Corsby and C. Edwards (eds.) *Exploring Research in Sports Coaching and Pedagogy: Context and Contingency*, pp. 13–21, Newcastle Upon Tyne: Cambridge Scholars Publishing.

Potrac, P. and Jones, R. (2009) 'Micro-political workings in semi-professional football coaching', *Sociology of Sport Journal*, 26: 557–77.

Potrac, P., Jones, R., Gilbourne, D. and Nelson, L. (2013) 'Handshakes, BBQs, and bullets: A tale of self-interest and regret in football coaching', *Sports Coaching Review*, 1: 79–92.

Potrac, P., Jones, R. and Nelson, L. (2014) 'Interpretivism', in L. Nelson, R. Groom and P. Potrac (eds.) *Research Methods in Sports Coaching*, pp. 31–41, London: Routledge.

Potrac, P., Mallett, C., Greenough, K. and Nelson, L. (2017) 'Passion and paranoia: An embodied tale of emotion, identity, and pathos in sports coaching', *Sports Coaching Review*, 6: 142–61.

Potrac, P. and Marshall, P. (2011) 'Arlie Russell Hochschild: The managed heart, feeling rules, and emotional labour: Coaching as an emotional endeavour', in R. Jones, P. Potrac, C. Cushion and L.T. Ronglan (eds.) *The Sociology of Sports Coaching*, pp. 54–66, London: Routledge.

Potrac, P., Smith, A. and Nelson, L. (2017) 'Emotion in sport coaching: An introductory essay', *Sports Coaching Review*, 6: 129–41.

Richards, A. and Ressler, J. (2016) 'A collaborative approach to self-study research in physical education teacher education', *Journal of Teaching in Physical Education*, 35: 290–5.

Ronglan, T.L. (2011) 'Social interaction in coaching', in R.L. Jones, P. Potrac, C. Cushion and L.T. Ronglan (eds.) *The Sociology of Sports Coaching*, pp. 151–65, London: Routledge.

Stanford University. (2019) *Social Inquiry (SI)*. Online. Available HTTP: <https://undergrad.stanford.edu/programs/ways/ways/social-inquiry> (accessed 12 March 2019).

Stewart, M. (2013) 'Understanding learning: Theories and critique', in L. Hunt and D. Chalmers (eds.) *University Teaching in Focus: A Learning-Centred Approach*, pp. 3–20, London: Routledge.

Thomas, J. (2000) *A Review of Research on Project-Based Learning*, San Rafael: Autodesk Foundation.

Ward, P.R. (2019) 'Trust, what is it and why do we need it?', in M.H. Jacobsen (ed.) *Emotions, Everyday Life and Sociology*, pp. 13–21, London: Routledge.

Wood, B. (2013) 'What is Social Inquiry?', *SET: Research Information for Teachers*, 2013: 20–8.

5

USING PROJECT-BASED LEARNING FOR THE GRADUATE STUDENT-COACH LEARNING STRENGTH AND CONDITIONING

Brian Gearity and Bettina Callary

Chapter objectives

By the end of this chapter, the reader should be able to:

1. Articulate an understanding of Project-Based Learning.
2. Identify essential facilitators and barriers to effective implementation of Project-Based Learning.
3. Draft an instruction plan using Project-Based Learning.

Brief chapter overview

In this chapter, we present an overview of concepts, research, and applications of Project-Based Learning (PBL). The first author, Brian, will elaborate on his experience using PBL in a graduate strength and conditioning (S&C) course. Brian has been honing PBL at three different universities for over 10 years with students from varying educational and social backgrounds. PBL can be a powerful instructional strategy to enhance critical thinking and professional judgment. We provide a tested framework for implementing PBL with university-level graduate students in an S&C course; however, PBL could be used in a variety of coach development contexts.

Why and when I use Project-Based Learning

When I first started teaching strength and conditioning (S&C) at the university level, I co-taught it with a professor of exercise science (thanks, Dr. Howley) to undergraduate students. We decided to have students design a year-long S&C program because, from my experiences as an S&C coach, this is a highly essential, and challenging to learn, aspect of coaching. Designing an S&C program was a challenging problem, which aligns with PBL (e.g. requires *creating a project/artifact* and addresses a *challenging problem*) (Tamim & Grant 2013). In the next section, while reviewing related PBL concepts and literature, we provide a framework for planning PBL with graduate students in an S&C course, which can be adapted by the coach developer for their context, including applications outside of S&C.

The essentials of Project-Based Learning

Definitions, essential components, and goals of PBL

PBL has gone by varying terms for over 100 years and is closely related to other strategies (e.g. problem–based learning, experiential learning). We propose differentiating PBL from *problem*-based learning by highlighting "project": The learning occurs while creating a deliverable. Markham, Larmer and Ravitz (2003) offer a formal definition of PBL as "a systematic teaching method that engages students in learning knowledge and skills through an extended inquiry process structured around complex, authentic questions and carefully designed products and tasks" (p. 4). Next, we describe five oft-mentioned essential components of PBL.

Lifelike or real-life challenging problem or driving question

Coaches are faced with the problem of enhancing athletes' performance, which encompasses designing and implementing physical training programs. Designing S&C programs integrates science from many disciplines, drawing heavily from biomechanics and physiology. Also, planning and implementing programs necessitates the consideration of cognitive–interpretive, pedagogical, and sociocultural issues (e.g. translating research to practice, reflecting on practice, working with varying and diverse athletes, coach to athlete ratio, facilities, and available equipment). Bereiter and Scardamalia (1993) talk about a *progressive problem* as an enduring central problem experienced in practice that prompts practitioners to reflect, reframe, and strategize solutions for better outcomes. In support of these issues, students often report to us, "I never knew S&C program design was so complex". Presenting a driving question to students in PBL is how to actualize this essential component.

Constructive investigations

PBL is tied to experiential learning or inquiry; coaches learn how to address (not always solve) problems and improve professional judgment over an extended duration. There are often huge differences between students new to S&C coaching and experienced S&C coaches; although more research needs to better understand this difference. We've seen students design leg workouts for young athletes that would take about three hours of non-stop, intense weightlifting movements! Students come into the classroom with preconceived notions of how to work out, which influences their S&C program design. Additionally, graduate students are always embedded in a research and theory-based curriculum, which takes time to comprehend and is continually changing.

Centrality to the curriculum

Most PBL theorists believe that the project should be central to the curriculum. Although some theorists identify that a project could be used that relies on students' existing knowledge, this seems in opposition to the previous component of PBL being a constructive investigation over time that *extends* student learning. Coach developers may use PBL while supplementing it with other instructional strategies. For example, within the scope of a project, students will benefit from direct instruction on a complex topic such as acute and chronic endocrine responses to exercise or instructing a sprinter's race distribution. In some cases, the project is central to – but not the only part of – the curriculum.

Autonomy

One of the proposed benefits of PBL is that it provides students with choice in how they go about finding answers to questions. Some research shows students are more motivated in PBL than other instructional strategies (Thomas 2000), but it's a bit simplistic to think that all students are highly intrinsically motivated because of the magic of PBL. So, while PBL is called a student-centered strategy and students are provided great autonomy, this is in comparison to other, more teacher-centered, approaches. In my own teaching of S&C, I permit students to select the sport they want to design a program for, but I encourage them to not select a sport they played extensively. I do this because most S&C coaches will typically work with athletes of many sports, and I want students to be able to design programs accordingly. Also, many collegiate athletes tend to merely reproduce what their collegiate S&C coach had designed for them. Reproduction is disastrous because it does not result in the need to engage in the critical, inquiry driven, problem-solving, project-creating process.

Reflection, collaboration, and holism

Some PBL theorists identify the centrality of reflection, collaboration, or holism (e.g. cognitive, affective, physical, and ethical domains) (Kokotsaki, Menzies &

Wiggins 2016). We've included these at the end because we don't find them to be inherently essential components of PBL. Reflection or Reflective Practice Theories (e.g. Kolb, Schön) are distinct from PBL because they focus on learning and problem solving in and outside of coaching practice and obtaining feedback, but do not culminate in the creation of a project and may not involve an enduring central challenge. Collaboration is often tied to PBL, but students could work individually on a project. In my graduate-level S&C course, students engage each other in discussion and peer review, but submit their own project. These discussions allow students to share different points of view on the same question posed, deepening their understanding and furthering reflection. Alternatively, students could work in groups on the same project, and the collaboration would lead to consensus on the problem as they work out how to best address the issue. Finally, project questions can focus on one or more "domains" such as developing coaches' cognitive or affective understanding of issues. While there are affective-ethical components to S&C program design that I bring up to the students (e.g. use of supplements or drugs, risk from poor exercise technique), these tend to be relatively peripheral features. Developing students' understanding of the physiological and biomechanical features of S&C are more salient to the project, and thus the students are required to dig deeper into these considerations. In the following section, we will revisit these essential components while providing a framework on how to create a PBL instructional strategy for graduate students studying S&C.

Tested framework and tips for developing PBL

We offer a three-step framework – design a driving question, map and manage the process, and create and perform assessments – as a guide to coach developers wishing to use PBL. Naturally the framework can be modified dependent upon the teacher's and student's skills, context, and purpose. We often prefer to sketch out step one, then three, and then work on step two. This is because we find it useful to know where we're going, and then a lot of time is spent on step two creating learning materials (which explains why step two is the longest section here). The process is recursive, which means an enduring re-visitation of all the steps, like the sport coach designing yearly, weekly, or daily practice plans!

Step one: driving question

Step one considers what the coach developer wants sport coaches (students, more generally) to know, do, or have an attitude toward at the end of the course, and how PBL facilitates achievement of course objectives. Before considering what kind of project might be appropriate, the coach developer needs to identify what the course is about (course description), what specific and measurable outcomes the students achieve (course objectives), and how the teacher, and student, know when the objectives have been met (assessment). It is imperative to think of these items altogether because proper *alignment* should occur, and does when the description, objectives, learning activities, and assessments fit together. Alternatively, a

62 Gearity and Callary

poorly aligned course would have items out of place, such as assessing a project with a multiple-choice quiz that tests basic comprehension or application.

Let's look at an example from my (Brian's) course for what we hope shows good alignment. Here is some of the exact info for a four-credit, ten-week graduate-level course taught fully online entitled "Strength, conditioning, and injury prevention program design".

Course description

This advanced-level course is designed to educate students on the scientific, theoretical, and practical foundations of strength, conditioning, and injury prevention. Students will learn how to design S&C programs to enhance athletic performance and reduce and lessen the severity of injury. This course is also intended to help students become familiar with the National Strength and Conditioning Association's (NSCA) Certified Strength and Conditioning Specialist exam, and position statements from several national governing bodies on athlete safety and physical performance.

Course objectives

1 Design an S&C program that could be used to improve athletic performance, reduce injury, or lessen the severity of injury.
2 Plan individualized S&C programs based on individual and environmental factors.
3 Identify scientific concepts related to acute and chronic adaptations to anaerobic and aerobic exercise.
4 Produce informational materials on drugs, nutrition, and supplements for numerous stakeholders.
5 Demonstrate proper exercise technique and offer effective instruction and feedback.
6 Distinguish between training systems (e.g. Olympic, powerlifting, body-building, sport training, etc.) and methods (e.g. resistance training exercises, speed drills, etc.).

The first two objectives are tightly linked to PBL, and these objectives are what we call higher-order thinking skills. The third objective is linked to the presentation portion of the project. Students are required to design an S&C program *and* present it to the class by creating and sharing a video of them justifying their program.

Driving questions

How would you design an S&C program to improve athletic performance and decrease or lessen the severity of injury? Are you really doing everything you can to design the best program?

These questions provide students a lifelike, challenging task to facilitate their own authentic knowledge construction. Students are told to increase athletic performance and lessen injuries and they construct their own knowledge, skills, and attitude. The second question prompts students' reflection. Rather than "just design a program", students are challenged to think about important features to consider. I also provide several prompts in a fuller description of the project to save time and energy, and this pre-instruction on many procedural issues will deepen student learning (Kokotsaki, Menzies & Wiggins 2016).

When crafting driving questions, keep in mind meeting the essential components of PBL and consider the course structure. If students need ample time (e.g. weeks or several hours) to engage in inquiry, reflection, revisions, etc., then structure the question and course accordingly. If the project is to facilitate higher-order, authentic thinking skills, then use a question that challenges coaches. It would be a mistake to write a problem that mimics a typical essay question, addresses something without the creation of some concrete artifact, or is merely theoretical or abstract.

We want to point out how we've considered the essential elements of PBL. That is, the project is a lifelike or real-life problem (yes, S&C and sport coaches design and implement programs) and the project is central to – but not the only – instructional approach in the curriculum (three course objectives are directly tied to PBL, students are assessed on this project worth about 40 percent of their grade, and other course activities and assignments indirectly support the project). One of the ways we, as coach developers, can help students learn this essential and complex task is to model how to write programs, share our experiences, and provide feedback and questioning to students. Merely lecturing to students to have them acquire content knowledge or preparing them for a national certification in S&C that is assessed by multiple-choice exams will not help students acquire the knowledge, skills, and attitude of a competent coach who can design an S&C program.

Step two: map and manage the process

Step two involves supporting student learning throughout the project. The role of the teacher in PBL is to facilitate and guide, not excessively tell. PBL theorists have warned of this because it is often a great shift from teacher-centered instruction to student-led inquiry (Tamim and Grant 2013). For example, when I (Brian) started teaching S&C courses, I was tempted to immediately correct a student's program. While I was a practicing S&C coach for more than 10 years and thought that I designed effective programs, I've come to appreciate there are multiple ways to design a program. Indeed, students have submitted S&C plans that are unique and reflect careful consideration of many factors, including evaluating knowledge and practices across scientific disciplines, contextual factors, and socio-ethical-legal concerns. Instead of seeking some sort of unattainable perfect program, I've shifted my thinking to seeking students who can exhibit sound professional judgment.

64 Gearity and Callary

Coach developers provide opportunities for practice and feedback to enhance students' ability to design S&C programs. In PBL, we anticipate students will experience challenges developing the project and we must determine: (a) whether to intervene or let the students attempt to figure things out on their own; and (b) how to intervene. As an example of my own epic failure, when I (Brian) first started teaching S&C courses, I required students to create a workout routine consisting of three to four days per week of training over 52 weeks! This was too much, and the projects lacked depth and a careful integration of science and practice. As fatigue set in (which it unanimously did), students did little more than copy and paste workouts from week to week. I've learned to favor quality over quantity. In my fifth year using PBL, when I taught the course on campus (as opposed to online), I started using 20-minute segments of class time to meet with students about their projects. For my online graduate S&C course, students are required to video conference with me to discuss their project. Students must bring drafts of their work and specific questions to ask. Do all students do as requested? Of course not. There are always 5–15 percent who basically bring nothing. Inevitably, the students who brought drafts receive more specific feedback and reflective questions from me, ask meaningful questions, and rather than addressing basic components, we're able to have a deep conversation about the project. For example, we might talk about how exercise frequency and loading should vary from exercise to exercise or set to set within a day, week, or month. I'm then able to query students on their knowledge, including scientific knowledge, of why and how the body adapts.

There are several smaller assignments that build on one another to formulate the entire project (e.g. macrocycles, split routines, athlete profile and needs analysis, microcycles, biomechanics of injury prevention, and several rounds of revisions). A quick caveat: The focus of the S&C course is resistance training, not speed, agility, or other components. I used to require students to do these components, but upon reflection, I decided it was too much to ask in one course. I have students sketch this part of the project last, and it does not carry the same weight during the assessment.

The rationale for breaking down the project into smaller, bite-sized assignments is to keep students on task and to provide ongoing feedback. The sequencing of these assignments is important. Over the years teaching, I've found that starting with how to design a macrocycle (year-round plan) is a good starting point. Without having to take into consideration all the minute details of designing months of workouts, by starting with the macrocycle, students can see how the S&C program goals are laid out throughout the year in tandem with the sport season. Students, as coaches and often former athletes, understand the sport season, and this inherent structure puts some boundaries on designing a macrocycle. When designing a macrocycle, students are introduced to many considerations, including how much time is available to train and the goals that will enhance performance the most (e.g. power or muscle size), and begin to question what is the best way to organize a plan. For every building-block assignment, I provide students with a template to use to save them time and save me from visually inspecting numerous different styles.

By providing a detailed template, one that I've revised multiple times, I am prompting students to consider more factors than they would otherwise. After students create a macrocycle draft and peer review a classmates' macrocycle, we will all collectively reflect, and students respond to a few questions I've offered about their design experience. The scaffolding allows me to provide a bit more feedback early in the course to check that students are on track and feel supported.

We then move on to designing split routines while continuing course readings such as position stands from the NSCA and the American College of Sports Medicine. Designing the split routine is relatively easier than the following activities, but puts into practice these readings that until now had just been conceptual.

One simple problem that I typically see at this point is that students may omit important muscle groups or assign an exercise frequency that doesn't match the athlete's abilities or goals. For example, some students have erroneously submitted split routines whereby a strength/power athlete, such as a rugby or American football player, exercises leg muscles just once per week. This is a good time to discuss this problem with the students before moving on to more complex tasks.

Next, students will complete an athlete profile and needs analysis. The athlete profile is almost too simple to begin with, because it is basic demographic and training background information. I pair it with the needs analysis to add complexity and because the student's initial needs analysis will need to be improved. Conducting a thorough needs analysis involves reviewing a wide breadth of research and literature on the physiology, biomechanics, and injuries in sport. I require students to select a position within a sport and a real or imaginary athlete. Specifying a position narrows the focus and reduces complexity. When we've prompted students with, "You're now the S&C coach for a famous athlete (e.g. LeBron James, Lionel Messi, Serena Williams)" or when they consider a real athlete they're currently coaching, it adds concreteness and a lifelike component. Although students are provided another template, I inform them to take more ownership and to adjust the template as needed to make it more practical and aesthetically pleasing.

While revising their macrocycles, students spend time on the biomechanics of injury part of the needs analysis, including finding empirical research, which was not previously required. The result is that students explore scientific journals and consider mechanisms of injury. It should be clear now that we introduce a relatively easier task before asking students to complete a more challenging task.

The next building block has students create four single workouts for a specific mesocycle goal (e.g. one sample workout for endurance, hypertrophy, strength, and power), which is done before the more complex assignment of creating a 12-week mesocycle. The next assignment is for students to design 12 weeks from their macrocycle. This is when students finally develop a draft of a program that must include three to four days per week of resistance training, including

66 Gearity and Callary

10 weeks of off-season training and two weeks of in-season training (hence, 12 weeks).

In addition to the templates provided, I also show students real-life programs I've collected from coaches at varying levels so they can compare pros and cons of program design, including aesthetics and function (e.g. if the program looks good, and if it is easy to understand and use).

I am careful to not provide examples of programs earlier in the process, because at this point, students are engaged in a constructive investigation whereby they analyze, evaluate, and create their own program and develop professional judgment. By having students select their own specific athlete and the components of the program over time, I also reduce copying and plagiarism. By providing a few examples, especially those from former students, I'm telling the current students that they are capable of excellent work and show the breadth of thought in the field.

Within each of these sequential activities, I follow a similar process – draft of a simple task, feedback from peers and instructor, whole course discussion, questions to promote reflection and metacognition (learning by their own thoughts and learning), and editing the draft toward a final product.

Developing a PBL toolbox for tune-ups

A few instructional tools we have used to support PBL are designed to promote reflection, collaboration, and holism by creating projects. Not all the tools need to be used, and coach developers can glean and transfer these tools to their own contexts.

Building a community of constructive peer reviewers

As students in our master's degree program, and because they constantly interact online and provide feedback to one another, I want to develop a strong sense of community. Because my students coach different sports, and some have S&C backgrounds, I leverage this by alternating peer reviewers and using group discussions. I will have students introduce themselves in a week one discussion board and provide them with suggestions on how to complete a peer review. To evaluate their peers' work, I require students to provide their qualitative feedback and complete a rubric I provide (presented in the next section), which sensitizes all students to think about how their own program meets the identified criteria.

Research requirement

I provide students with a mini-lesson on how to use the library database, because I require research integrated into their projects. Some students will have already completed a graduate research course, while others have not. Again, I partner students to complement their strengths and weaknesses.

Addressing S&C gaps

Many students often omit athletic testing, or a test battery, from early drafts of their projects. By implementing some sort of mini-lesson on testing, students consider why, what, and how to test. This activity can also be linked to the research component by discussing how researchers quantify and measure variables, and how that likely influences program design (e.g. the standardization and quantification required of experimental designs likely affects how scientist-coaches design S&C programs).

Especially if they were *not* an athlete, never had an S&C coach, nor regularly engaged in a structured S&C program, having students go to the gym and perform their own designed microcycles can promote learning. Some students are quick to write grueling workouts without understanding how training volume matters. For example, I have witnessed several occasions when students draft programs for novice to intermediate athletes containing 8–12 leg exercises of four to six sets each with a load between 60–80 percent. If this doesn't strike you as too much, we leave it to the reader to head to the gym for some experiential learning!

While S&C program design is heavily influenced by physiology and biomechanics, integrating the physical sciences with social and behavioral sciences promotes a greater awareness of actual coaching practice. For example, reminding students about how injury can cause athletes to suffer poor mental health or how too much stress causes illness can be a powerful reminder and motivator to students to learn how to prevent injuries and how program design (e.g. work to rest, athlete autonomy, engagement of injured athletes) and implementation affects athletes holistically. Sometimes students think S&C is just writing reps and sets on paper, and they forget that as a coach they will be influencing real lives.

Step three: create and perform assessments

Evaluating a graduate-level S&C project

We close out our framework with step three: Create and perform the assessments. We think it useful to do step one and three together, even if just sketching out assessments early without finalizing them. The reader can glance back at the objectives presented earlier to check how those verbs (e.g. design, identify) will be assessed by the following rubrics. Without this alignment and clarity, it's likely that coach developers will send mixed messages to students, resulting in poorer projects. Once the coach developer decides the elements, criteria, and scale for assessment, they can go back to their course description and objectives to determine if there is proper alignment.

Assessment should show how well students solved or addressed the driving question and engaged in constructive inquiry. Because the driving challenge in this course was designing and justifying an S&C program, I decided that the final project would consist of an S&C program manual and would be assessed by a corresponding rubric (Table 5.1) and a sport coaching clinic-like presentation and its corresponding rubric (Table 5.2).

Formative and summative assessment are essential as they affect student learning and ultimately the final course grade. One particularly effective type of formative assessment is to have students submit drafts of components of a project for peer review and instructor feedback. I use parts of the final rubric (i.e. Table 5.1) early in the course, and I have students use this to peer review each other's work, which provides them with detailed and clear expectations of how quality can range on a project. However, for their initial draft submissions, students do not earn points based on the final rubric, but on whether they've submitted the assignment on time, with good-faith effort, and addressed most of the required elements. My intent is to promote iterative inquiry, dialogue, and clarity on high standards without the excessive focus on "earning points" or "passing the course".

Students also learn to articulate strong rationales for their decision-making, which helps them on the final presentation. Because sport coaches justify their training practices at clinics, to employers, or to parents and administrators, they need to learn how to present a strong and convincing argument. An early and weak rationale might be, "That's the way we did it when I was an athlete", "I took the example from the book and used that", or "I saw it on a popular website". Stronger rationales reflect sophisticated reasoning, empirical support, and the integration of multiple and often competing demands such as, "Research shows that athletes at this position tend to possess more muscle mass, and based on several studies, we are more likely to develop this mass through multiple sets of multi-joint exercises of a moderate to heavy load", or "This athlete plays multiple sports and doesn't have much time to train with me. So, I decided that when they're with me they will perform highly technical exercises to learn proper technique".

In our online learning management system (e.g. Canvas), I can enter written feedback and a video of me providing verbal feedback. Students are also required to view each other's manuals and presentations, and to post their feedback, questions, and replies to each other via the online discussion board.

One additional assessment I use often (e.g. usually weekly) is a metacognitive assignment called a "wrapper". My wrappers are typically three to five questions that tap into each student's unique thought process including struggles and successes of learning, comprehension of course concepts, and what they need from me to facilitate their learning. Students often reply with a few sentences per question, and they're awarded effort points for completion. By collecting this information, I promote the students' reflection, know where I need to spend my time to support their learning, and often ward off problems before it's too late to

TABLE 5.1 Strength and conditioning program manual rubric

Elements	Criteria		
Usable and professional	S&C manual is professional looking, usable, and contains proper standard English grammar.	S&C manual is mostly professional looking, mostly usable, or contains few standard English grammar errors.	S&C manual is mostly unprofessional looking, mostly unusable, or contains several standard English grammar errors.
Scale	8–10 points	4–7 points	0–3 points
Athlete profile	Athlete profile is presented and contains all essential components.	Athlete profile is vague or missing a few components.	Athlete profile is unclear or missing several components.
Scale	9–10 points	6–7 points	0–5 points
Needs analysis	Thorough and detailed explanation of athlete and sport physiological, biomechanical, and injury analysis.	Mostly thorough and detailed explanation of athlete and sport physiological, biomechanical, and injury analysis.	Partial or superficial explanation of athlete and sport physiological, biomechanical, and injury analysis.
Scale	9–10 points	7–8 points	0–6 points
Macro- and meso-cycles	Annual plan is fully completed and accurate, per sport schedule and governing body rules. Training volume matches the respective mesocycle's goals. Development is informed by strong research and reasoning. Use of time is sensible and equitable to meet goals.	Annual plan is fully completed and mostly accurate, per sport schedule and governing body rules. Training volume closely matches the respective mesocycle's goals. Development is informed by some research and reasoning. Use of time is mostly sensible and equitable to meet goals.	Annual plan is partially completed or somewhat accurate, per sport schedule and governing body rules. Training volume somewhat matches the respective mesocycle's goals. Development is informed by weak research and reasoning. Use of time is somewhat sensible and equitable to meet goals.
Scale	27–30 points	21–26 points	0–20 points
Microcycles	All components of training are included, richly described, and highly likely to achieve stated goals.	Most components of training are included, described, and likely to achieve stated goals.	Some components of training are included, described, and unlikely to achieve stated goals.
Scale	27–30 points	21–26 points	0–20 points
Exercise selection and progression	Exercise selection and progression is highly likely to achieve stated goals.	Exercise selection and progression is likely to achieve stated goals.	Exercise selection and progression is unlikely to achieve stated goals.
Scale	9–10 points	7–8 points	0–6 points

TABLE 5.2 Clinic presentation rubric

Elements	Criteria		
Verbal delivery, flow, and enthusiasm	Coach introduced him/herself, provided a good attention getter, appeared or sounded genuinely energetic throughout, and provided a formal conclusion, including a question-and-answer opportunity.	Coach omitted one or two of the following: Introduction of him/herself, a good attention getter, appeared or sounded genuinely energetic throughout, and provided a formal conclusion, including a question-and-answer opportunity.	Coach omitted two or more of the following: Introduction of him/herself, a good attention getter, appeared or sounded genuinely energetic throughout, and provided a formal conclusion, including a question-and-answer opportunity.
Scale	8–10 points	4–7 points	0–3 points
Use of instructional aids	Instructional aids (e.g. slides, content description and image), font size and style, and quality and quantity of information facilitated learning and enhanced presentation.	Instructional aids (e.g. slides, content description and image), font size and style, and quality and quantity of information mostly facilitated learning and enhanced presentation.	Instructional aids (e.g. slides, content description and image), font size and style, and quality and quantity of information somewhat facilitated learning and enhanced presentation.
Scale	13–15 points	9–12 points	0–8 points
Use of time	Use of time fell within allotment and was allocated effectively to present vital information.	Use of time fell within allotment and was mostly allocated effectively to present mostly vital information.	Use of time fell outside allotment or was somewhat allocated effectively to present somewhat vital information.
Scale	9–10 points	6–8 points	0–5 points

Explanation	Explanation of S&C program was richly described and based on thorough review of research and astute practical observations; justification for program components was provided, as well as why other methods were not selected.	Explanation of S&C program was described and based on mostly thorough review of research and practical observations; justification for program components was mostly provided, as well as why other methods were not selected.	Explanation of S&C program was omitted or may have been described based on some or haphazard selection of research or limited practical observations; justification for program components was omitted or somewhat provided, as well as why other methods were not selected.
Scale	27–30 points	21–26 points	0–20 points
*Appearance and delivery	Clothing and appearance was professional and non-verbals facilitated understanding.	Clothing and appearance was somewhat sloppy or unprofessional, or non-verbals were somewhat distracting or failed to facilitate understanding.	Clothing and appearance was sloppy or unprofessional, and non-verbals were distracting or failed to facilitate understanding.
Scale	4–5 points	1–3 points	0 points

*If the presentation is in person or the presenter appears in a video (often in an online course), then this element could be assessed.

intervene. In total, these forms of assessment show students' growth over time and provide a map for their professional development.

Personal reflections and wishful thinking

I wish we could have athletes to implement our students' projects. Designing and implementing S&C programs with current athletes would add realism to PBL. Nurses work with mannequins, then real patients, while teachers teach real students, and the trade fields are rife with learning in action (e.g. learning how to change a tire by changing a tire). Unfortunately, getting access to current athletes and "experimenting" on them with students' projects is nearly impossible. In addition to protecting the health and safety of athletes, many clubs, schools, or organizations are not welcoming to the idea of novice student-coaches tinkering with their athletes.

Activities for coach education

1 Consider coaches you're working with and what problems they're likely to experience. Can you identify a driving question whereby using PBL would be a good fit as an instructional strategy?
2 Facilitate small-group (three to four people) discussions with coach developers about their experiences designing and implementing PBL.

   a Was the project defined and implemented as a lifelike challenge?
   b Was support, feedback, and learning materials provided along the way to help complete the project?

3 Communicate with like-minded practitioners to gain insight on how others have used PBL and share ideas. For example, at the University of Denver's free, open access listserv devoted to coach education: https://listserv.du.edu/mailman/listinfo/coach-educator

Additional resources

1 The Buck Institute for Education (BIE) hosts an informative website solely devoted to using PBL: www.bie.org
2 Purdue University publishes an academic journal titled: *The Interdisciplinary Journal of Problem-Based Learning* (IJPBL) at: http://docs.lib.purdue.edu/ijpbl/ − although the journal focuses on *problem-based* learning, there are many papers on *project-based.*

Bibliography

Bereiter, C. and Scardamalia, M. (1993) *Surpassing Ourselves: An Inquiry into the Nature and Implications of Expertise*, Chicago: Open Court.

Kokotsaki, D., Menzies, V. and Wiggins, A. (2016) 'Project-Based Learning: A review of the literature', *Improving Schools*, 19: 267–77.

Markham, T., Larmer, J. and Ravitz, J. (2003) *Project Based Learning Handbook: A Guide to Standards-Focused Project Based Learning for Middle and High School Teachers*, Novato: Buck Institute for Education.

Tamim, S.R. and Grant, M.M. (2013) 'Definitions and uses: Case study of teachers implementing Project-Based Learning', *Interdisciplinary Journal of Problem-Based Learning*, 7: 72–101.

Thomas, J.W. (2000) 'A review of research on Project-Based Learning', *The Autodesk Foundation*. Online. Available HTTP: <www.bie.org/images/uploads/general/9d067 58fd346969cb63653d00dca55c0.pdf> (accessed 14 June 2018).

6

REFLECTIVE PRACTICE TO ENHANCE COACH DEVELOPMENT AND PRACTICE

Clayton R. Kuklick and Michael Kasales

Chapter objectives

By the end of this chapter, the reader will be able to:

1 Explain the core concepts of reflective practice (RP) as they relate to experiential learning in graduate studies in sport coaching.
2 Describe various instructional strategies for coaches that utilize RP to facilitate reflection on experiences.
3 Identify enablers and barriers to effective RP implementation in graduate-level courses.

Brief chapter overview

In this chapter, we offer a "learning through experience" framework that explains how coaches use reflective practice to deepen their knowledge, so that coach developers can better understand how to construct meaningful learning experiences in graduate-level courses. We draw upon Schön's work on reflective practice (1983) to show how coaches learn by reflecting on their experiences in an experiential learning process, how RP can be used to facilitate deep reflection and learning, and how to use RP to create instructional strategies in two different graduate-level contexts.

Why and when I use RP and experiential learning

Clayton has done much work with applying RP as an instructional strategy in a variety of university-based courses in the Master of Arts in Sport Coaching program at the University of Denver (DU). Michael has researched and applied Kolb's (2015) work on experiential learning to practicum courses in the same program. We both have experiences facilitating ten-week online graduate-level core courses and practicums in the sport coaching program. In these courses, tasks and assignments are designed to facilitate learning by reflecting on experiences linked to theoretical, scientific, and ethical aspects of coaching for the purposes of enhancing student-coaches' reflective abilities, knowledge, skills, and attitudes toward effective coaching. Higher education coach development curricula often present quality knowledge in the sports sciences, psychological, sociological, and technical and tactical aspects of sport, which are drawn from the research on what knowledge is needed to be an effective sports coach (Cassidy, Jones & Potrac 2004). Yet, coaches often cite formal coach education curricula as a having a low-level impact on their coaching practices, which suggests a disconnect between how the content is presented in courses and how coaches apply knowledge (Abraham & Collins 1998; Irwin, Hanton & Kerwin 2004). In comparison, coaches often cite acquiring knowledge through reflection on experiences as being more applicable and meaningful to their coaching (Irwin, Hanton & Kerwin 2004; Nash & Sproule 2012; Wright, Trudel & Culver 2007). In essence, the mere presentation of knowledge is not enough to create meaningful learning experiences that deepen and broaden coaches' knowledge. So, as coach developers, we create instructional strategies that leverage reflection on real-world experiences to bring meaning and application to knowledge, theories, and literature presented in the courses. In the following sections, we highlight the main concepts of RP and offer descriptive insights for creating RP instructional strategies.

The essentials of reflective practice

Definitions, essential components, and goals of RP

Reflective practice, theorized by Schön (1983, 1987), is an experiential learning theory that explains how practitioners learn through their experiences in professional practice. Schön explains how the process of reflecting on experiences builds upon and deepens practitioners' current knowledge and critical thinking abilities. Schön theorized that meaningful and deep learning occurs by engaging in a reflective cycle that begins with identifying a problem and then actively generating and experimenting with strategies to overcome the problem. Of critical importance to Schön's work is that deeper levels of meaning, learning, and thinking are encountered when practitioners reflect on problems that are experienced in highly contextualized and personalized scenarios that they are directly involved in. The main concepts of RP include role frames and reflective conversations.

Role frames

A role frame (RF) is described as a coach's lens in which they view and interpret coaching. Mainly, RFs are grounded by a coach's previous experiences, the current knowledge they possess, their education, and other influencers that guide their interpretation and attention to certain things that happen in their coaching. For example, a coach may tend to focus on tactical aspects of their sport, developing relationships, discipline, or winning (Gilbert & Trudel 2001; Kuklick, Gearity & Thompson 2015). The main focal points of a coach's RF will typically dictate the subtle problems that they experience; or in contrast, their RF may cause them to miss or not consider certain situations as a problem, which results in squandered learning opportunities.

Reflective conversations

Reflective conversation (RC) is described as the reflective cycle that creates meaningful learning experiences whereby knowledge is constructed and built upon. The RC begins with *appreciation*, which means that the coach sets a problem determined by their RF. Once the coach appreciates the problem, they will engage *action*, which is when strategies are generated with the intent to overcome the problem. These strategies may be generated by engaging in critical thinking; collaborating with other coaches; using books, research, or previously used strategies developed in the past; or drawing upon new perspectives and theories (Gallimore, Gilbert & Nater 2014; Gilbert, Gilbert & Trudel 2001; Gilbert & Trudel 2001; Irwin, Hanton & Kerwin 2004). Action also includes the process of experimenting with a strategy in an attempt to overcome the problem. From here, a coach may perceive that their strategy worked or didn't work based on their RF. If the strategy is perceived as not being effective, the coach *re-appreciates* the same problem, and therefore experiments with something new and then re-evaluates the outcome again. Or, as a result of the experimentation, the coach may also appreciate another subtle problem that needs solving. However, when a satisfactory outcome is perceived, the RC is concluded. Engaging in multiple cycles of a RC often creates greater learning experiences in comparison to single loop cycles whereby a satisfactory outcome is perceived on the first try (Schön 1983; Gilbert & Trudel 2001; Kuklick, Gearity & Thompson 2015).

Thus far, we've been writing about experiential learning, in which reflection plays a key role. Therefore, it is worthwhile to briefly discuss Kolb's (2015) work regarding experiential learning to help us reinforce and clarify what we really mean by learning through experience by way of reflection. Kolb thought that learning is fundamentally about discovery through direct contact in order for the experience to be meaningful. In other words, experiential learning is learning by doing, as opposed to learning from instruction and lecture, or merely thinking through the reflective cycle rather than actively doing it. In relation to RP, Kolb's theorizing helps to understand how deeper levels of knowledge and meaning are generated from actively doing and putting the reflective cycle to work, rather than thinking through the RP process. Of critical importance for coach developers is to create RP instructional strategies that seek to get student-coaches to actively do, try out, and experiment with their reflections in their immediate coaching contexts. In the following sections, we provide practical examples of how to create instructional strategies informed by RP in our graduate-level core and practicum courses.

Instructional strategies to facilitate reflection in core courses

Typically, graduate student-coaches are actively coaching while they are learning theoretical concepts in graduate courses. In this section, we provide a step-by-step process for how to embed RP into a practical application assignment (PAA) in order to help student-coaches connect the content from a core course (i.e. motor learning and pedagogy) to application by way of reflection. The PAA could be used multiple times in a course, or broken down into components whereby one part of the PAA is built upon each week throughout the course.

Step one: using content and case studies to expand role frames

The PAA is dependent on some sort of content being delivered. A motor learning course contains various content areas including understanding how athletes interpret stimuli to produce movement responses, evaluating learning vs. performance, pedagogical models, different feedback approaches, practice structures to enhance learning, etc. Typically, a content area is presented each week, along with case studies that show how the content applies in relation to identifying or solving coaching problems. For example, a hypothetical case may be presented of a coach experiencing a problem related to an athlete learning to read and react to a certain situation and how they used their knowledge of motor learning to solve the problem. The content and case study examples are a prelude to the PAA, which guides student-coaches' RFs toward attending to this content in their coaching experiences.

Step two: facilitating the problem setting

After content has been delivered, the PAA begins with two approaches that can be used to set a problem. One option is to start with a question that prompts the student-coaches to reflect upon a coaching problem (i.e. appreciation) in relation to a content area (e.g. feedback) in their coaching. If coaches are in a "down period" or off-season when they are not actively coaching, we provide them with the caveat that they can identify a problem in their past or future coaching experiences. A second approach we often use to set the problem is by tasking the student-coaches to do a self-reconnaissance, whereby they take a three-minute video of themselves coaching so that they can review how their feedback approach, as it would be in motor learning, influences athletes. This approach might read, "Student-coaches should provide a three-minute video of themselves conducting a coaching session with athlete(s). Student-coaches should review the video and identify a problem in relation to [content area, e.g. feedback]". When taking a video of a coaching session might not be applicable to the content, snapshot pictures or audio recordings could be used instead.

Step three: setting the stage for articulating the problem

Once problems have been identified, the student-coaches need to reflect on what strategies may enable them to overcome their problems (i.e. action). The caveat for coach developers here is that it's imperative that student-coaches engage in the praxis (i.e. the application of theory into practice) of coaching by understanding what their problems are and why they are considered problems (i.e. theory); otherwise, they will not be able to generate appropriate ideas and strategies to solve them (i.e. practice). Thus, student-coaches must be prompted to explain the variables or roots of their problems. Some student-coaches struggle with this, and therefore may need to acquire more information about their problems. Coach developers are encouraged to help student-coaches by providing or directing coaches with resources. This part of the assignment might read:

> Now that a problem has been identified, articulate the different variables of the problem by listing out four bullet points explaining why this is considered a problem. Note: If you are short on listing out four bullets, a deeper understanding of the problem may be needed. You can resort back to the content from the course; look in the library for research, books, or theories that you think are relevant; discuss the problem with another coach; ask athletes; or look to the resources provided in the syllabi.

Now that student-coaches understand how and why their problems are considered problems in the first place, we turn to schemes to solve them.

Step four: facilitating three schemes to solve problems

In this step of the PAA, the goal is to facilitate multiple ways in which a problem can be solved (i.e. action). This can be a challenge – in our experience, student-coaches' RCs are stopped sometimes because they do not engage in reflection on a multitude of possible strategies. This may occur because student-coaches have limited knowledge in the areas needed to solve their problems.

If student-coaches think of one strategy off the top of their head that does not work after experimentation, they may quit trying to solve their problems thereafter. So, we note that it is important for coach developers to task student-coaches to construct at least three ways or schemes to solve their problems. If they can't initially think of at least three schemes to overcome a problem, they are then reverted to obtaining more ideas by resorting back to the content or other related resources provided by coach developers, or by spinning off one of their initial ideas to create a new strategy.

Step five: constructing the decision-making task

Once multiple strategies have been generated, student-coaches might be caught in deciding which strategies to implement (i.e. action). For this part of the assignment, student-coaches are tasked with completing DECMATs or decision-making matrices (see Figure 6.1) to help identify which strategies would best overcome their problems by filling in relative values for the importance of different factors to consider. We have found through experience that this part of the PAA works best when student-coaches are provided with a template spreadsheet

---

DECMAT

Directions: A DECMAT is a way to help make the best decision on which strategy to implement to solve a coaching problem. Complete the following steps to determine which strategy would be best to use to solve a problem. The scores will automatically generate.

1. List strategies in the gray column. Please do not prioritize your strategies.

2. List important factors in the factors row; add or remove columns, where appropriate. Please do not prioritize your factors.

3. Assign relative values to each factor in the relative values row (e.g. a 4 would be twice as important as a 2).

4. Assign objective 0–100 scores for how the strategy fulfills each factor (i.e. a 100 means a guarantee or extreme level of confidence, and a 0 means a very poor or low level of confidence). Assigns scores for each factor and each strategy.

5. Strategies with the higest scores in the far right column should be considered.

Relative Values	3	1	5	2	11
	27%	9%	45%	18%	100%
Factors	Factor: Athletes' performance	Factor: Equipment needed	Factor: Influence on relationships	Factor: Time spent	Score
Strategies					
Strategy	50	80	30	50	44
Strategy	40	35	30	100	46
Strategy	25	1	80	50	52
Strategy	60	100	50	1	48
Comments:					

FIGURE 6.1 DECMAT

80 Kuklick and Kasales

with formulas that automatically calculate the importance of the relative values for each factor and strategy. Examples for how to create DECMAT templates are provided in the additional resources section at the end of the chapter.

Step six: planning an evaluation strategy

Sometimes student-coaches may feel uncertain that problems are solved, or if they aren't solved, they may not be sure what went wrong, which can limit student-coaches from engaging a second loop of an RC. As part of the PAA, student-coaches develop plans for evaluating if each strategy worked or didn't work. That is, they need to develop what (e.g. looking at technique errors, communication, reaction times, scores, stops), how (e.g. observation rubrics, quantitative numbers, video, surveys), and when (e.g. immediately, two weeks, after practice, during practice, outside of practice) they are going to evaluate their implemented strategies. Ideally, it would be great for student-coaches to develop their own evaluation plans, however, it's useful for coach developers to provide some examples and resources that could be modified to meet student-coaches' needs.

Step seven: prep for action

Finally, coach developers should consider when and how they want student-coaches to directly implement their strategies for overcoming problems. Student-coaches will have different problems that take different amounts of time to solve, and in most graduate courses, coach developers are moving on to new content areas in the next week. As mentioned previously, student-coaches can get halted in their reflective cycle, which impedes meaningful learning. To overcome the issue, we use a problem-solving tracking chart that seeks to keep the reflective cycle flowing. The chart is filled out by student-coaches, which keeps track of problems that are in progress, have been solved, or are in a second round of RC throughout the course. Additionally, student-coaches take notes and monitor their progress of overcoming their issues. Typically, this part of the PAA is submitted at any time in the course after student-coaches have implemented their strategies and evaluation plans, or at the end of the course as a collection of PAAs to allow time for problems to be solved. We use a reflective practice rubric that evaluates the process of reflection rather than the outcome, which helps provide feedback to coaching students who might be merely evaluating their strategies as successful without being immersed in the reflective processes.

Instructional strategies to facilitate reflection in practicum courses

We now transition into showing how assignments and tasks in a practicum course can be informed by RP in a variety of different aspects of coaching. In the components listed in the following sections, we provide descriptions of the practicum course's assignments and tasks associated with RP. These assignments and tasks are a bit different from core courses, because in practicum, the problems that student-coaches reflect upon are wide open and based in their coaching experiences rather than being guided by a specific content area. As such, student-coaches reflect on problems associated with administrative duties, athletes' performance and learning of techniques and tactics, disciplining athletes, interactions with coaches or parents, and team cohesion, among others. In the following sections, we describe six main RP components of the practicum course.

Component one: active coaching

The practicum course's foundation is based on the idea that student-coaches need to be actively engaged in coaching in order to participate in learning through experience, which provides a foundation for subsequent reflective activities. Student-coaches are required to complete a minimum of five hours per week of hands-on coaching at approved practicum sites; however, many complete well over the requirement. This requirement provides student-coaches with real-world experiences working with athletes, other coaches, or administrators from which the course is designed to facilitate the active experimentation of strategies generated from reflecting on encountered problems. While coaching, student-coaches are accountable for adhering to the roles and responsibilities determined by their site leads. As coach developers, we typically do not provide any site-specific responsibilities or roles in which student-coaches must engage in an attempt to mitigate any conflict with site leads.

Component two: the reflective autobiography

Reflective autobiographical writing is one of the first assignments that student-coaches in our practicum course complete. Student-coaches are provided an autobiography worksheet which captures their experiences across various stages of their life (i.e. childhood, early adolescence, late adolescence, early adulthood, and mid-adulthood), four different social influences (i.e. family, school, athletic, and life in general), and their current coaching values. In this assignment, student-coaches describe their life experiences, how these social forces affect how and why they coach, and their guiding principles that inform their coaching practices, or, in other words, their RFs. The intention is to bring awareness to how student-coaches' previous experiences inform their current coaching practices and the problems that they may or may not look to solve. To facilitate this awareness, student-coaches are prompted to reflect upon their autobiography by discussing the limitations and strengths of their knowledge generated from their previous experiences and how these experiences focus their attention to certain problems, while missing others, which is done through an online discussion board. Additionally, other student-coaches are assigned the coach's autobiography worksheet to review and provide alternative perspectives, with the intent to

82 Kuklick and Kasales

show how they may look to solve certain problems and not others. For example, student-coaches who are focused on how athletes respond to their very detailed and strict instructions might realize that this focus is generated from how they were once coached, and therefore may miss problems to learn from outside of this aspect of coaching. Without such realizations, problems that could initiate RCs might not be realized because student-coaches' current RFs are restricted to identifying problems and generating strategies based on the previous ways they were coached. As a developmental tool, at different points in the course (i.e. middle and end) student-coaches are prompted in discussion boards to revisit their values and RFs in relation to their autobiographies to see if they remain consistent or have changed as new knowledge is created in the remaining nine weeks of reflective activities.

Component three: reflective storytelling assignments

The reflective storytelling assignments involve student-coaches identifying coaching problems, understanding those coaching problems, and developing ways to resolve them at their respective practicum sites. There are five different reflective storytelling assignments conducted throughout the course, which are based on pre-formatted worksheets that contain prompts designed to progress student-coaches through RCs. Table 6.1 contains each assignment's descriptions and the prompts for their associated worksheets. The worksheets are used to provide some structure to follow whereby each assignment and its respective worksheet builds on the previous by progressively scaffolding the steps of a RC for student-coaches to draw upon. Additionally, the assignments' consistent structure reduces coach developers' burden with viewing and interpreting multiple formats, which allows for more time and effort to be spent providing meaningful feedback to student-coaches. For each assignment, student-coaches complete their worksheets and submit their stories into the discussion board for all students to view. An additional set of prompts are provided to facilitate student-reviewers' feedback in the discussion board, which cue them to evaluate the logic of the responses on the worksheet, describe their own perspectives on the problems, critique the theories that help explain problems, and offer other strategies that could help resolve them. In these ways, the feedback from student-reviewers serves as a way of facilitating RCs by collaborating and generating ideas to solve problems realized at practicum sites. Student-coaches are instructed to work through the same problem for each of the worksheets until the problem is solved, to ensure they comprehend the components involved with reflecting on complex experiences.

Component four: readings and discussion boards for facilitating reflection

Each week, student-coaches read a variety of coaching-related scholarly articles to broaden their understandings of coaching. These readings do not address

TABLE 6.1 Reflective storytelling assignment examples

Assignment	Purpose	Directions	Worksheet
RP storytelling assignment 1	To initiate student-coaches' RCs by identifying coaching problems in their coaching experiences, and to gain better understandings for student-coaches' problems and RFs by rationalizing the connection between their problems and their previous experiences detailed in their autobiographies.	Using worksheet 1, complete the following prompts to tell a story about a coaching experience. Post your story in the discussion board.	Worksheet 1 prompts: 1 Provide a concise summary of a current coaching problem. 2 Explain why this is the problem important to you. 3 Provide the first-person story of how the problem occurred (i.e. explain what, who, when, where, to explain the conflict in action). 4 Explain what the outcome would look like when the problem is resolved. 5 Using the autobiography, speculate why you are challenged by the problem.
RP storytelling assignment 2	To tap deeper into RCs by prompting student-coaches to identify an existing theory or to construct a personal theory of human behavior to help explain why their current coaching practices did not produce the intended outcome, thus resulting in a problem.	Using worksheet 2, complete the following prompts to tell a story about a coaching experience. You may use the same problem from the previous worksheet or use a new problem. Post your story in the discussion board.	Worksheet 2 prompts: 1 Provide a concise summary of a current coaching problem. 2 Explain why the problem is important to you. 3 Provide the first-person story of how the problem occurred (i.e. explain what, who, when, where, to explain the conflict in action). 4 Identify an existing theory or construct a personal theory of human behavior to help explain the problem. 5 Describe two or three strategies that could be used to overcome the problem related to the theory described in prompt 4, and the affects suspected to be achieved.
RP storytelling assignment 3	To help student-coaches see their coaching problems from a new view or perspective than initially realized, which in turn will help with the strategy generation processes in student-coaches' RCs.	Using worksheet 2, copy and paste your responses for items 1–3 from last week. For items 4 and 5, develop new ways of looking at your problem. Post your story in the discussion board.	See worksheet 2 prompts in this column.

(*Continued*)

TABLE 6.1 (Continued)

Assignment	Purpose	Directions	Worksheet
RP storytelling assignment 4	To facilitate RCs by prompting student-coaches to implement strategies and to describe the changes that have occurred in their stories.	Using worksheet 3, complete the following prompts to tell a story about a coaching experience.	Worksheet 3 prompts: 1 Provide a concise summary of a current coaching problem. 2 Explain why the problem is important to you. 3 Provide the first-person story of how the problem occurred (i.e. explain what, who, when, where, to explain the conflict in action). 4 Identify an existing theory or construct a personal theory of human behavior to help explain the problem. 5 Describe two or three strategies that could be used to overcome the problem related to the theory described in prompt 4, and the affects suspected to be achieved. 6 Implement one of the strategies and describe the changes in the story as a result of implementing the strategy. 7 Evaluate the strategy with evidence to support the claim that the problem has been solved or unsolved, and provide a future course of action.
EL storytelling assignment 5	To provide student-coaches with opportunities for unsolved problems to be revisited using new views to understand and resolve problems, or to facilitate new learning experiences by engaging new RCs if the previous problems have been solved.	If your problem from your last assignment has been solved, use worksheet 3 to explain a new coaching problem based on your current experiences. If your problem was unresolved from last week, use worksheet 3 and copy and paste your responses for items 1–3 from last week. For items 4–7, develop new ways of looking at your problem and potential solutions. Post your story in the discussion board.	See worksheet 3 prompts in this column.

technical or tactical coaching subjects, but serve to inform student-coaches on various psychological and sociological concepts, different coaching methodologies, and some intrapersonal and interpersonal attributes required of coaches. Such readings might encompass the case study research of John Wooden (Gallimore & Tharp 2004), Pat Summit (Becker & Wrisberg 2008) and Phillip Fulmer (Gearity, Callary & Fulmer 2013). After student-coaches complete the readings, they answer several prompts in a discussion board that aim to connect the reading's content toward how it can help with identifying new problems and develop new strategies that might otherwise go unrealized. It is critical that coach developers create prompts that are specific to the readings and are relevant to student-coaches' experiences, while keeping RP concepts in mind. To do so, we start with the key theoretical components and takeaways from the reading, and then create a series of prompts that focus student-coaches on each of the RC components. Such prompts might include describing how a key insight from the reading influences student-coaches' views of current coaching situations, what new knowledge was created from the article, what problems they now realize in their immediate coaching from the reading, what the author or studied coach would say regarding current coaching problems, and what new strategies can be generated from the reading that can be used to solve problems.

Component five: mentor-coaches

Each week, student-coaches are asked to meet with an assigned mentor-coach. We recruit mentor-coaches based on their years of experience, level of education, area of expertise, and willingness. Mentor-coaches are provided expectations for their role, which includes being asked not to "teach" course content, but rather facilitate RCs by providing perspectives on student-coaches' experiences and identified problems, and by collaborating on strategies to solve them. Student-coaches, on the other hand, are instructed to not discuss specific coursework, but rather direct the meetings based on their current coaching experiences and identified problems. We added these expectations due to student-coaches asking for help understanding course content, rather than using the mentor-coaches to facilitate RCs. While student-coaches are asked to submit brief synopses of what problems and strategies they discuss, in many cases as coach developers, we don't know the specific components of the meetings. However, the mentor-coaches' instructions, at the very least, are implemented to facilitate a better understanding of coaching experiences, explore new ways of looking at coaching problems, or collaborate on ideas to better implement strategies to solve problems. In the feedback we have received, student-coaches often cite their most influential learning experiences in the practicum course being produced from their interactions with mentor-coaches that facilitate reflection.

86 Kuklick and Kasales

Component six: reflective journaling

After each academic week, student-coaches prepare and submit reflective journals. The reflective journal is comprised of two parts. Part one includes student-coaches detailing their total number of hours spent in games, practices, preparation, meetings, and professional development, and their perceived effects of specific coaching activities. The aim of part one is to facilitate reflection by recording information about their completed coaching experiences where problems may occur. Sometimes, vague entries such as "this was a busy week" or "I felt like I did really well this week" are provided, and, in our estimation, are not sufficiently detailed to describe experiences encountered during the week. So, feedback and examples should be provided by the coach developer to ensure detail. The second component of the reflective journal is where student-coaches answer questions directed toward bringing awareness to what they have learned from engaging in reflection on their past week's coaching experiences. Such questions might include: What have I learned? How have I learned? How do I feel about what I have learned? How could I have learned more? What actions can I take to learn more in the future? The reflective journal is turned in as a discreet assignment, is not reviewed by fellow student-coaches, and only the coach developer provides feedback to student-coaches, which allows the reflective journal to contain personal thoughts they may be unwilling to share with the entire class (e.g. ethical conflicts, specific athlete concerns). At a minimum, the reflective journaling assignment helps student-coaches recognize ongoing learning opportunities generated from the other weekly assignments that were informed by Schön's RP (1983, 1987).

Personal reflections and wishful thinking

The reality is that student-coaches have different previous and current experiences, which interact with the depth and breadth of knowledge created from reflection. After getting to know many student-coaches in our courses, we wish we could place them in specific coaching scenarios that we know would offer new learning experiences. Those particular contexts would pose different problems that are in conflict with their previous or current experiences and provide a great reflective learning opportunity. While we do use role play to stage certain scenarios where problems are exposed, in the future we could utilize virtual reality to provide lifelike scenarios that might initiate reflection on problems that coaches normally would not experience.

Activities for coach education

1   Develop a reading and discussion post assignment that aims to engage coaches in RP. Provide a description of the reading and explain the purpose, directions, and prompts.

Reflective practice for coaches **87**

2   Take an instructional strategy described in this chapter and apply it to a coach development context outside of a graduate-level coach development course. Explain how the instructional strategy would be implemented in the new context, and the differences between approaches.

3   Search and explore an educational research study that has used RP to facilitate learning. Critique the approach and provide an example of how the approach would be used as an instructional strategy in a graduate-level sport coaching course.

Additional resources

1   *The Quality Toolbox* by Nancy Tague (2005) contains a variety of tools for generating ideas, determining root causes of problems, and decision-making that can be used in relation to RP and experiential learning. An additional resource specific to creating decision-making matrices (i.e. DECMATs) can be found at: http://asq.org/learn-about-quality/decision-making-tools/overview/decision-matrix.html

2   *The Theory of Experiential Education* by Karen Warren (1995) offers a collection of articles and experiential learning theoretical tools that can be used by coach developers to assist in constructing experiential learning curricula.

Bibliography

Abraham, A. and Collins, D. (1998) 'Examining and extending research in coach development', *Quest*, 50: 59–79.

Becker, A.J. and Wrisberg, C.A. (2008) 'Effective coaching in action: Observations of legendary collegiate basketball coach Pat Summitt', *The Sport Psychologist*, 22: 197–211.

Cassidy, T., Jones, R. and Potrac, P. (2004) *Understanding Sports Coaching: The Social, Cultural and Pedagogical Foundations of Coaching Practice*, London: Routledge.

Gallimore, R., Gilbert, W. and Nater, S. (2014) 'Reflective practice and ongoing learning: A coach's 10-year journey', *Reflective Practice*, 15: 268–88.

Gallimore, R. and Tharp, R. (2004) 'What a coach can teach a teacher, 1975–2004: Reflections and reanalysis of John Wooden's teaching practices', *The Sport Psychologist*, 18: 119–37.

Gearity, B.T., Callary, B. and Fulmer, P. (2013) 'Learning to coach: A qualitative case study of Phillip Fulmer', *Journal of Coaching Education*, 6: 65–86.

Gilbert, W.D., Gilbert, J.N. and Trudel, P. (2001) 'Coaching strategies for youth sport: Part 1: Athlete behavior and athlete performance', *The Journal of Physical Education, Recreation & Dance*, 72: 29–33.

Gilbert, W.D. and Trudel, P. (2001) 'Learning to coach through experience: Reflection in model youth sport coaches', *Journal of Teaching in Physical Education*, 21: 16–34.

Irwin, G., Hanton, S. and Kerwin, D.G. (2004) 'Reflective practice and the origins of elite coaching knowledge', *Reflective Practice*, 5: 425–42.

Kolb, D.A. (2015) *Experiential Learning: Experience as the Source of Learning and Development*, 2nd edn, Upper Saddle River: Pearson Education.

Kuklick, C.R., Gearity, B.T. and Thompson, M. (2015) 'Reflective practice in a university-based coach education program', *International Sport Coaching Journal*, 2: 248–60.

Nash, C. and Sproule, J. (2012) 'Coaches perceptions of their coach education experiences', *International Journal of Sport Psychology*, 1: 33–52.

Schön, D.A. (1983) *The Reflective Practitioner: How Professionals Think in Action*, New York: Basic Books Inc.

Schön, D.A. (1987) *Educating the Reflective Practitioner: Toward a New Design for Teaching and Learning in the Professions*, San Francisco: Jossey-Bass.

Tague, N.R. (2005). *The Quality Toolbox*, 2nd edn, Milwaukee: ASQ Quality Press.

Warren, K., Sakofs, M. and Hunt, Jr., J.S. (eds.). (1995) *The Theory of Experiential Education: A Collection of Articles Addressing the Historical, Philosophical, Social, and Psychological Foundations of Experiential Education* (3rd ed.), Dubuque: Kendall Hunt.

Wright, T., Trudel, P. and Culver, D. (2007) 'Learning how to coach: The different learning situations reported by youth ice hockey coaches', *Physical Education & Sport Pedagogy*, 12: 127–44.

7

WARMING UP TO RACE

A case study approach to develop engaged athletes

Jim Denison and Nathan Kindrachuk

Chapter objectives

By the end of this chapter, the reader will be able to:

1 To discuss how case studies can be used as an instructional coach development strategy within a graduate-level coaching program to address a specific problem or concern facing a coach.
2 To illustrate how coach-controlled warm-ups can restrict and limit athletes' decision-making capabilities.
3 To demonstrate how case studies, as an approach to coach development and learning, align with the reality of coaching as highly context specific.

Brief chapter overview

In this chapter, we illustrate how the use of case studies can be an effective coach development strategy to support and enhance coaches' practices. More specifically, we discuss how the first author (Jim), who was the second author (Nathan)'s supervisor for his master's thesis in coaching, collaborated to explore how various warm-up protocols used within a high-performance swimming context could be designed differently to increase athlete engagement. We further justify our use of case studies as an effective coach development strategy given the "nature" of coaching as a complex and context specific activity. Accordingly, through a case study approach, a coach developer could support a coach's development by focusing on issues and concerns that matter most to a coach given their particular coaching context.

Why and when we use Case Study

Jim served as the coach developer and worked closely with Nathan as part of his master's thesis to help him learn how to problematize his use of warm-ups as a high-performance swim coach. As a professor in coach education at the University of Alberta, Jim has written extensively about the idea of problematization as a core coaching competency (Denison, 2019). Briefly, to problematize as a coach means to question one's *normal* or *everyday practices* by considering any *unintended consequences* they might be having. In addition, as a former high school and university endurance running coach, Jim also brought to this collaboration a strong understanding of many of swimming's coaching norms given the strong emphasis both sports have on conditioning as the basis of athlete development and performance.

At the time of our collaboration, Nathan, in addition to being a graduate student, was the head coach of a large community swim club in Edmonton, Alberta. His squad of swimmers consisted of seven males and seven females between 14–18 years old. The genesis of our coach development collaboration was Nathan's concern that due to the strong coach-controlled nature of his warm-ups – *a normal, everyday practice* – his swimmers were not developing important skills related to decision-making and engagement – an *unintended consequence* resulting from this normal, everyday practice. This resulted in a case study set up by Jim whereby he and Nathan met weekly over an eight-week period to discuss how Nathan's "normal" warm-ups could be compromising his intentions to develop more athlete-centered practices, and subsequently, how he could change his warm-ups to support such an aim.

The case of warm-ups

For Nathan, every training session that he coached began the same way. He gathered his swimmers around the whiteboard on the side of the pool to explain the purpose of the upcoming training session. His explanation included a focus on the group's training plan in the current week of training and how it fit with the seasonal training plan. Further, in his whiteboard explanation, Nathan told his swimmers how the warm-up he had designed (usually 30–45 minutes) connected with the technical goals of the training session and the main set of the training session. The warm-up, technical goals, and main set were the aspects of his training sessions that were always present in his program, as is consistent with conventional swim coaching practice.

Despite the technical soundness of Nathan's warm-ups, and the well-supported rationale he always presented to his swimmers to explain how he determined the specific elements of his warm-ups, they were not necessarily always enacted by his swimmers seamlessly. Yes, many of his swimmers dove into the pool and began their warm-up when he told them to, but many were also hesitant. They would stare at the water, sometimes for two or three minutes, dreading the cold transition into the pool. This made Nathan anxious and stressed: "How can I be considered an effective coach if the athletes are not following my plan, including how they begin their practice?" After all, it was Nathan's National Coaching Certification Program (NCCP) training that explained to him how his swimmers must use time efficiently to achieve the technical and physiological goals in training that he had determined (Swimming Canada 2013, 2016).

The discomfort and doubt that Nathan experienced on the pool deck when his swimmers began their warm-ups late, and the pressure he felt to adhere to NCCP and Swimming Canada coaching practices, led him to ask: "What is wrong here?" As part of his master's degree, Nathan completed a course with Jim, where he was exposed to the work of Michel Foucault (1995) and the idea that problems in sport experienced by athletes can sometimes have to do with how coaches control their athletes' training and development (Lang 2010; McMahon, Penney & Dinan-Thompson 2012; Rinehart 1998).

As Nathan reflected on his warm-ups, and in line with Foucault's (1995) concept of docility, he realized how strongly he was micro-managing his swimmers. He controlled in detail every aspect of their warm-ups: Where and when it exactly occurred, how long it exactly took, and what it exactly entailed. In this way, his fixed warm-up protocol had eliminated the opportunity for his swimmers to make any decisions concerning how best to warm up, based on their own particulars. For example, were they coming off a bad night's sleep or nursing a minor injury? And according to Foucault, it is this type of strict control by a more powerful other (e.g. a coach) over others' thoughts and movements that can render individuals docile, a state defined by apathy, passiveness, and disengagement (Denison 2007).

The fact that all of his athletes had some "particulars" unique to them when they arrived at practice led Nathan to consider how he might change his warm-up protocol so that it could be less coach-controlled – and as a result, more athlete-centered. With this aim in mind, Nathan teamed up with Jim to begin to problematize his warm-up practices from a Foucauldian perspective. That is, the purpose of our collaboration was to develop new coaching practices that would provide Nathan's swimmers with the warm-up they needed to be successful in the pool, but not limit them through predetermined warm-up protocols and parameters. Accordingly, the instructional strategy that we will discuss is how our collaboration, as a type of case study intended to solve a very specific problem, led Nathan to change his normal warm-up routines to become more athlete-centered.

The essentials of case study

Definitions, essential components, and goals of coach development through case study

Coach education courses are integral aspects of provincial, national, and international coach development programs. Despite the intent to support coaches' learning, many coach education courses offered through formal organizations such as the NCCP are viewed by coaches as limited and not very useful (Mallett,

Trudel, Lyle & Rynne 2009; Nelson, Cushion & Potrac 2013). Specifically, these programs have been critiqued by researchers who have shown the importance and effectiveness of more informal or non-formal types of coach education such as mentorship, actual coaching experience, and conversations with other coaches, none of which are driven by a pre-established curriculum (Cassidy, Potrac & McKenzie 2006; Cushion, Armour & Jones 2003; Cushion & Nelson 2013; Piggott 2012). In other words, coaches learn in ways other than through formal coach education courses, and these ways can be very valuable to their development.

One way that could be used to develop coaches – in particular, within a graduate program in coaching where it is possible for a student/coach to work one on one with a professor/coach developer – is a case study. Such an approach allows for a coach to tap into a specialist's knowledge, which in the case of our example here concerned a specific sociological concept Nathan found interesting and relevant to his coaching context following the course he took with Jim, that of docility and how athlete engagement can be compromised by a coach's strict and controlling protocols. Moreover, as coaching is much more than a technocratic activity, many sociologically informed coaching researchers have described the actual act of coaching as a complex and messy reality (e.g. Cassidy, Jones & Potrac 2009; Jones & Turner 2006). And importantly, this "messy reality" is something that cannot be accounted for by coach development strategies that are based on educating large groups. For this reason, case studies, especially when they can be arranged as a one-on-one collaboration, have a great deal to offer coach developers.

A further rationale for using a case study as the instructional strategy that informed this specific coach development intervention is the strong connection between Foucault's (1995) concept of docility and athlete learning as an embodied and reciprocal process that is very much shaped by the "learning culture" a coach fosters (Barker-Ruchti 2019). More specifically, such an understanding of learning and development rejects the idea that all people are independently experiencing the same set of meanings (Avner, Jones & Denison 2014; Markula & Silk 2011). Rather, people experience life in dynamic, fractured ways that do not produce consistent, universal understandings. Accordingly, a fixed coach development curriculum that is not case specific in its design and delivery will be unable to account for the vagaries of human experience and meaning, such as the particulars of Nathan's team and his individual swimmers' unique backgrounds and embodied histories (Flyvbjerg 2006).

A further assumption related to teaching and learning that supports the idea of using case studies is the view of power not as hierarchical, but as relational. This view of power recognizes how power functions in fluid, dynamic, and sometimes subtle ways, rather than in a top-down or predictable manner (Avner, Jones & Denison 2014; Markula & Silk 2011). Accordingly, collaboration needs to become central to the process of teaching and learning with the aim of creating specific instructional strategies that recognize how learning is a reciprocal process as opposed to the objective transmission of knowledge from teacher to learner or expert to novice. Again, this points to the strength of the case study as a coach development instructional strategy, as it is much easier in a one-on-one collaborative setting for a coach developer to modify learning outcomes and learning activities to take into consideration a coach's perspective and views with an eye toward change.

It was the idea of change, therefore, and the importance of Nathan feeling confident and capable to break away from his fixed understanding of how his swimmers' warm-ups should look and function that was a critical learning outcome associated with our coach development collaboration. More specifically, the change that Nathan was interested in making through his work with Jim was to learn how to design and implement warm-ups that could support the development of his swimmers' engagement, awareness, and decision-making, and avoid making them docile.

Instructional strategies to facilitate case study

Our coach development collaboration involved weekly meetings for eight consecutive weeks that lasted between 60–90 minutes. These meetings took place in a neutral public meeting room on the campus of the University of Alberta that allowed for uninterrupted conversations. To kick off our collaboration, Nathan, based on his understanding of docility that he learned in his university course, described for Jim his newfound awareness of his athletes' disengagement and their struggles to begin their warm-ups. It was then through the specific constraints that Foucault (1995) outlined contributed to docility – namely, the strict control and organization of space, time, and movement by another over others' development and performance – that enabled Nathan and Jim to brainstorm possible solutions to the unintended consequences Nathan had begun to notice emerging from his tightly prescribed warm-ups – his problematization of one of his normal, everyday practice.

Based on this initial brainstorming in our first meeting, and Jim's probing, prompting, and clarifying Foucault's (1995) understanding of docility, Nathan devised a number of specific changes to his warm-ups. In other words, our case study was built on using a specific theory to guide what Nathan was both noticing and changing about his practices. It is in this way that we found theory to be crucial to our case study, as it allowed us to focus our conversations and intentions for change in very direct and clear ways. For example, Nathan became very aware of the unintended consequences of following a precise timetable to determine when to do *everything* in practice, as well as arranging his athletes in the same place or in the same way, and also never modifying the way he planned a sequence of drills or exercises. In all of these examples, the potential for athletes to become docile, and as a result not be as engaged and motivated as they could be, is quite high due to the lack of consideration being given to the athletes' difference, needs, preferences, or experiences.

For our subsequent seven meetings, we followed a specific process. At the beginning of each meeting, Nathan brought a summary of his field notes that included his reflections from a previously implemented Foucauldian-informed "new" warm-up. We then discussed Nathan's reflections, including what he could do next to further problematize his normal use of warm-ups by applying ideas based on Foucault's analysis of the conditions that tend to make people docile – the strict control and organization of space, time, and movement.

We would now like to provide examples of three situations when Nathan made changes to his warm-up routine based on his work with Jim: Training session warm-ups, in-season competition warm-ups, and peak competition warm-ups.

Typically for his training session warm-ups, and through his strict, scientifically informed instructions and feedback, Nathan would do his best to ensure that his swimmers were moving in time with each other so that they all completed their warm-up at the same time. However, by problematizing his control of time and efficient group movement, such that his swimmers all moved in the same way as a well-oiled machine, Nathan designed a training session warm-up that allowed his swimmers to make their own decisions concerning the duration and intensity of their warm-up based on how they felt after arriving at the pool.

To communicate these new intentions for his warm-up, Nathan utilized the whiteboard on the pool deck – an aid he normally used to write down *one* warm-up option. In this case, however, he used the whiteboard to present to his swimmers *multiple* warm-up options listed under three categories: Core Body Temperature Elevation, Flexibility, and Technical Proficiency. Under each category, Nathan provided three to five possibilities for achieving that outcome, and he instructed his swimmers that that they could mix and match any of the options listed to design their own warm-up as long as they drew from all three categories. This change, as Nathan commented on in his field notes, allowed his swimmers "to exert some ownership over their decision-making and also to possibly complete a different set of warm-up exercises than their peers, potentially improving the quality of their warm-up".

During in-season competition warm-ups, Nathan typically controlled, down to the meter, the volume his swimmers swam so they were, in his words, "properly warmed up for a race". However, through our collaboration, Nathan reconsidered the importance of determining and tracking his swimmers' warm-up volume so tightly. Instead, the day before his team's first in-season competition, he held a classroom session after practice to discuss with his swimmers how they are all likely to have their own personal "ideal performance state" prior to a race. He further explained how this state is unlikely to be reached by everyone with only one acceptable warm-up volume as determined by him. It was in this way that Nathan was encouraging his swimmers to swim only as far as they needed to as part of their warm-up in order to feel ready to perform optimally. Reflecting on this change, Nathan observed in his field notes:

Case study for coach development **95**

This change allowed the swimmers to swim the volume of warm-up that they thought was best for their bodies based on the race they were preparing for. For example, was it a sprint or a distance event, was it their first race of the day or their third? In which case, shouldn't the volume swum reflect that?

As is very normal in high-performance swim contexts, during peak competition warm-ups, coaches and swimmers become increasingly focused on hitting very specific and tightly prescribed performance outcomes. Accordingly, at peak competitions, Nathan typically established a clear timetable for his swimmers to follow to prepare for their races that included everything from when they should wake up, eat, arrive at the pool, and warm up. His new Foucauldian-informed peak competition warm-up that resulted from our discussion, however, led to Nathan foregoing the use of such a detailed, yet ironically also very generalized, timetable. Instead, each swimmer held a conversation with Nathan the day before the competition to discuss how to approach their pre-race routine including their warm-up plan. Nathan commented: "The precision of this new swimmer-led plan was far less specific and detailed than the one I would normally design, but the swimmers certainly seemed committed to it and very excited to execute it".

Nathan further noticed that these swimmer-led peak competition warm-up timetables "allowed the swimmers to try new strategies to prepare for races that they would not have previously had the chance to try. This gave them opportunities to learn about their bodies and their capabilities in new ways". In other words, through this change, Nathan observed that his athletes began to seek out ways of preparing to race that might be unique to their needs on that particular day.

Personal reflections and wishful thinking

Nathan underestimated how stressful it would be when he implemented coaching practices that challenged his "normal" coaching, which was usually informed by strict sport science protocols without any regard to how such protocols can make athletes docile. For example, Nathan's modifications to his in-season competition warm-ups meant that he was unable to track the volume that each one of his swimmers completed. Nathan's discomfort with this was largely because these warm-ups appeared to him to be less productive than when he assigned the volume to be swum.

Without implementing a warm-up that was based on a fixed volume, a dominant norm in swimming coaching cultures (Mujika et al. 1995), Nathan felt unstable in his knowledge and expertise as a coach. In fact, despite the purpose of letting go of the strict calculation of his swimmers' warm-up volume to reduce the constraints he normally imposed on his athletes, he still counted the distance that a handful of his swimmers completed in their warm-ups because of his discomfort with not knowing this precise number. Upon further reflection through conversations with Jim, it was no surprise that Nathan had internalized such a dominant coaching practice as tracking his swimmers' volume given his 15 years of exposure to high-performance swimming contexts and the overwhelming influence that exercise physiology has had over swim coaches' thinking and decision-making.

Another challenge Nathan faced when implementing his new warm-up routines was the time it demanded from him. In all the examples we presented, Nathan needed to take more time, either to think of other warm-up options to present to his swimmers, or to meet with them individually to discuss their warm-up preferences. The demands of such one-on-one work are often why coaches prescribe general programs for their athletes, or make all the decisions about training themselves.

But while these increased time demands indeed made Nathan's job harder, he believed that in the long run, the benefits would be worth it for two reasons. First, he was convinced that greater athlete engagement would transfer over to improved performances, given the unpredictable nature of swimming races and the importance of swimmers being able to make decisions quickly and to adapt immediately to changing circumstances without being able to consult their coach. Second, he believed that the increased amount of time he needed to invest early on in helping his swimmers learn how to tailor their warm-ups to their own particular needs would eventually save him time micro-managing the details of his training program and free him up to have more in-depth and meaningful conversations with his swimmers about their specific desires, ambitions, and goals, and, of course, their insecurities and anxieties. In this way, his role could begin to transition from being a technical program manager to a learning facilitator.

With respect to our reflections on the case study approach itself, time was also a relevant concern. For us to meet weekly over such a long period required a significant level of commitment that might not be possible for many coaches or coach developers. This is one of the major reasons why coach development is – for the most part – organized in large group settings: It makes the transmission of knowledge and ideas more efficient.

However, when working from a Foucauldian perspective, which problematizes various norms such as prioritizing efficiency, the case study approach is particularly beneficial. For example, for a coach to challenge any number of dominant ways of thinking and believing can be very disconcerting and easily lead one to question taking such a path (Denison, Mills & Konoval 2015; Mills & Denison 2013). Therefore, due to the pressure to conform that a coach might experience, case studies as a coach development strategy can work especially well, given how much personal support a coach is likely to need to coach in a way that might not be perceived by others, and even to themselves, as normal and/or effective. For Jim, this has been the most important reason to adopt case studies as his preferred method of coach development.

Activities for coach education

Based on all that we have written in this chapter concerning our use of case studies as a coach development strategy, we believe the following three steps can serve as a guide for a coach developer to begin using theoretically driven case studies as part of their instructional toolkit. The steps below illustrate this using Foucault's (1995) idea of docility, but there is no reason why these steps could not be modified to incorporate any specific theoretical concept.

1   Collaborate with a coach to *identify a normal coaching practice* that might be making the coach's athletes docile. For example, the coach could be prompted to identify a specific practice whereby they might strictly control how they organize what they have their athletes do within a very regulated timeframe.
2   Ask the coach to think of some *unintended consequences* or *problematic effects* that they think could result from the practice they identified in step one. For example, a coach who prescribes very specific instructions with regards to sets and reps might begin to notice, with the help of their coach developer, that such strict protocols actually make it less likely, not more likely, that their athletes challenge their limits as much as they could in favor of simply completing the sets and reps the coach assigned. And such an outcome can be disastrous for a coach intent on their athletes learning how to push through the pain and discomfort that almost always accompanies hard training.
3   Discuss with the coach how it might be possible to *avoid* or *prevent* the effects they came up with in step two from occurring through their use of some specific pedagogical methods or new coaching practices or strategies. For example, in what ways could time become more flexible? Or how could players be organized into different groups, or indeed use different spaces to carry out some of their training? And what about finding ways to support and encourage athletes to explore their limits of exhaustion in practice instead of simply completing an assigned workout?

Additional resources

1   For coach developers to further understand what it could mean to design a case study to enable a coach to begin to problematize her coaching based on Foucault's (1995) concept of docility, we recommend reading a three-part blog post series that Jim wrote with Dr. Joseph Mills, his former Ph.D. student and now a practicing coach developer based in Calgary, Alberta. This blog post series offers a number of example problems coaches often face with respect to docility and how they can be solved following the steps we outlined in the previous section. This blog post series can be found at www.mcmillanspeed.com

Bibliography

Avner, Z., Jones, L. and Denison, J. (2014) 'Poststructuralism', in L. Nelson, P. Potrac and R. Groom (eds.) *Research Methods in Sports Coaching*, pp. 42–51, London: Routledge.

Barker-Ruchti, N. (ed.). (2019) *Athlete Learning in Elite Sport: A Cultural Framework*, London: Routledge.

Cassidy, T., Jones, R. and Potrac, P. (2009) *Understanding Sports Coaching: The Social, Cultural and Pedagogical Foundations of Coaching Practice*, 2nd edn, London: Routledge.

Cassidy, T., Potrac, P. and McKenzie, A. (2006) 'Evaluating and reflecting upon a coach education initiative: The CoDe of rugby', *The Sport Psychologist*, 20: 145–61.

Cushion, C., Armour, K. and Jones, R. (2003) 'Coach education and continuing professional development: Experience and learning to coach', *Quest*, 55: 215–30.

Cushion, C. and Nelson, L. (2013) 'Coach education and coach learning', in P. Potrac, W. Gilbert and J. Denison (eds.) *The Routledge Handbook of Sports Coaching*, pp. 359–74, London: Routledge.

Denison, J. (2007) 'Social theory for coaches: A Foucauldian reading of one athlete's poor performance', *International Journal of Sports Science & Coaching*, 2: 369–83.

Denison, J. (2019) 'What it means to 'think outside the box': Why Foucault matter for coach development,' *International Sport Coaching Journal*, 6: 354–358.

Denison, J., Mills, J.P. and Konoval, T. (2015) 'Sports' disciplinary legacy and the challenge of "coaching differently", *Sport, Education and Society*, 22: 772–83.

Flyvbjerg, B. (2006) 'Five misunderstandings about case-study research', *Qualitative Inquiry*, 12: 219–45.

Foucault, M. (1995) *Discipline and Punish: The Birth of the Prison*, New York: Vintage Books.

Jones, L. and Turner, P. (2006) 'Teaching coaches to coach holistically: Can problem-based learning (PBL) help?', *Physical Education and Sport Pedagogy*, 11: 181–202.

Lang, M. (2010) 'Surveillance and conformity in competitive youth swimming', *Sport, Education and Society*, 15: 19–37.

Mallett, C., Trudel, P., Lyle, J. and Rynne, S. (2009) 'Formal vs. informal coach education', *International Journal of Sports Science & Coaching*, 4: 325–33.

Markula, P. and Silk, M. (2011) *Qualitative Research for Physical Culture*, Basingstoke: Palgrave Macmillan.

McMahon, J., Penney, D. and Dinan-Thompson, M. (2012) 'Body practices-exposure and effect of a sporting culture? Stories from three Australian swimmers', *Sport, Education and Society*, 17: 181–206.

Mills, J. and Denison, J. (2013) 'Coach Foucault: Problematizing endurance running coaches' practices', *Sports Coaching Review*, 2: 136–50.

Mujika, I., Chatard, J.C., Busso, T., Geyssant, A., Barale, F. and Lacoste, L. (1995) 'Effects of training on performance in competitive swimming', *Canadian Journal of Applied Physiology*, 20: 395–406.

Nelson, L., Cushion, C. and Potrac, P. (2013) 'Enhancing the provision of coach education: The recommendations of UK coaching practitioners', *Physical Education and Sport Pedagogy*, 18: 204–18.

Piggott, D. (2012) 'Coaches' experiences of formal coach education: A critical sociological investigation', *Sport, Education and Society*, 17: 535–54.

Rinehart, R. (1998) 'Born-again sport: Ethics in biographical research', in G. Rail (ed.) *Sport and Postmodern Times*, pp. 33–48, Albany: State University of New York Press.

Swimming Canada. (2013) 'Level 3 senior coach evaluation guide: Portfolio A, B & C training and competition'. Online. Available HTTP: <www.swimming.ca/content/uploads/2015/09/senior-coach-evaluation-guide-mar2014-en.pdf> (accessed 16 February 2016).

Swimming Canada. (2016) 'NCCP programs'. Online. Available HTTP: <www.swimming.ca/en/nccp-programs/> (accessed 13 June 2016).

8

TEACHING WITHIN A SOCIAL CONSTRUCTIONIST AND CRITICAL FRAMEWORK

Developing student-coaches in a graduate university program

Chris Cushion

Chapter objectives

By the end of this chapter, the reader should be able to:

1 Understand an approach to teaching student-coaches inspired by social constructionist critical theory.
2 Position this teaching approach in relation to other approaches.
3 See how this approach can shape educational tasks and activities to produce critical thinking and reflexivity in student-coaches.

Brief chapter overview

This chapter outlines the key tenets of a social constructionist and critical framework applied to teaching student-coaches in a graduate program. The purpose is to give "intellectual anchors" that support thinking about coaching, teaching, and research about coaching from this perspective. A constructionist perspective to teaching means positioning the student-coaches, as well as me, the tutor, as relational and sociohistorical entities that can only be understood in context and as reflexive. The teaching approach in this case is more than merely passing on "survival tips", "tricks of the trade" (Cushion, Ford & Williams 2012), or pre-packaged knowledge. Instead, the approach highlights how the program looks to critical reflection that focuses on probing sociocultural distortions, coaching ideology

100 Cushion

> and taken-for-granted coaching cultures and systems. To this end, the chapter outlines teaching strategies, student tasks, and activities underpinned by the assumptions of the approach that reach into the student-coaches' realities.

Why and when I use a social constructionist and critical framework

I have been working with student-coaches on university graduate degree programs for 20 years. This experience includes working with students undertaking a "coaching course" within a more general sport-related program, and more recently with students enrolled on specific graduate "sport coaching" programs. During this time, my teaching approach for graduate coaching students has carried with it an assumption that as coaches, they must confront multiple and layered issues in their working lives to implement change. Importantly, this assumption means that simply having "knowledge" of coaching and its applied principles is insufficient, and that coach development involves more than simply providing coaches with a "toolbox" of skills and professional and theoretical knowledge (Cushion, Armour & Jones 2003; Lyle & Cushion 2017). This teaching approach requires that student-coaches are provided with a host of knowledge, understanding, practices, strategies, coherent arguments, and – crucially – critical thinking. While drawing on social constructionist assumptions, the development of critical thinking is a cornerstone of the approach and runs through the program that includes drawing on work from Brookfield on critical theory in education and Mezirow on transformative learning.

Far from being benign activities, coaching practice, coach education, and coaching research always contain and advance values and agendas – and support certain approaches to coaching practice and coaching research. Moreover, the nature of coaching practice is often taken for granted and assumed but, in reality, *is* ill-defined and under-theorized. The approach to teaching, as well as the wider graduate program, takes both a critical and a reflexive stance toward coaching practice and research, and in undertaking this task, theory provides both necessary and useful "thinking-tools". Hence, uncovering theoretical layers alongside theoretical debate is an important activity that features in all teaching and assessment throughout the program. This acts as a springboard for discussion and prompts coaches to question the relationships among philosophical assumptions, coaching perspectives, learning and instructional theory, coaching practice, and coaching research. My teaching approach equips student-coaches with an awareness of their own beliefs and assumptions about coaching that also addresses the social, cultural, and political complexities of coaching research and practice. Underpinning the approach to teaching is providing an environment whereby the student's coaching practice and the coaching practice of others, as well as different approaches to research, can be interrogated and assumptions made explicit.

The essentials of a social constructionist and critical framework

Definitions, essential components, and goals of SC and CF

An important starting point for the program, and of this approach, is the assumption that coaching practice and its research are always "infected" by the values and beliefs of its community – that coaching practice and research is not objective or neutral (Lyle & Cushion 2017). Thus, when setting out student-coaches to investigate and understand coaching research and practice, it must be recognized that coaching situations and approaches are already permeated by the interpretations, beliefs, and intentions of practitioners – coaches' experience and knowledge (including student-coaches) have already been shaped by historical and cultural circumstances. In other words, coaching research and practice has an underlying paradigm, or "philosophy", a theoretical framework that guides – implicitly or explicitly – all activities. In this case, a philosophy or paradigm are worldviews that define the nature of the world, the individual's place in it, and the possible relationships to that world and its parts (Schuh & Barab 2007) – it is concerned with the nature of knowledge and the nature of reality. Theoretical perspectives have their roots in philosophy and will differ according to their underlying assumptions and will incorporate, for example, models of practice, standards, rules and techniques, and methods consistent with the view of reality the paradigm underpinning it. Paradigms are seldom made explicit in coaching theories and practice, but nevertheless, structure perceptions and shape subsequent coaching practice.

In terms of student-coaches researching and understanding their coaching practice and the practice of others, it is important that they gain an awareness of the emergence of a range of approaches and advocates arising from varying theoretical and paradigmatic perspectives. These perspectives attempt to understand athlete and coach learning and coaching practice – as well as offering frameworks to guide coaching interventions and designing and researching coaching (for an overview, see, for example, Cushion et al. 2010; Cassidy, Jones & Potrac 2016). Coaching, however, remains a "hybrid discipline", and will reflect its own theoretical and practical struggles, as well as being a proxy for wider debate over "turf" and what constitutes legitimacy in practice and research (Lyle & Cushion 2017). Therefore, our program and approach is structured to help the student-coaches be aware of these struggles, but also show that they are an integral part of these struggles.

An important part of our approach is to give the student-coaches what Windschitl (2002) terms "intellectual anchors" to support their thinking about coaching, research, and their position in relation to these. To this end, our teaching introduces and develops ideas relating to social constructionism, the idea that the student-coaches' social realities are constructed and meanings and actions of individuals produce particular meanings – meaning therefore is constructed

102 Cushion

and requires both a constructing and constructed self. The process of construction requires something to construct (coaching), a constructing subject (coach, researcher), and a social context that constructs the coach (Alvesson & Sköldberg 2009). The student-coaches therefore come to recognize coaching knowledge is historically and culturally specific; language constitutes rather than reflects reality, and is a pre-condition for thought and a form of social action – the focus on learning and teaching in this case is in interaction processes and social practice (Young & Collin 2004). Thus, ontologically, reality exists through interpretations, and in a constructionist or sociocultural perspective, society and an individual's relationship to society have a primary role in the shaping of that reality (Schuh & Barab 2007; Prawat & Floden 1994). Importantly, as Young and Collin (2004) suggest, constructionism is more than "constructing" knowledge, but positioning within the historical and cultural location of that construction.

This instructional strategy assumes that coaching changes as knowledge changes only as both products and producers of social states and interactions – where multiple perspectives are paramount, and practice is structured through language and strategic action. Taking a social constructionist teaching approach requires that I posit that knowledge has both individual and social components, and is sustained by social processes linked to knowledge (Young & Collin 2004) whereby knowing is distributed in the world, among objects and individuals. This means that during sessions with student-coaches, knowledge creation is a shared experience, rather than an entirely individual experience (Prawat & Floden 1994).

Such a perspective challenges views of learning to coach as a linear, unproblematic transfer of knowledge (Cushion, Ford & Williams 2012), as the program attempts to readily embrace sociocultural and complex views of learning and allows an exploration of alternative pedagogical approaches. In particular, this means a shift to a more interactive, complex, and unpredictable learning environment. My role in this approach is repositioned to stand back and observe more, act as a facilitator, be less directive, attempt to see the big picture, and give consideration about when and how to contribute. Therefore, to develop student learning, I may be required to scaffold, question, guide, advise, de-brief, converse, or offer heuristics or conceptual structures to engage the student-coaches' learning. In turn, the student-coaches are encouraged to be an active part of the context and explore the articulations between their experiences, the experiences that they are exposed to, conceptual understanding, pedagogical practices, and the wider cultural and political realities of coaching.

Borrowing from Mezirow (1997), this approach is cognizant of understanding how coaches construct knowledge and learn through a critically reflective process wherein the student-coach will assess previous understanding to determine whether those assumptions hold in the present situation (see also Stodter & Cushion 2016). Learning in this approach occurs by adding to or transforming old meaning and perspectives or constructing new meaning. According to Mezirow (1997):

A significant personal transformation involving subjective reframing, that is, transforming one's own frame of reference, often occurs in response to a disorienting dilemma through a three-part process: critical reflection on one's own assumptions, discourse to validate the critically reflective insight, and action.

(p. 60)

My teaching approach uses this model of learning to develop practice by linking perspectives on constructionist assumptions, critical thinking, and transformative learning. The purpose is to move student-coaches to consider critically coaching viewed as instrumental rationality as a means to a given end.[1] The term "instrumental rationality" is often used to conceptualize and critique cognitive and behavioral approaches to coaching practice and reflects a need to control and manipulate the external environment. This remains a dominant view in coaching, whereby practice is said to be driven by "instrumental rationality" – that is, the manipulation and control of the environment, prediction about observable events, and a coaching reality based on empirical knowledge means that coaching is governed by technical rules. Instrumental rationality remains highly influential in informing coaching practice and research, coaching curricula design, and coach education, and – it could be argued – is a pervasive ideology. Challenging this ideology means that I position coach development not as a rational process of information processing, problem solving, and decision-making applied to issues of practice, but to a more critically reflective and intuitive approach. To do this involves looking at coaching situations as integrated wholes rather than discrete parts, and encouraging the student-coaches to become more involved with the process rather than act as detached observers. The essentials of this approach, therefore, attempt to foster constructionist, critical, transformative, and context-aware development to link student-coaches' new knowledge (gained through practice or research) to their previous experiences, contexts, and practice.

Using a social constructionist and critical framework across a graduate program

Design and planning

The overall design of the program draws on principles of learning, including those of Eraut (1994: 13), who suggests that, to be effective, learning should consider and include: (a) an appropriate combination of learning settings; (b) time for study, consultation, and reflection; (c) the availability of suitable learning resources; (d) people who are prepared (i.e. both willing and able) to give appropriate support; and (e) the learner's own capacity to learn and take advantage of the opportunities available. In addition, Armour's (2010) notion of the "learning coach" is also useful. Drawing on professional development discourses, Armour points to John Dewey's (1958) work as an important reminder that the design and

104 Cushion

management of every learning opportunity needs careful consideration, because the nature and quality of any current learning experiences influence how understanding and learning in subsequent experiences will occur. That is, the principle of continuing of experience (Dewey 1958) whereby "every experience both takes up something from those which have gone before and modifies in some way the quality of those which come after" (p. 27). Therefore, the teaching approach must ensure that each block of activity through the program considers learning activities that are designed and organized in ways that build on coaches' existing understandings, but more importantly, extend their capacity to engage in ongoing learning.

In addition, as part of this principle, an important pedagogical emphasis is also to allow student-coaches to develop broad, abstract conceptual reasoning – that can be applied to consider broad questions impacting coaching practice. Therefore, design involves developing broad and structured tasks that that avoid rushing to an overly narrowing focus on the particulars of practice because critical thinking can be obscured by the personal and the particular (Brookfield 2009). Consequently, all learning activities attempt to encourage a broader look at claims made by various groups, including coaches and researchers, and also consider the basis for comparison – that is, what the possible interpretations are and how they might be constrained or determined by a particular social group or context. Importantly, the student-coaches' learning experiences are designed to arouse curiosity, thereby creating favorable conditions for ongoing learning (Armour 2010). This is without becoming fixated on the "particular puzzles" of the student-coaches' own practice as these puzzles are not what Brookfield (2009: 6) describes as "procedural kinks or pedagogic tangles" of our own making. Instead, coaching situations are seen as politically sculpted situations that can illustrate something of the contradictions and problems within sporting systems. That is, social reality is not just something that is constructed through the interpretations of individuals – the social structure, as well being the product of the meaning and actions of individuals in the social structure, produces particular meaning that limits and constrains action. Thus, this approach to teaching engages critically with the influence of broader social forces.

Delivery

Within coaching research and practice, interpreting, explaining, and meaning making are acts in which we engage, whether or not we set out deliberately to do so, or whether or not we use particular terms to describe what we're doing (Brookfield 2009). As Brookfield (2009) suggests, all learners are participants in particular conceptions of the world, and therefore contribute to sustain a conception of the world or to modify it through new modes of thought. The key point here is to challenge student-coaches with the idea that theory is a restrictive professional discourse – though theorizing in social science is elaborate and sophisticated, it can be subject to critical scrutiny (Brookfield 2009). Theory

Teaching research and critical thinking **105**

is always in the midst of any of the student-coaches' practice, research, action, judgment, and decisions. Therefore, my teaching approach must be transformative in the sense that it provides student-coaches with the capacity to be increasingly comprehensive and discriminating in understanding and illuminating what is observed, experienced, practiced, and researched. To this end, I aim to enable a reading of theory that facilitates student-coaches to name and rename their experiences to challenge existing reasoning and judgment. Student-coaches are exposed to a range of theoretical approaches and ideas, and encouraged to use them as tools to explore their coaching practice. I encourage methodological eclecticism – method does not define paradigm, so the student-coaches are asked to experiment with aligning different coaching "methods" to different theoretical understanding with different contexts, and then analyze and re-analyze their own and others' experiences. The emphasis or approach will be valid, depending on context, and how this is pursued will depend on the unique and complex configuration of coaching and the student-coaches' own positionality and experience. To apply methodological and theoretical understanding while at the same time taking a self-critical perspective is, as Brookfield (2009) suggests, a sign of a commitment to critical practice – and hence this critical approach moves beyond the abstract and into the student-coaches' realities.

The delivery of the program is in "blocks" – mindful of the principles underlying the design (e.g. an appropriate combination of learning settings, time for study, consultation and reflection, building learning capacity). The delivery has four core "coaching blocks", and these consider in turn: (a) "coach learning and coaching philosophy"; (b) "coaching process and coaching models"; (c) "coaching practice and pedagogy"; and (d) "coach development". Interspersed with these are units that address research methods and areas of applied sport science (psychology, physiology, and biomechanics). The aim of this mixed approach to the program content is to provide a level of reflection for the student-coaches in the core coaching modules, which means investigating the way in which the theoretical, cultural, and political context of their individual and intellectual involvement affects interaction with what is being researched, read, and practiced across the whole program.

The aim is also to develop reflexivity; that is, "ways of seeing which act back on and reflect existing ways of seeing" (Clegg & Hardy 1996: 4). This encourages student-coaches' metatheoretical reflection and becomes a form of enquiry in its own right. Being reflexive in this case involves considering coaching through multiple levels of research, method, and theory, while being reflective is focused on a specific method or level of interpretation (Alvesson & Sköldberg 2009). Such reflexive interpretation requires considerable effort from the student-coaches, and tutor guidance, but invokes a breadth and variety of ways to considering coaching. The point being to draw out and illustrate that there is no self-evident, simple, or unambiguous rules or procedures for coaching, and that the crucial ingredient is the student-coaches' judgment, intuition, and ability to "see" and point something out. The examples in Tables 8.1–8.3 illustrate some

106 Cushion

of the tasks the student-coaches are asked to complete: They all have common key features, in that they are asked to consider empirical material in a variety of forms (e.g. accounts, observations, and other empirical materials). From this, the students will be asked to write and then discuss an interpretation of the material in relation to both their particular practice, but also to coaching more broadly (e.g. consider underlying meanings). Some students, through their writing, can engage in more critical interpretations (e.g. ideology, power, social reproduction), but this is more likely to occur during the in-class discussions where I may share alternative interpretations and reading around the area and introduce additional reading that offers a more critical stance (e.g. on power and surveillance). These discussions also include shared reflections on language and authority (e.g. claims to authority, selectivity of voice) (Alvesson & Sköldberg 2009).

In addition to formal theory or technical knowledge, coaches need to employ practical knowledge, as well as understand how they use these to construct an understanding of practice (Cervero 1992). Therefore, student-coaches benefit from case history examples or stories from other coaches illustrating their lived experiences (Christensen 2011; Carless & Douglas 2011). Student-coaches also derive examples, metaphors, case studies, stories, and scenarios directly from their

TABLE 8.1 Task linking to coach learning

Reading	Task
1 Cassidy, T., Jones, R. and Potrac, P. (eds) (2009) 'Reflection,' in *Understanding Sports Coaching*, 2nd Edn, London: Routledge.	In 500 words, answer the following questions: Identify one or two
2 Mallet, C. (2010) 'Becoming a high performance coach: Pathways and communities', in J. Lyle & C. Cushion, *Sports Coaching Professionalisation and Practice*, London: Elsevier.	moments in your coaching when you have "learned from experience". What did you learn, why, and
3 Cushion, C.J., Armour, K.M. and Jones, R.L. (2003) 'Coach education and continuing professional development: Experience and learning to coach', *Quest*, 55: 215–30.	how do you know you have learned from this? Evaluate the strengths and weaknesses of the reading
4 Gilbert, W. and Trudel, P. (2001) 'Learning to coach through experience: Reflection in model youth sport coaches', *Journal of Teaching in Physical Education*, 21: 16–34.	in this task.
5 Richards, P., Mascarenhas, D. and Collins, D. (2009) 'Implementing reflective practice approaches with elite team athletes: Parameters of success', *Reflective Practice*, 10: 353–63.	
6 Culver, D. and Trudel, P. (2006) 'Cultivating coaches' communities of practice: Developing the potential for learning through interactions', in R.L. Jones (ed.) *The Sports Coach as Educator*, London: Routledge.	

TABLE 8.2 Task linking to conceptualizing the coaching process

Reading	Task
1 Abraham, A., Collins, D. and Martindale, R. (2006) 'The coaching schematic: Validation through expert coach consensus', *Journal of Sport Sciences*, 24: 549–64.	In 500 words, write a critical review of Abraham et al.
2 Cushion, C. J., Armour, K.M. and Jones, R.L. (2006) 'Locating the coaching process in practice: Models "for" and "of" coaching', *Physical education and Sport Pedagogy*, 11: 1–17.	Consider your coaching process and practice in light of the reading. How do the different approaches discussed
3 Côté, J. and Gilbert, W. (2009) 'An integrative definition of coaching effectiveness and expertise', *International Journal of Sports Science and Coaching*, 4: 307–23.	capture your coaching? Come prepared to discuss your findings.
4 Lyle, J. (ed.) (2002) 'The coaching process', in *Sports Coaching Concepts: A Framework for Coaches' Behaviour*, London: Routledge.	
5 Lyle, J. (ed.) (2002) 'Modelling the coaching process', in *Sports Coaching Concepts: A Framework for Coaches' Behaviour*, London: Routledge.	
6 Lyle, J. (ed.) (2002) 'A proposed model for coaching', in *Sports Coaching Concepts: A Framework for Coaches' Behaviour*, London: Routledge.	

TABLE 8.3 Task relating to understanding conceptions of coaching practice

Reading	Task
1 Saury, J. and Durand, M. (1998) 'Practical knowledge in expert coaches: On-site study of coaching in sailing', *Research Quarterly for Exercise and Sport*, 69: 254–66.	In 500 words, summarize the evidence supporting the claims made in the reading.
2 Jones, R.L. and Wallace, M. (2005) 'Another bad day at the training ground: Coping with ambiguity in the coaching context', *Sport Education and Society*, 10: 119–34.	Consider and interpret your coaching practice in light of ONE of the articles (1–4). Come prepared to discuss your findings. Then read:
3 Bowes, I.M. and Jones. R.L. (2006) 'Working at the edge of chaos: Understanding coaching as a complex, interpersonal system', *The Sport Psychologist*, 20: 235–45.	Cushion, C.J. (2007) 'Modelling the complexity of the coaching process', *International Journal of Sport Science and Coaching*, 2: 395–401.
4 Jones, R.L. (2007) 'Coaching redefined: An everyday pedagogical endeavour', *Sport Education and Society*, 12: 159–73.	Highlight the key points from the argument developed and consider these in light of your coaching
5 Lyle, J. (2002) 'Coaching practice', *Sports Coaching Concepts: A Framework for Coaches' Behaviour*, London: Routledge.	practice, and coaching experience. Come prepared to discuss your findings.

108 Cushion

coaching practice. The process of developing, for example, case studies from their own experiences enables student-coaches to do what Cervero (1988) has suggested, and "become researchers of their own practice" (p. 56). To develop improvements in practice, the most effective means are practitioner's dialogue, reflection and theory building where knowledge is generated and constructed from "new examples, understandings and actions" (Cervero 1988: 158). The key to developing new meaning is by being transformative, whereby meaningful learning results in student-coaches crafting their own idiosyncratic significance for new information, making learning new and more relevant through its application to their context. To this end, the assessment tasks ask students to outline and share their process, while contributing to the case studies of coaching in the program.

A crucial aspect of the delivery of the program – and aligning the design principles – is to create opportunities for student-coaches to speak with others. Communities of practice (CoPs) (Lave & Wenger 1991) have been advocated as a means to understand and structure coach learning (Cushion 2006; Culver & Trudel 2006, 2008). However, while the rhetoric of CoPs is appealing, the reality of student-coaches' lives makes them difficult to sustain beyond the classroom (Culver & Trudel 2006; Gilbert, Gallimore & Trudel 2009), because the nature of the student-coach's day-to-day coaching routines and regularities largely promotes coach isolation (Gilbert & Trudel 2006). Within the program, the student-coaches work in groups, and push one another to discuss coaching beyond an instrumental level. That is, discussions are more than merely passing on "survival tips" or "tricks of the trade" (Cushion, Ford & Williams 2012). Instead, aligning with the assumptions of the approach, the program looks to what Mezirow (1991) describes as systemic critical reflection that focuses on probing sociocultural distortions, "external ideologies . . . or other taken for granted cultural systems" (Mezirow 1998: 193). These discussions require me to provide some structure and direction, and are linked to relevant reading. For example, descriptions of coaching practice may be linked to ideology with a structured question: "What are the elements of the dominant ideology in coaching in your sport?" Or, around power: "What aspects of your reading on power were most resonant for you?" Some care is required with this, as moving student-coaches out of their "comfort zone" can, in effect, be experienced as threatening and even oppressive for some student-coaches – having the opposite effect to that intended, and in fact shutting down conversation.

Evaluation and reflection

Student-coaches' early work in the program shows that the philosophical roots and assumptions of their practice are not clearly articulated. Neither are they able to easily "pin down" the philosophical assumptions that exist, often implicitly, in empirical material about coaching. The reality of this suggests that an instrumental approach remains the dominant element in coaching whereby such perspectives form a subtle, but coherent, set of rationalities and techniques that underpin coaching practices, coach education and coaching research (Lyle & Cushion 2017). Interestingly, this dominant ideology means that student-coaches can resist or dismiss a more critical approach that highlights issues such as conformity to dominant ideologies, one-dimensional thinking, or notions of power, control, and surveillance. The result can be a confusion that limits the development of the student-coaches' conceptual "repertoire" and the growth (and acceptance) of different approaches to understanding and doing coaching.

Since the program develops critical thinking and provides a theoretical grounding or foundation to coaching practice, I evaluate the success of this approach not only on student-coaches' engagement with the concepts, but also how they are able to demonstrate (through dialogue, activity, and assessment) sharper boundaries between theoretical categories and concepts – not whether they agree or disagree with such. In line with Mezirow (1991), learning can be considered reflexive or non-reflexive. Non-reflexive learning is learning without a critical element. As Habermas (1975) suggests, "non-reflexive learning takes place in action contexts in which implicitly raised theoretical and practical validity claims are naïvely taken for granted and accepted or rejected without discursive consideration" (p. 15). This can be contrasted with reflexive learning that is tinged with criticality; that is, questioning and challenging everyday practices and social arrangements. Importantly, this approach recognizes that an individual's reflective capacities are always culturally bounded (Brookfield 2009). The approach in this chapter attempts to develop reflexive learning and normalize critical skepticism within the student-coaches. As Fendler (2003) argues, we should maintain a "skeptical and critical attitude about what we do", and it is not my role or that of the program to become simply a "technology that reproduces (dominant) assumptions" (p. 23) about coaching.

This approach also seeks to develop the student-coaches' repertoire of interpretations, so as not to limit possibilities or prioritizing certain interpretations over others. The student-coaches (and the program) therefore are also evaluated in terms of an ability to develop creativity. This is considered in class tasks and in program assessment, as, for example, being able to see different aspects, theoretical sophistication, theoretical breadth, and variation; and the ability to reflect at a metatheoretical level. Encouraging student-coaches to consider empirical material that is disparate or has several interpretations encourages the possibility of multiple interpretations to enhance reflection and develop what Norén (1990) describes as an empirically grounded imagination.

Personal reflections and wishful thinking

It is important to resist the expectations and dominance of instrumental rationality in coaching and, to an extent, in schooling. So, the approach in our program is based on broad principles derived from a specific theoretical underpinning rather than precise details and "best practice", a recipe of activities of "what works" and rigid control of all aspects of the student-coach experience. Over different iterations

110 Cushion

of the program, I have tried to increase the opportunity to open up more spaces and possibilities for creativity, reflexivity, and critical thinking. I am attempting to enable student-coaches to develop the oft-cited "sociological imagination" and to question coaching structures and understand their position in coaching.

While a more "social" and critical approach to coaching has gained ground in recent years, the curricula offered in many coach education programs still looks unbalanced with the privileging of certain approaches and disciplines, perhaps because they seem to offer quick fixes and seductively simple steps for student-coaches to follow. Perhaps this is inevitable as part of the "growing pains" of coaching and coach education as a subject area, but it leaves the field impoverished. As has been attempted through the approach to student-coach development described in this chapter, a re-imagining of coach education is required that does not have as its first step a particular discipline, but instead has a focus on coaching practice in the social world. Such an approach perhaps offers the potential to transcend a disciplinary-based curriculum and ground coach education in the realities of coaching practice.

Activities for coach education

1   To teach differently, the historical, social, and contextual aspects of coaching need to be critically considered. The following questions can assist with this process:

    a   What underlying theory guides your current teaching in coach education?
    b   What assumptions does this theory make about coaching practice and coaching knowledge?
    c   How might these assumptions and the teaching approach constrain or enable student-coaches' development?

2   Map out your current coach education curriculum – what is the basis for the knowledge that underpins the curriculum? From this perspective, what is the purpose of coach education, and how might this address structural factors, such tradition, habit, and coaching customs? How might a critical perspective help student-coaches address these?

Additional resources

Carr, W. and Kemmis, S. (1986) *Becoming Critical: Education, Knowledge and Action Research*, London: Routledge.

Note

1   Coaching in this sense is viewed as complex but open to analysis; the complexity is penetrable and regarded as susceptible to control. Theory, from this perspective, is something that is applied to practice, and coaching is cast as an applied science – "coaching science".

Bibliography

Alvesson, M. and Sköldberg, K. (2009) *Reflexive Methodology: New Vistas for Qualitative Research*, 2nd edn, London: Sage.

Armour, K.M. (2010) 'The learning coach . . . the learning approach: Professional development for sports coach professionals', in J. Lyle and C. Cushion (eds.) *Sports Coaching Professionalization and Practice*, pp. 243–53, London: Elsevier.

Brookfield, S.D. (2009) *The Power of Critical Theory for Adult Learning and Teaching*, Berkshire: Open University Press.

Carless, D. and Douglas, K. (2011) 'Stories as personal coaching philosophy', *International Journal of Sports Science and Coaching*, 6: 1–12.

Cassidy, T., Jones, R.L. and Potrac, P. (2016) *Understanding Sports Coaching: The Social, Cultural and Pedagogical Foundations of Coaching Practice*, 3rd edn, London: Routledge.

Cervero, R.M. (1988) *Effective Continuing Education for Professionals*, San Francisco: Jossey-Bass.

Cervero, R.M. (1992) 'Professional practice, learning, and continuing education: An integrated perspective', *International Journal of Lifelong Education*, 11: 91–101.

Christensen, M.K. (2011) 'Exploring biographical learning in elite soccer coaching', *Sport, Education and Society*, 19: 204–22.

Clegg, S. and Hardy, C. (1996) 'Some dare to call it power', in S. Clegg, C. Hardy and W. Nord (eds.) *Handbook of Organisation Studies*, London: Sage.

Culver, D.M. and Trudel, P. (2006) 'Cultivating coaches' communities of practice: Developing the potential for learning through interactions', in R.L. Jones (ed.) *The Sports Coach as Educator: Re-Conceptualising Sports Coaching*, London: Routledge.

Culver, D.M. and Trudel, P. (2008) 'Clarifying the concept of communities of practice in sport', *International Journal of Sports Science and Coaching*, 3: 1–10.

Cushion, C.J. (2006) 'Mentoring: Harnessing the power of experience', in R.L. Jones (ed.) *The Sports Coach as Educator: Re-Conceptualising Sports Coaching*, pp. 128–44, London: Routledge.

Cushion, C.J., Armour, K.M. and Jones, R.L. (2003) 'Coach education and continuing professional development: Experience and learning to coach', *Quest*, 55: 215–30.

Cushion, C.J., Ford, P. and Williams, A.M. (2012) 'Coach behaviour and practice structures in youth soccer: Implications for talent development', *Journal of Sport Sciences*, 30: 1631–41.

Cushion, C.J., Nelson, L., Armour, K., Lyle, J., Jones, R.L., Sandford, R. and O'Callaghan, C. (2010) *Coach Learning and Development: A Review of Literature*, Leeds: Sports Coach.

Dewey, J. (1958) *Experience and Education*, New York: The Macmillan Company.

Eraut, M. (1994) *Developing Professional Knowledge and Competence*, London: Falmer Press.

Fendler, L. (2003) 'Teacher reflection in a hall of mirrors: Historical influences and political reverberations', *Educational Researcher*, 32: 16–25.

Gilbert, W., Gallimore, R. and Trudel, P. (2009) 'A learning community approach to coach development in youth sport', *Journal of Coaching Education*, 2: 1–21.

Gilbert, W. and Trudel, P. (2006) 'The coach as a reflective practitioner', in R. Jones (ed.) *The Sports Coach as Educator: Re-Conceptualising Sports Coaching*, pp. 113–27, London: Routledge.

Habermas, J. (1975) *Legitimation Crisis*, Boston: Beacon Press.

Lave, J. and Wenger, E. (1991) *Situated Learning: Legitimate Peripheral Participation*, Cambridge: Cambridge University Press.

Lyle, J. and Cushion, C.J. (2017) *Sport Coaching Concepts: A Framework for Coaching Practice*, 2nd edn, London: Routledge.

Mezirow, J. (1991) *Transformative Dimensions of Adult Learning*, San Francisco: Jossey-Bass.

112 Cushion

Mezirow, J. (1997) 'Transformation theory out of context', *Adult Education Quarterly*, 48: 60–2.

Mezirow, J. (1998) 'On critical reflection', *Adult Education Quarterly*, 48: 185–98.

Norén, L. (1990) 'Om fallstudiens trovärdighet', FE-rapport, Department of Business Administration, Göteborg University.

Prawat, R.S. and Floden, R.E. (1994) 'Philosophical perspectives on constructivist views of learning', *Educational Psychologist*, 29: 37–48.

Schuh, K.L. and Barab, S.A. (2007) 'Philosophical perspectives', in J.M. Spector, M.D. Merrill, J. van Merrienboer and M.P. Driscoll (eds.) *Handbook of Research Educational Communications and Technology*, pp. 69–82, New York: Lawrence Erlbaum Associates and Taylor Francis Group.

Stodter, A. and Cushion, C.J. (2016) 'Effective coach learning and processes of coaches' knowledge development: What works?', in P.A. Davis (ed.) *The Psychology of Effective Coaching and Management*, pp. 35–52, New York: Nova Science Publishers.

Windschitl, M. (2002) 'Framing constructivism in practice as the negotiation of dilemmas: An analysis of the conceptual, pedagogical, cultural, and political challenges facing teachers', *Review of Educational Research*, 72: 131–75.

Young, R.A. and Collin, A. (2004) 'Introduction: Constructivism and social constructionism in the career field', *Journal of Vocational Behavior*, 64: 373–88.

SECTION 2

Coach development strategies in organizations

9

SOCIAL LEARNING IN COMMUNITIES AND NETWORKS AS A STRATEGY FOR ONGOING COACH DEVELOPMENT

Diane Culver, Erin Kraft, and Tiago Duarte

Chapter objectives

By the end of this chapter, the reader should be able to:

1   Provide the theoretical underpinnings of social learning theory to guide learning communities and networks.
2   Discuss examples of social learning in sport (including barriers and challenges).
3   Describe ongoing research using a social learning approach, along with practical steps to facilitate social learning.

Brief chapter overview

In this chapter, we discuss the evolution of Wenger-Trayner's[1] social learning theory; our research and experiences planning, promoting, and assessing social learning spaces; and practical tools for coach developers to facilitate coach development using this approach. Practically, an organization interested in learning communities should enable a coach developer to promote and assess social learning initiatives aligned with its strategic goals. A coach developer could reflect on and ask the following questions: In what learning activities are coaches engaging? What have they learned? Have they tested what they learned in practice? What were the results? Has that changed their practice, identity, or the community?

Why and when I use social learning

My (Diane) initial cultivation of a community of practice (CoP) was, to our knowledge, the first example of a social learning intervention for coach development (Alpine skiing and athletics; Culver & Trudel 2006). Since then, we have studied social learning in various sport spaces, including youth sport and the National Collegiate Athletic Association (NCAA). Recently, we are taking a landscape of practice (LoP) approach for parasport coach development (wheelchair curling and para-athletics). Furthermore, two of the authors (Diane and Erin) are conducting an evaluation for a social learning program in Alberta, Canada aiming to create gender equity and leadership development for women in sport.

The essentials of social learning

Definitions, essential components, and goals of social learning

Social learning theory

For many disciplines, including coaching and teaching, learning has been considered an individual activity, commonly removed from actual practice (Wenger 1998). This is so despite the work of Vygotsky, who died in 1934 but was not widely known outside of Russia until the late 1970s. Vygotsky theorized that we are innately social beings who learn from others (Vygotsky 1987). Indeed, the assumptions underlying social learning theory (SLT) are that humans are fundamentally social beings, learning is at the core of our existence, and as we learn, we become – hence, develop our identity. Therefore, identities, as well as meanings, are produced through our interactions with the world (Wenger 1998). These interactions take place in social learning spaces.

Social learning spaces

Social learning spaces are "places of genuine encounters among learners where they can engage their experience of practice" (Wenger 2009: 2). These include anything from one-on-one conversations to mentorships, personal and professional networks, learning communities, project teams, and communities of practice (CoPs). In social learning spaces, participants engage in interactions focused on "both their experience of practice and their experience of themselves in that practice" (Wenger 2009: 3). In this chapter, after continuing our brief story of the development of SLT, we will focus on coach development through participation in various social learning spaces, mostly networks and CoPs. Networks and CoPs are considered different aspects of "the social fabric of learning" (Wenger, Trayner & De Laat 2011: 9). The network aspect relates to "a set of nodes and links with affordances for learning, such as information flows, helpful linkages, joint problem solving, and knowledge creation" (p. 9). The CoP aspect involves members who share an identity and collective intention to advance knowledge about their practice.

In the early 1990s, during the first phase of SLT, the anthropologists Lave and Wenger (1991) studied human learning in certain practice-focused communities and published the monograph *Situated Learning*. This concept challenged the accepted, decontextualized model of learning whereby the application of knowledge is separated from the actual learning. Learning was reframed as a context specific social engagement, with the traditional apprenticeship model as the example. In the second phase of SLT, Wenger (1998) expanded on this approach, studying the concept of communities of practice (CoPs).

Communities of practice

The definition of a CoP is: "Groups of people who share a concern, a set of problems, or a passion about a topic, and who deepen their knowledge and expertise in this area by interacting on an ongoing basis" (Wenger, McDermott & Snyder 2002: 4). There are three essential characteristics of a CoP (Wenger-Trayner & Wenger-Trayner 2015). The *domain* is what makes the CoP relevant to its members, who share common ground and a commitment to certain competencies as defined by the CoP. This implies that they identify with the CoP. The *community* implies that members interact with each other by engaging in various activities related to their shared domain and practice, such as reflecting on, sharing, and co-creating knowledge. However, this does not imply that the members engage in their practice together. The *practice* involves the co-creation and sharing of a repertoire of resources such as tools, stories, and ways of doing and talking about their practice. The development, sharing, and upkeep of this knowledge is always specific to the local practice. The practice element of CoPs is about the knowledge contribution to the practice. It is important to dispel certain myths about CoPs, such as that they are harmonious, consensual, and involved in the reproduction of existing practices. In fact, a healthy CoP is one in which ambiguity and heterogenous opinions are welcome. This phase of SLT has played an influential role in our current culture of coach development, in that several empirical studies have nurtured CoPs in specific coaching contexts to promote learning and development.

Landscape of practice

As SLT continues to evolve it is scaling up from the community level to the level of the whole landscape of a practice. The concept of landscape of practice (LoP) has been recognized as an important perspective for building learning capability across organizations and professions. Given that the complete body of knowledge of any one profession is almost never understood to be housed within a single CoP, LoPs are defined as "a complex system of communities of practice and the boundaries between them" (Wenger-Trayner & Wenger-Trayner 2015: 13). This third phase of the SLT broadens the scope of a CoP and considers the LoP and the many learning opportunities between and at the borders of communities (Wenger-Trayner et al. 2017). This systems approach has been at the forefront of our research in the parasport and women in sport domains. Rather than fostering an individual CoP, our studies encompass a range of actors from those central to the community to others participating at the boundaries. To illustrate this point, and its implications for knowledge transfer, we will refer to the Alberta Women in Sport Leadership program. The program aims to help sport organizations achieve gender equity. This program involves a central CoP consisting of 12 leaders of sport organizations and five mentors. Recently, at a sport forum during the Canada Games, numerous sport leaders presented posters they had developed about their initiatives to transfer knowledge from the CoP to the greater coaching community. Wenger-Trayner et al. (2017) would refer to the posters as "boundary objects", enabling learning to extend beyond the CoP and the individual sport organizations to the greater landscape. Additionally, three of these women sport leaders participate in a Nationwide Status of Women Canada CoP, providing further learning opportunities across the landscape.

Goals: co-creating knowledge and empowering coaches

Considering the vast landscape of sport, as this book does, it is impossible for any single form of coach development to meet the needs of every coach. In the case of the youth sport domain, learning communities and networks allow coaches to be more intentional in their selection of coaching practices in fields (e.g. skiing, soccer) where available information is abundant. In these cases, the social learning spaces allow coaches to make meaning of information and subsequently create new knowledge applicable to their particular practices. In other coaching contexts, coaches are especially disadvantaged in their access to learning opportunities, making this instructional strategy appropriate for creating learning opportunities where they may not otherwise have existed. Over the past few years, our University of Ottawa research group has planned, promoted, and/or assessed (at varying stages, as this research is ongoing) various CoPs. Following, we will provide a description of what has been or may be achieved through these social learning interventions.

Facilitator and community members

As an instructional strategy, social learning spaces are driven by a learning agenda focused around the needs of those in the space. Thus, there are often no specific experts or knowers in the community, but rather, there is a group of people, with varying degrees of expertise, learning together. As such, the traditional roles of teacher and student do not apply. However, the role of a facilitator does play an important role in the ongoing engagement of a community. While

Social learning in communities and networks **119**

leadership can be distributed throughout the community and rotated, leadership is required to maintain the focus on learning (see Culver & Trudel 2006).

Learning communities in practice

The following section provides specific examples of empirical research to illustrate examples of CoPs as learning communities and networks. The key coaching disciplines from our empirical research referenced here can be categorized into three domains (coaching contexts): Youth sport (alpine skiing, soccer, and karate), parasport (paracycling, wheelchair curling, and para–athletics), and women in sport (NCAA, Alberta sport organizations). In terms of community, the three contexts included a variety of community members dependent on their goals, including: Youth sport (coaches, head coaches, coordinators, and mentors), parasport (coaches, integrated support team, Canadian Paralympic Committee, and Own The Podium),[2] and women in sport (sport administrators, coaches, provincial sport organization representatives, Coaching Association of Canada). As for practice, the youth sport domain collaborated to share best practices and to create local knowledge, whereas the parasport domain was interested in knowledge construction for context-specific practices, and minimizing isolation considering the geographical vastness of Canada and the relatively few opportunities to interact with others about para-coaching. Finally, the women in sport domain, sharing many similarities to the parasport domain, saw a focus on the empowerment of women and their allies, seeking to provide them with confidence and the tools necessary to promote change (gender equity and leadership development) in their practices and organizations. Please refer to Table 9.1 for an overview of the communities we nurtured and/or assessed.

While the following sections are neatly separated, the reader should keep in mind that social learning spaces are communities of enquiry in which design, planning, and delivery processes are usually cyclical in nature. An important aspect of this is that the participants are involved in the decisions made regarding the learning activities.

Designing and planning

In order to illustrate the design and planning of learning communities, we will rely heavily on cases from alpine skiing and wheelchair curling. While the idea to share and co-create knowledge at the local level is a major aspect of learning in communities, these two initiatives came at this from different angles. For instance, on one hand, the alpine CoP (Culver & Trudel 2006) was composed by youth coaches who worked in the same ski club. Skiing is a mainstream sport with a wealth of resources available to its coaches. Therefore, one of the challenges these coaches face is how to narrow down the types of information that are relevant at the local level. On the other hand, the wheelchair curling coaches have so few resources specific to their context that they need to be very creative

TABLE 9.1 Overview of the communities nurtured and/or assessed

Learning community	Number of members	Context	Meeting format	Facilitator(s); role	Incentives to participation besides learning
Wheelchair curling	20	From high-performance (HP) to developmental coaches from seven different provinces	More online than in-person	Researcher, non-member of the wheelchair curling (WC) community; nurtured and assessed	Professional development (PD) credits
Para-athletics	14	From HP to developmental coaches from four provinces	More online than in-person	Researcher, non-member of the para-athletics community; nurtured and assessed	Networking opportunity and PD
Women in sport	18	Women leaders and allies in sport organizations across one province	More online than in-person	Project leader and researcher, non-member of CoP; Researcher is assessing the CoP and developing a model	Opportunity to develop and implement gender equity projects for sport organizations/ access to mentors
NCAA women in sport	8	HP coaches and allies from the same university but different sports	All in-person	Coaches belonging to the community; research assessed	Access to colleagues and mentors
Ski coaches	17	U11–12 coaches from the same club	All in-person	Researcher member of the community; nurtured and assessed	
Karate	9	Instructors from the same club	All in-person	Researcher member of the community; nurtured and assessed	
Soccer	5	Youth coaches from the same club	All in-person	Researcher non-member of the community; nurtured and assessed	
Paracycling	5	HP coaches and HP directors from three provinces	One in-person	Researcher non-member of the community; failed to nurture	

Social learning in communities and networks **121**

in finding ways to solve their coaching issues. In many cases, the trial-and-error approach can be extremely frustrating and even put their athletes at risk of injury due to an unsuccessful tinkering process. Collaborative efforts to share and co-create specific parasport coaching knowledge attenuates this.

Both initiatives utilized constructivist views of learning in which the learner is at the center of the process, which should also provide value to the coaches from the start. To achieve that goal, the skiing CoP facilitator designed the meeting format to address a practical question. A few days before the first meeting, she asked the coaches to be prepared to share "three things that he or she had learned from their coaching practice in the days leading up to the meeting". In doing so, the coaches were engaged in learning that was narrowly linked to their daily practice. The discussions and subsequent solutions or suggestions (e.g. best practices) could then be applied and experimented with immediately by the coaches as they returned to their athletes on the slopes. It took the skiing CoP a few meetings to get used to the process, but once the ski coaches started to share their lessons, the facilitator stepped back as the coaches took ownership of the meeting. The design, and therefore the format, of the meetings stayed fairly consistent throughout the season. The coaches described it as a sort of laboratory in which individual and collective reflection led to changes in coaching practice and improvements in athlete outcomes. During the second phase of this project, the facilitator nurtured a different CoP of ski coaches from the same club. This time was during summer, and the shared domain was slightly different since the coaches were not with their regular teams, making the application of new learning less evident. The learning agenda was different, and the coaches, who were all very experienced, ended up sharing stories that were more about their professional life and the challenges related to being a ski coach. Every CoP will be different, given that the learning agenda depends on the CoP members and where they are in their lifelong learning. The design of the wheelchair curling CoP took a different direction. The facilitator conducted an in-depth interview to map the coaches' learning interests and sources. Based on our interviews, we identified that the coaches appreciated learning during training camps mainly because of access to more experienced coaches who are part of the National Team Program (NTP), as well as Sport Services and Sport Medicine (SSSM) specialists. These findings shaped the design of the learning activities. For instance, there were four types of group meetings, including meetings only with coaches to discuss their common issues, webinars with NTP coaches to discuss strategy and athlete benchmarks, webinars with SSSM experts to discuss a certain topic, and webinars with participant coaches who were knowledgeable in a certain field (e.g. fundraising). All these meetings were based on the interests determined from the interviews or expressed during previous meetings.

A common question regarding the curation of learning communities is the role played by the facilitator. In these two cases, they were very distinct. Diane (facilitator) was an expert in the sport of skiing, being a former competitor and high-performance coach who worked with the Canadian and New Zealand national programs. Such an insider perspective gave her the legitimacy to engage with the coaches as an expert member of that community. While her participation could be seen as one of authority, she focused her efforts on leaving the spotlight and allowing the coaches to direct the agenda. Tiago was almost on the other end of the spectrum because he was neither a member of the wheelchair curling nor the curling communities; his "fresh" eyes allowed him to explore the landscape and question the status quo of the sport. Since the CoP comprised coaches from so many provinces, Tiago organized online meetings and in-person ones during a few specific competitions he attended where he organized events for the coaches. While Diane's involvement diminished as the group meetings progressed and the coaches felt more comfortable with the group activities, Tiago's involvement increased as the coaches expressed their interest in exploring specific topics that required him to find and invite in experts from outside the learning community. These examples show that just as each community has its own identity, so the role of facilitator varies.

Delivering

When it comes to delivering activities for a CoP, there are considerable negotiations that must take place to meet the needs of as many community members as possible. It is important to note that not every community member is required to participate in every activity and meeting to maintain their membership. At times, some members may not consider an activity relevant to their needs, and may decide to abstain. Additionally, other issues such as time and location may not permit every member to participate fully.

The coaches' organizations play an important role in nurturing a CoP. Throughout Wenger's work, he and colleagues proposed that CoPs are an effective way to develop members of any given organization and supporting these initiatives should be in alignment with the organization's strategies. Therefore, different types of support should be provided. For instance, Curling Canada afforded access to many resources such as: (a) technology software to conduct the meetings; (b) human resources (SSSM providers and NTP coaches); (c) professional development credits to coaches who attended meetings and webinars; and (d) financial resources to plan social gatherings and allow Tiago to attend two national championships. These resources were viewed as strategic for the organization, since the athlete pathway for parasport is often shorter than in able-bodied sport. There are instances in which able-bodied athletic individuals (e.g. athletes or soldiers) acquire a disability, and with an understanding the training required to excel, it is not uncommon that they fast track to high-performance parasport. Thus, providing developmental coaches with access to the most up-to-date terminology and knowledge about the sport better positions them to identify such individuals and to provide a higher quality service for them. The following are examples of discussion topics that may be considered when delivering activities.

Online or in-person

The geographical proximity of members of any CoP is a factor that affects the way the meetings are designed and delivered. There are a few considerations that coach developers should reflect on before choosing the preferred medium of interaction. For online interactions, there are free alternatives for hosting meetings for small groups if funding is not available. However, our experience has been with paid platforms (e.g. Zoom, Skype, Adobe Connect, GotoMeeting). Many sport organizations already have accounts with such video conferencing programs; if not, the question of who will fund the meeting software must be addressed. Since the curling coaches live in seven different Canadian provinces and meet face-to-face only a few times every winter, an online platform was the only viable way to bring them together regularly. For in-person interactions, coach developers will need to address who organizes and pays for the space, food, and beverages. For instance, the ski coaches worked at the same club and were able to meet in person, thus a face-to-face approach was used and many other interactions among the coaches were observed outside of the meetings as they worked together on the mountain.

Creating an online space for sharing (e.g. GetAssist, Basecamp, Slack) also allows for posting meeting recordings, allowing those who were not in attendance access to the recorded content. In the wheelchair curling CoP, coaches who viewed the recorded events and reflected on a few targeted questions were awarded professional development credits, as if they attended the webinars. As well, these types of platforms allow for important continued discussion following activities.

Scheduling

As previously discussed, many CoPs include members from across a variety of locations and time zones. Trying to find a date and time that is convenient for most CoP members is essential. Sending out a poll (such as a Doodle poll) in advance with a selection of dates and times may assist with the process. Scheduling is also more successful when there is buy-in from the sport organizations and administration. For example, in the soccer CoP, the administration chose to schedule other meetings at the same time as CoP meetings, creating barriers for participation. Whereas with the para-athletics CoP, an insider played a significant role in promoting the CoP meetings and collaborating with the research team to propose potential activity dates that would fit well with the coaches' competitive schedules.

Finding experts

Some meetings may focus on facilitated discussions, while others may include a presentation from an expert to create context specific learning opportunities for a given CoP. We have found it useful to encourage CoP members to ask specific questions or recommend topics to the expert in advance so that the expert may cater their presentation to the needs of the CoP. As well, allotting more time than the traditional ten minutes at the end of the presentation for the members to ask additional questions to the expert may be effective for learning.

Challenges

Some consistent issues we have faced in cultivating and sustaining optimal learning in the CoPs are related to internet access, accommodating coaches' individual needs, working across time zones, and position turnover. To accommodate, we regularly send out Doodle polls before scheduling a meeting and take time zones into account, integrate some in-person meetings, and ask for help from others when necessary (e.g. e-mailing a coaches' spouse or partner who has internet access when the coach does not). In sport, turn-over and funding are systemic barriers that may affect the capabilities of a CoP.

The following section will discuss our evaluations of CoPs to assess the value created (or not) from these activities and meetings.

Evaluating

Our methods for evaluating learning communities have changed and grown over the years, along with the development of new assessment tools. In this section, we will describe our initial attempts to assess CoPs and then address our more recent attempts utilizing an evolving framework specifically geared toward planning, promoting, and assessing social learning spaces. In the latter instance, we have used quite rigorous methods for assessments, as we are in an academic context. However, the tools mentioned ahead may be applied to other sport coaching contexts so that coach developers may assess the value gained in learning communities and going forward modify activities according to the evolving needs of coaches.

In my (Diane's) earlier assessments of CoPs (youth sport), data were primarily collected through qualitative interviews and participant observations, and analyzed using thematic analysis. Wenger, Trayner and De Laat (2011) developed an assessment framework specifically for communities and networks titled the Value Creation Framework (VCF). This framework provides a way to assess community members' perceptions of value gained (or not) in a social learning space. The initial framework consisted of five main value cycles – *immediate, potential, applied, realized,* and *transformative* value (see Wenger, Trayner & De Laat 2011 for definitions of each value). We have found this framework to be useful, both as a guide to continue fostering learning and as a means to show evidence of value created (or not). First, we have assessed CoPs to keep us abreast of what is working and what may be adjusted to promote further learning according to the CoP members' collective and individual needs. Second, having evidence of perceived value gained provides data for stakeholders and other key actors wishing to see the return on their investments. In one of our first studies using this framework, community members participated in three interviews with the primary investigator (coaches of women's teams in the NCAA; Bertram, Culver & Gilbert 2017). The analysis of the community members' stories and experiences of participating in their CoP allowed for the assessment of their perceived value created. The VCF provides specific indicators for each value cycle (for examples of indicators, refer to Wenger, Trayner & De Laat 2011).

More recently, Wenger-Trayner et al. (2017) developed an additional two cycles (*strategic* and *enabling* value) which explore value created through interactions (e.g. quantity and the quality of these) with stakeholders and other actors who may influence and support the ongoing social learning efforts of the community (for definitions of these cycles, refer to Wenger-Trayner et al. 2017). These two forms of value have become more significant in our more recent work (parasport and women in coaching), as the number of CoP members have increased and diversified (e.g. moving from a small community of coaches to communities with multiple organizations).

In our ongoing program evaluation of a social learning initiative with Alberta sport organizations (women in sport), both the data generation and the analysis to assess this CoP are taking a landscape approach. The landscape approach aims to assess both the learning and value created through the CoP, as well as the value created at the borders of the CoP (e.g. with individuals outside of the CoP) and across the landscape. Our first point of data generation in this evaluation was collected through a short online survey (e.g. "What are some ways the CoP could function differently to support the outcomes of my organization's project?"). The purpose of the survey was to ask the participating members if the CoP was functioning optimally in order for them to meet their goals, aligning with the iterative nature of designing, delivering, and assessing a CoP. A consolidated version of the anonymous results was then provided to the CoP facilitators so that they could adjust the CoP accordingly. Subsequently, Erin conducted one-on-one, semi-structured interviews with each CoP member. In addition to answering interview questions, each member completed the Value Creation Story and Personal Value Narratives templates found in the VCF (refer to Wenger, Trayner & De Laat 2011 for both templates). These templates are tools designed to prompt participants to reflect on their experiences of the CoP, which are then analyzed and assessed for value gained according to all seven cycles.

Outside of higher education contexts, a coach developer may also choose to reflect on the growth of the community, and may consider asking the following questions: In what learning activities are coaches engaging? What have they learned? Have they tested what they learned in practice? What were the results? Has that changed their practice, identity, or the community? These reflections could serve as more of an informal assessment to maintain an awareness of the ever-changing needs of the community.

Personal reflections and wishful thinking

The wheelchair curling community has continued its investment in the CoP for a second year, signaling strong buy-in. All our projects have resulted in positive value for coaches. It seems that the coach development community is now recognizing the importance of adding social learning initiatives to the spectrum of coach development opportunities.[3] The upscaling of SLT to include the landscape perspective will enable a systems approach to coach development. A systems approach to coach development would strive to align learning activities with the broader objectives of a whole organization, or sport community. It would spread the onus for coach development across the landscape and include funders and other important stakeholders. For example, a high-performance director would schedule in certain social learning activities for coach development when distributing the yearly training plan template to coaches (see following for examples), in the same way that major competitions are indicated. This would indicate to coaches and organizations that coach development should involve more than individual coach activities, and that coach learning should not only be sought in the presence of other coaches but can include a variety of other people from the landscape (see Chapter 10). Additionally, a systems approach would have sport funding tied to such planning and require sports to provide evidence of the value created for individual coaches, organizations, and even athletic performance.

Activities for coach education

1   Identify coaches' learning networks and landscape (e.g. influential people, sources of knowledge, National Sport Organizations, Provincial Sport Organizations, etc.). We have used various techniques to accomplish this: Timelining, concept mapping, and mind mapping. Sometimes we have produced these maps on the basis of interviews with the coaches, and other times we have handed the coaches a paper to do this themselves and backed this up with a clarification interview. This exercise raises awareness of possible learning sources and opens the pathway for designing learning opportunities with these key stakeholders.

    a   Divide coaches into small groups and have them negotiate the top three learning needs of the whole group.
    b   All small groups negotiate and then write their top three learning needs on post-its and place them on a wall.
    c   Each coach then receives three stickies.
    d   Have the entire group of coaches walk around the room and place a sticky on their individual three most important learning needs.
    e   Use totals to determine which learning needs are collectively most important, and plan activities accordingly.

Additional resources

1   Wenger-Trayner, E. and Wenger-Trayner, B. (2018) *Communities of practice handbook*, May, version 5.0.
2   Wenger, E., Trayner, B. and De Laat, M. (2011) *Promoting and assessing value creation in communities and networks: A conceptual framework*. Report 18, Ruud de Moor Centrum, Open University of the Netherlands.

Notes

1 Etienne Wenger married a renowned learning consultant named Beverly Trayner in 2012. They both now take the surname Wenger-Trayner.
2 Federal government organization supporting high-performance sport in Canada.
3 The International Council for Coaching Excellence (ICCE) is organizing an event about learning communities and networks for international coach developers before the ICCE Global Coaching Congress in 2019 in Tokyo, Japan.

Bibliography

Bertram, R., Culver, D.M. and Gilbert, W. (2016) 'Creating value in a sport coach community of practice: A collaborative inquiry', *International Sport Coaching Journal*, 3: 2–16.
Bertram, R., Culver, D.M. and Gilbert, W. (2017) 'A university sport coach community of practice: Using a value creation framework to explore learning and social interactions', *International Journal of Sports Sciences and Coaching*, 12: 1–16.
Culver, D. and Trudel, P. (2006) 'Cultivating coaches' communities of practice: Developing the potential for learning through interactions', in R. Jones (ed.) *Re-Defining the Coaching Role and How to Teach It: New Ways of Thinking About Practice*, pp. 97–112, London: Routledge.
Lave, J. and Wenger, E. (1991). *Situated Learning: Legitimate Peripheral Participation*, Cambridge: Cambridge University Press.
McMaster, S., Culver, D.M. and Werthner, P. (2012) 'Coaches of athletes with a physical disability: A look at their learning experiences', *Qualitative Research in Sport, Exercise and Health*, 4: 226–43.
Nelson, L.J., Cushion, C.J. and Potrac, P. (2006) 'Formal, nonformal and informal coach learning: A holistic conceptualisation', *International Journal of Sport Science and Coaching*, 1: 247–59.
Vygotsky, L. (1987) 'Thinking and speech', in R.W. Rieber and A.S. Carton (eds.) *The Collected Works of L.S. Vygotsky, Vol. 1: Problems of General Psychology*, pp. 37–285, New York: Plenum.
Wenger, E. (1998) *Communities of Practice: Learning, Meaning, and Identity*, Cambridge: Cambridge University Press.
Wenger, E. (2009) 'Essays on social learning capability: Four essays on innovation and learning in social systems', in *Social Innovation*, Sociedade e Trabalho, Lisbon: MTSS/GEP & EQUAL.
Wenger, E., McDermott, R. and Snyder, W.M. (2002) *Cultivating Communities of Practice*, Boston: Harvard Business School Press.
Wenger, E., Trayner, B. and De Laat, M. (2011) *Promoting and Assessing Value Creation in Communities and Networks: A Conceptual Framework*, Rapport 18, Ruud de Moor Centrum, Open University of the Netherlands.

Wenger-Trayner, E., Fenton-O'Creevy, M., Kubiak, C., Hutchinson, S. and Wenger-Trayner, B. (eds.). (2014) *Learning in Landscapes of Practice: Boundaries, Identity, and Knowledgeability in Practice-Based Learning*, London: Routledge.

Wenger-Trayner, E. and Wenger-Trayner, B. (2015) *Introduction to communities of practice: A brief overview of the concept and its uses*. Online. Available HTTP: <wenger-trayner.com/introduction-to-communities-of-practice/> (accessed 5 December 2018).

Wenger-Trayner, B., Wenger-Trayner, E., Cameron, J., Eryigit-Madzwamuse, S. and Hart, A. (2017) 'Boundaries and boundary objects: An evaluation framework for mixed methods research', *Journal of Mixed Methods Research*, 1–18.

10

TRAVEL-BASED LEARNING

Study Tours for high-performance coaches

Diane Culver, Darren Holder, and Steven B. Rynne

Chapter objectives

By the end of this chapter, the reader should be able to:

1   Develop the case for why International Coach Study Tours might be valuable for high-performance coaches (HPCs).
2   Understand the design and delivery of a high-performance Study Tour by a major sporting organization.
3   Discuss means of evaluating the value created through such a Study Tour.

Brief chapter overview

In this chapter, we tell the story of the International Coach Study Tour (Study Tour), an ongoing coach development strategy designed and delivered by Cricket Australia (CA) for its national-level coaches. By exposing these coaches to cultures of excellence in other performance domains, CA hopes to encourage their HPCs to expand their horizons and to become innovators in their practice.

Why and when I use travel-based Study Tours

The overarching Study Tour aims were to shift the culture and perception of coaching in cricket, create cultures of excellence, and inspire continuous learning for coaches in high–performance environments. The Study Tours typically last seven to ten days, and involve visits to multiple organizations renowned for performance excellence. Following the initial Study Tour, Cricket Australia (CA) invested in two subsequent HPC Study Tours and a Leadership Tour. The second author, Darren, is the elite coaching manager for CA and was the person responsible for conceiving of and organizing the Study Tours. The first and third authors have been involved as coach development researchers, assisting mostly with the evaluations of the tours through a collaborative inquiry framework, which is "a way of structuring adult learning experiences" (Bray, Lee, Smith & Yorks 2000: 16).

The essentials of travel-based Study Tours

Definitions, essential components, and goals of TBST

The role of the coaches was to participate in every activity as a motivated learner. Preparatory materials, formulated and provided by the coach developers (CDs), took the form of study diaries and workbooks. There was also a variety of priming materials supplied, such as various readings and short video clips (see Additional Resources at the conclusion of this chapter).

The CDs led the Study Tours and fulfilled a variety of functions, from driving vehicles and speaking to hosts ahead of time to confirming logistics, general bookings, and travel arrangements. In terms of impact on coach learning, the CDs facilitated discussions among the high-performance coaches (HPCs) in support of reflection and applied learning. Being the leaders in the design and concept development, the CDs were best placed to introduce the HPCs to their hosts and outline content to be investigated during interactions. The CDs also had the benefit of observing the HPCs during the Study Tour and assessing their ability to comprehend principles that could be adapted for implementation into their practice. CDs also posed challenging questions and helped make meaning across the sites.

Educating HPCs

Learning to coach is a complex, lifelong process, particularly for HPCs (Milistetd, Peniza, Trudel & Paquette 2018). Evidence indicates that the HPC pathway is idiosyncratic (Rynne, Mallett & Tinning 2010; Werthner & Trudel 2009), which complicates coach development opportunities for HPCs. That is, the current trend of a learner-centered approach, which demands that the experiences of the learner be taken into consideration when designing learning opportunities, is confounded when the idiosyncratic pathways of HPCs are considered. Therefore, when faced with a group of HPCs, a coach developer would be hard pressed to design a series of activities to satisfy the numerous needs of a diverse group.

Sport coaches report learning much from experience and observation (Trudel & Gilbert 2006). The nature of such constructivist learning opportunities conforms to both learner-centered and situated approaches to learning, wherein learning is a function of the learner engaging in the activity and context in which the learning occurs (Lave & Wenger 1991). A substantial body of literature exists regarding such approaches for general workplace learning (e.g. Billett 2014), as well as coach development (e.g. Araya, Bennie & O'Connor 2015; Culver & Trudel 2006). Given CA's objective to broaden the thinking of its HPCs regarding innovative practices, Darren decided that the opportunity to observe and interact with those involved in different high-performance (HP) cultures, and to reflect on and discuss these encounters, would create an appropriate context for workplace learning. Because many of the HPCs on the Study Tour were often opponents, it was the hope that their displacement from the cricket world into other HP cultures would facilitate shared reflections.

Assessing the learning

We applied a specific framework to evaluate the success of the Study Tour and to guide future Study Tours. The Value Creation Framework (VCF; Wenger, Trayner & De Laat 2011; Wenger-Trayner et al. 2017) was formulated to promote and assess the learning value created within the varying social learning spaces (see also Chapter 9). Following the Study Tours, the VCF, comprising seven value cycles (immediate, potential, applied, realized, transformative, enabling, and strategic), guided the interviews used to assess the Study Tour participants' learning. The analysis of the interview transcripts involved looking for indicators of the seven value cycles (Wenger, Trayner & De Laat 2011; Wenger-Trayner et al. 2017). Table 10.1 provides sample quotations from the coaches which support the value created in the different cycles.

Doing the Study Tours

The organizational circumstances were favorable for the creation of the Study Tour. In 2015, at the same time the CDs were looking for opportunities to further HPC development, CA commissioned independent consultants to conduct a review and benchmarking assessment of its men's and women's high-performance programs. The report noted "the role and status of coaches remains misunderstood, unclear and under-valued . . . it is also a widely accepted view that some coaches are not open enough to outside input and that this is also holding back the performance progress of the sport". The CDs used this opportunity to secure organizational support for the Study Tour, because it had the potential to address both the issue of the HPCs feeling undervalued and the view that the progress of sport performance was hindered by the narrow thinking of some HPCs. CA agreed that CDs would identify high-achieving coaches committed to learning and provide this group with a distinctive learning opportunity. The tour of foreign environments known for performance excellence would broaden and challenge the thinking of the HPCs, as well as create positive visibility for the investment within and beyond CA.

132 Culver, Holder, and Rynne

TABLE 10.1 Sample value created for the different cycles

Value cycle	Coach evidence – quotations
Immediate	Being in and around the other coaches confirmed my coaching outlook and knowing I'm on the right track and something I'm ready for.
Potential	No plan in particular about how to implement this, but it will start by reviewing current practices. Will have a lesson plan for each session, followed by a review session: What worked well? What didn't? What do we need to improve?
Applied	[I've] made clear changes to giving staff clear roles and trusting them with these roles . . . [I'm] delegating roles more often, particularly the planning roles.
Realized	Some athletes were initially skeptical of the exercise, but soon were very involved and were actively creating games that may not have even showcased their strengths, but they were very enthusiastic to be involved.
Transformative	[I question what] success will look like, if players start making their own decisions on-field and appreciate being put out of their comfort zones in trainings.
Enabling	Feel valued from CA. The general feeling from all the coaches on tour, including myself, could not believe how much the company values its employees by investing this money to take us on a trip.
Strategic	I actually spoke at our annual general meeting and I talked about the plight of the team and then I finished by saying "for what it's worth, this was my experience" [on one part of the tour].

Numerous conversations took place to examine Study Tour programs that had occurred with other high performing national sport organizations. These programs included specific coach immersion at Olympic Games, up to one cycle in advance of HPCs taking responsibility for athletes and teams representing at international events. Facilitated by the Australian Institute of Sport (AIS), these Study Tours and visits to other major international sporting events (e.g. the Australian Open) provided valuable insight for the design and implementation of our tours. Additionally, the Australian Football League (AFL) and Australian Football League Coaches Association (AFLCA) hosted off-season Study Tours for HPCs to both the United States and Europe to coincide with major sports leadership forums. These were informative in terms of the people, places, and events of interest. Finally, individual franchise teams from the National Rugby League (NRL) and AFL developed off-season trips for their senior performance staff to access comparable environments in the USA and Europe.

The CDs commenced planning of the Study Tour by leveraging domestic and international relationships afforded through the status of CA (i.e. it is a high-status sport with global reach). In addition, the CDs made use of their personal networks locally and globally developed over many years of work, consultancy, and continuing professional development. Of direct and critical relevance to this initiative was the foundational involvement of university researchers/CDs, meaning that CA could garner input with respect to the program design, implementation, facilitation, review, and evaluation.

While consideration was given to a variety of international locations, the Study Tours were undertaken in the United States due to the density of performance environments. That is, the Study Tour could access a variety of elite performance organizations and/or personnel with relative convenience. Additionally, the CDs felt that taking the HPCs into a context where cricket was not well-known would remove their "star status". This ego-free environment for learning would allow the HPCs to ask questions and share their knowledge, lack thereof, and appetite for learning.

Despite senior management within CA being kept abreast of the planning, we needed formal endorsement of the proposal, as it had not been part of the annual schedule of events forecasted in the previous budget cycle. Darren needed to align the Study Tour goals with the strategic priorities of the organization and to support the funding request with regular and persuasive communication with the key decision-makers. Following extensive reviews and reporting on the inaugural Study Tour, a budget was established to resource future iterations on a "business as usual" basis. Using the VCF provided a way of demonstrating the significant investment that CA was making in the HPCs' development.

Designing and planning

The coaches considered for inclusion in the Study Tours were existing HPCs working at national or international levels of CA. They were chosen by applying distinctive selection criteria to an already existing "depth chart" of more than 40 elite coaches within the sport. A panel of seven high-performance personnel across Australian cricket provided independent assessment of the potential participants. These personnel made assessments in relation to professional workload and existing commitments, capability to be a future Australian head, assistant, or specialist assistant coach (or future state/domestic franchise/international franchise/international head coach), potential as a long-term coaching asset of the sport, capacity for growth, and ability to learn and share with others. The types of HPCs invited included existing leaders of national programs, state and domestic franchise head coaches and assistant coaches, of both male and female programs. Nineteen cricket HPCs, along with five HP staff (including the CDs), toured in three separate iterations. Since their involvement, more than half of this group have progressed to more senior roles with domestic or national programs.

CA partnerships and continuing professional development activities with the cricket community – and with a variety of organizations, institutions, and individuals – afforded the CDs with leads for proposed visit locations. In addition, it was imperative that the HPCs were engaged in decisions around what they would learn in the development of the Study Tour, as they would ultimately benefit and ideally be advocates of the experience. However, while the HPCs were committed to the Study Tour idea from the outset, they were unable to contribute significantly to the initial design of the program. As one coach stated, "I don't know what I don't know". His subsequent suggestion was "surround us with quality people and have as many head coaches around the group and part of the group as possible". These comments governed the design of the Study Tour. Various locations were subsequently identified to provide access to performance settings in six major domains: Professional sport, college (development) athletics, media, arts and entertainment, education, and industry. These settings had either direct relevance to coaching and performance, or to the principles that underpinned the Study Tour aims.

In line with the overarching Study Tour aims, four areas of development guided Darren's eventual selection of site visits: Innovation, sustainable success, cultures of excellence, and next practice. "Innovation" was a major reason for the inclusion of San Francisco, California and the Bay Area in each of the Study Tours. It is the only location featured on all tours. It enabled the coaches to interact with entities such as Google, Facebook, Twitter, Stanford University, and the San Francisco Giants. As an example of innovation, the HPCs were involved in a discussion with a team of engineers at Google. Following a brief introduction from Google innovation executives, personnel from Google and the Study Tour were paired to explore their role and function within their respective teams, uncovering principles that stand true across domains and are needed for teams to function effectively. This led to deeper conversations around the collective goal of the Google team, the roles of individuals within a collective and their contribution of expertise to the team, and an ensuing presentation detailing work in progress. We were then able to see this come to life with a driverless car demonstration and the associated explanation.

"Sustainable success" and "cultures of excellence" were features of the visits to the New York Yankees, San Antonio Spurs, ESPN, NFL, Notre Dame University, Toyota, and UCLA.

Sustainable success was evident in the evolution of the ESPN business and its ability to transform with the changing media landscape, while acquiring new business through the commitment to its ethos, "ESPN: The Worldwide Leader in Sports". Contributing to the ongoing and sustainable success of their model, the HPCs were privy to its practice of exploring new frontiers in sporting markets and platforms combined with a dedication to learning and staying true to the stories of the past. Creating cultures of excellence was a key interest for many of the HPCs, and Toyota served as a tremendous representation of this theme. Much has been written on "The Toyota Way" and their "Kata"; however, to hear from a senior executive enabled the HPCs to gain first-hand insight into the practice and how this permeates their business. In the intimate surrounds of the vehicle museum, HPCs observed a short presentation, followed by a question-and-answer session to explore topics such as the management structure, development programs, succession planning, marketing strategy, and brand positioning. Most striking was the unwavering commitment and discipline to plan projects so thoroughly that every possible scenario was considered. For example, if there was a 12-month period to develop a product from concept to production, Toyota would spend the first 11 months planning every detail, testing it over and over to mitigate all errors and flaws. Then, the final month would be spent finalizing the product to ready it for market. Furthermore, as an example of the priority placed by all staff on efficiency, no meeting lasts longer than 15 minutes – seven minutes to present a plan, and eight minutes for colleagues to interrogate the proposal and its outcome. Numerous coaches in this Study Tour have since adapted the lessons learned from Toyota into their everyday practice. For example, one HPC now ensures that meetings of performance staff have clarity of purpose and are limited to 15 minutes. A further example is the planning process for major international events whereby a strategy for success is established well before the actual performance, enabling testing and refinement over an extended period of time.

Finally, "next practice" was prioritized through encounters with the Cirque du Soleil, Chicago Cubs, Major League Soccer, Red Bull Media House and Performance Lab, prominent authors, and academics. Red Bull Media House in Los Angeles was a particular highlight for the HPCs, particularly because the Red Bull brand is synonymous with high-end talent across multiple performance domains. Spending time with High Performance Director Andy Walshe, as well as observing and discussing the experiences of Red Bull talent as they encounter various challenges in "performing under pressure" camps, served the purpose of expanding the horizons of the HPCs. This learning experience demonstrated that HPCs should step away from the game from time to time and create situations to disrupt their athletes' sense of comfort in their daily environment. Unsettling these daily rhythms is a focus at Red Bull; however, risk is always measured and supported with expertise surrounding any new task or environment. The facility also provides a variety of cutting-edge technologies and training systems so talent can be exposed to protocols, both predictive and descriptive, well before they become mainstream.

Key elements of the Study Tour as an instructional strategy are the educational workshops with an internationally renowned academic in sport coaching, in which the HPCs reflected on the interactions and observations afforded them during the Study Tour. In addition, the workshops created a deeper level of thinking from the HPCs as they made meaning of the visits and encounters throughout the Study Tour. By exploring the aforementioned themes in a systematic and deliberate way, the HPCs are encouraged to gain an understanding of the principles that underpin best practice. This process of seeking out the principles that are foundational to the performance and success of the people and organizations encountered on tour also applies to the themes of innovation, sustainable success, and cultures of excellence. Darren strategically positioned these sessions toward the conclusion of stimulus visits for maximum effect. This culminating experience of the Study Tour, a series of targeted workshops blended with social learning in a natural setting, brings together the situated experiential learning and establishes a platform for better coaching as the HPCs return to their daily environment with new ideas, stronger processes, and a better understanding of what quality coaching looks like.

A central learning tool utilized as a reference point for HPCs on the Study Tours is a comprehensive study diary and workbook. This document requires considerable preparation as it contains everything pertaining to the Study Tour, including:

- Complete itineraries for each participant.
- Overall schedule and visit details.
- Times and locations.
- Personal profiles and contacts.
- Book reviews and learning goals for each coach.
- Preparation strategies.
- Effective observation and interaction checklists.
- Background information on locations, history, culture, customs, and major sports.
- City briefs.
- Comprehensive summaries of tour sites.
- Daily learning intentions and themes.
- Daily observation and interaction recording tools.
- Questions for reflective thoughts, additional insights, and perspectives.
- Summary notes.

The workbook and diary serve as both a record of the thoughts of each individual through his or her lens, and also a physical record of the thoughts of others shared in the reflective sessions. It becomes a basis for future practice and a resource to reflect upon as a memory of the learning moments and what is required to continually improve.

Specific work of the lead coach developer

The preparation for, engagement in, and review of the Study Tour involved substantial work for the lead CD. The following lists provides examples of some of the tasks performed by the lead CD.

Prior to the Study Tour:

1   Initial garnering of support internally.
2   Engagement with individuals and host organizations to secure services and confirm intentions (including making sure they understand cricket and scale, purpose and intention, etc.).
3   Identification and invitation of possible coach participants (including internal liaison and screening).
4   Collaborative development of individual coach learning goals (including consultation with HP managers to align with previously developed PD plans

Travel-based learning **137**

and learning goals), pre-tour briefings, and provision of pre-tour primers for coaches.

5 Development of Study Tour diary/workbook.

During the Study Tour:

1 Troubleshooting changes of plans and logistics.
2 Stimulating reflections and supporting learning throughout.
3 Organizing media opportunities.

After the Study Tour:

1 Activation of post-tour surveys, including working with the researchers to use the VCF.
2 Follow-up with all visited organizations.
3 Engagement in research project.
4 Development and presentation of summary reports.
5 Development of next Study Tour.

Personal reflections and wishful thinking

The principle benefits to CA of this collaborative inquiry approach to Study Tours include:

1 The theoretical basis that provided a bedrock for action. A good theory can be practical, informing, as in this case, an evidence-based practice.
2 The use of the VCF helped CA internally by assisting individuals (CDs) and the organization (CA overall) in documenting the value. This is important because it counters the notion of these Study Tours being mere "junkets".
3 The Study Tours opened the doors for the revisiting of sites, both for future Study Tours and individuals.
4 The Study Tours allowed for the meaningful collaboration with international scholars, leading to numerous extensive continuing professional development episodes for a wider spectrum of the HP coaching community.
5 The collaboration positions cricket differently and addresses the initial rationale to elevate the status and value of the coach in cricket (i.e. presence at research conferences – domestic and international profile in research).

In keeping with the collaborative inquiry approach, we identify overall benefits of involvement for the researchers:

1 The Study Tour program provides researchers in coach development with a site for research; for us and our students.

138 Culver, Holder, and Rynne

2 Such projects allow us, as applied researchers, to have direct impact on coaches and sport organizations.
3 This project has fostered enduring relationships, with the potential for future grants and practical placements for our students.

What might be modified

In order for us, as coach developers, to continue garnering support for future Study Tours, certain aspects of the research component might be modified:

1 Future research should capture changes over time. A return to the HPCs six months or a year after their Study Tour would provide a deeper understanding of the impact of the Study Tour on coaching practice. Seeking the perspectives of athletes and others, as well as observational data of the HPCs in practice, could help support our understandings of value created (or not) by Study Tour participation.
2 The VCF is a useful tool for assessing value, and going forward, it can be used not just to evaluate a Study Tour, but to plan additional tours. Starting with the VCF as a planning tool would entail getting as much information ahead of time about the aspirations of the different constituents. For instance, CDs (including researchers, as the case may be) can ask HPCs what immediate, potential, applied, and realized value they would hope to get out of participating in a Study Tour. The HPCs should also be asked a "blue sky" question such as "One year from now, what would be the greatest thing that could result from your participation in the Study Tour?" The same questions can be asked of sport administrators. Then, with these in mind, the tour planners (i.e. CDs) should examine what kinds of strategic conversations they need to have to be sure that the tour objectives are aligned with specific aims of the HPCs and the sport organization. Furthermore, the CDs should consider what enabling factors will support the accomplishment of these aims (i.e. what needs to be in place for success?). Based on this information, the CDs need to think about what kinds of indicators could be used to support the eventual evaluation of the tour's success, and who needs to be made aware of the tour outcomes as evaluated.

For Darren, the lead CD, the Study Tours have been an amazing experience, both professionally and personally. Professionally, the tours were considered by CA as so successful that he was asked by CA to organize a tour for its senior executives and leaders of the performance unit which included the head coach and captain of the national men's team. Personally, he has been recognized beyond his sport; he was asked to organize and lead a Study Tour for a group of golf HPCs. As the Study Tours have evolved, the idea of cross-pollination by involving HPCs of other sports has been implemented, and this could be further developed. The participation of a researcher on an actual Study Tour would also likely provide

Travel-based learning **139**

a deeper understanding of the learning that occurs, and provide the basis for a more complete story.

Activities for coach education

1 CDs can use the following activity entitled "Bringing Your Study Diary to Life – What's Your Story?" to help coaches understand their learning during a Study Tour. Write a story of your Study Tour experience highlighting: a) the most memorable observation; and (b) the most useful or interesting interaction, and why? For each point, be sure to include:

   a Describe it in detail.
   b What skills or knowledge were inherent?
   c Why was it so impactful?
   d What are the underlying principles that make it valuable?
   e How does this connect to the culture of the team/club/sport/ organization?

2 CDs can ask the tour participants: What are the compelling questions (two to three only) that you would like to answer that have been generated from these Study Tour experiences?

3 To help tour participants transfer their learning from a tour into their practices, CDs can ask them to submit a dated, written reflection on the following questions: Are there any concrete actions that you can commit to that help to optimize, and create alignment and clarity for the way you do things? What needs to happen to progress these actions (responsibility, timeline, support, barriers, etc.)?

Additional resources

1 Ermeling, B.A. (2012) 'Improving teaching through continuous learning: The inquiry process John Wooden used to become the coach of the century', *Quest*, 64: 197–208.

2 Gilbert, W. (2017) *Coaching Better Every Season*, Champaign: Human Kinetics.

3 McAdams, D.P. (2016) *The mind of Donald Trump*, The Atlantic. Online. Available HTTP: <www.theatlantic.com/magazine/archive/2016/06/the-mind-of-donald-trump/480771/>.

4 Marshall, K. (2018) *How vulnerability became sport's winning weapon*, The Sydney Morning Herald. Online. Available HTTP: <www.smh.com.au/sport/how-vulnerability-became-sport-s-winning-weapon-20180514-p4zf72.html>.

5 Reid, J. (2011) *'Moneyball' is compelling but leaves out much of the real story*, The Washington Post. Online. Available HTTP: <www.washingtonpost.com/sports/nationals/moneyball-is-compelling-but-leaves-out-much-of-the-real-story/2011/10/11/gIQAMA1cdL_story.html>.

6 Following are samples of YouTube clips provided to HPCs as primers related to planned Study Tour interactions:

a David Epstein – www.youtube.com/watch?v=8COaMKbNrX0
b Adam Grant – www.youtube.com/watch?v=fxbCHn6gE3U
c Malcolm Gladwell – www.youtube.com/watch?v=ziGD7vQOwl8
d Moneyball – www.youtube.com/watch?v=-4QPVo0UIzc
e Wade Gilbert – www.youtube.com/watch?v=rZ_matZKgDY
f Andy Walshe – www.youtube.com/watch?v=zgDJmnS_61w

Bibliography

Araya, J., Bennie, A. and O'Connor, D. (2015) 'Understanding performance coach development: Perceptions about a postgraduate coach education program', *International Sport Coaching Journal*, 3–14.

Billett, S. (2014) 'Learning in the circumstances of practice', *International Journal of Lifelong Education*, 33: 674–93.

Bray, J.N., Lee, J., Smith, L.L. and Yorks, L. (2000) *Collaborative Inquiry in Practice*, Thousand Oaks, CA: Sage.

Culver, D. and Trudel, P. (2006) 'Cultivating coaches' communities of practice: Developing the potential for learning through interactions', in R. Jones (ed.) *Re-Defining the Coaching Role and How to Teach It: New Ways of Thinking about Practice*, pp. 97–112, London: Routledge.

Lave, J. and Wenger, E. (1991) *Situated Learning: Legitimate Peripheral Participation*, Cambridge: Cambridge University Press.

Milistetd, M., Peniza, L., Trudel, P. and Paquette, K. (2018) 'Nurturing high-performance sport coaches' learning and development using a narrative-collaborative coaching approach', *LASE Journal of Sport Science*, 9: 6–38.

Rynne, S.B., Mallett, C.J. and Tinning, R. (2010) 'Workplace learning of high performance sports coaches', *Sport, Education and Society*, 15: 315–30.

Trudel, P. and Gilbert, W. (2006) 'Coaching and coach education', in D. Kirk, M. O'Sullivan and D. McDonald (eds.) *Handbook of Physical Education*, pp. 516–539, London: Sage.

Wenger, E., Trayner, B. and De Laat, M. (2011) *Promoting and Assessing Value Creation in Communities and Networks: A Conceptual Framework*, Rapport 18, Ruud de Moor Centrum, Open University of the Netherlands.

Wenger-Trayner, B., Wenger-Trayner, E., Cameron, J., Eryigit-Madzwamuse, S. and Hart, A. (2017) 'Boundaries and boundary objects: An evaluation framework for mixed methods research', *Journal of Mixed Methods Research*, 1–18.

Werthner, P. and Trudel, P. (2009) 'Investigating the idiosyncratic learning paths of elite Canadian coaches', *International Journal of Sport Science and Coaching*, 4(3): 433–450.

11

A "PERSONAL LEARNING COACH" FOR HIGH-PERFORMANCE COACHES

A companion to reflect and learn from one's own coaching practice

François Rodrigue and Pierre Trudel

Chapter objectives

At the end of this chapter, readers should be able to:

1 Understand the rationale for proposing a new actor, entitled "personal learning coach", to support high-performance sport coaches in their lifelong learning journey.
2 Outline the essential components of narrative-collaborative coaching, the approach that guides the conversation between a personal learning coach and a high-performance coach.
3 Conceptualize the use of narrative-collaborative coaching in their own professional practice.

Brief chapter overview

In this chapter, we first argue that current coach education programs and other teaching initiatives somewhat prepare coaches to assume their role; however, they are not suited to help experienced high-performance (HP) coaches in their lifelong learning journey. Second, we introduce the personal learning coach (PLC) as a new actor to help HP coaches learn from their actual coaching practice. By using a narrative-collaborative coaching

(NCC) approach, the PLC becomes a learning companion in the co-creation of knowledge for the coach's coaching practice. Third, we present the procedure used by the first author to conduct NCC with five university team sport coaches. Finally, we conclude by sharing our reflections on the role of PLCs in sport.

Why and when I use a personal learning coach

In an attempt to foster the development of their coaches, national governing bodies and sport federations have developed coach education programs. The content of these programs varies in order to adapt to the specific needs of different coaching contexts. For coaches, who begin to coach at the high-performance level, some organizations might offer a more individualized program (Rodrigue, He & Trudel 2015). The process will usually start with a committee, composed of administrators and coach developers, conducting an audit meeting with a high-performance (HP) coach to identify gaps between the coach's perceived and actual competencies, and those of an "ideal HP coach". An individual learning plan is then charted to correct these weaknesses. The committee then assigns a coach developer or a mentor to supervise the implementation.

Over the years, we have acted – and continued acting – as coach educators, facilitators, mentors, and consultants for different sport organizations while researching coach development. While we recognize the positive impact of the coach education programs currently in place for incoming coaches, we observed that HP coaches are often isolated after certification. There is a piece missing in the sport system to support HP coaches in their lifelong learning journey. Our combined experiences enable us to suggest an initiative to optimize the development of HP coaches: "Personal coaching for HP sport coaches".

The essentials of narrative-collaborative coaching

Definitions, essential components, and goals of NCC

Experienced coaches, who are adequately certified and still want to learn from their ongoing coaching practice, need a companion to participate in a reflective process that leads to the co-creation of knowledge useful for their current and emerging challenges – just in time – rather than someone to tell them what to do. We have named that learning companion a "personal learning coach" (PLC). What differentiates PLCs from other actors helping sport coaches in their development is that PLCs base their work on narrative-collaborative coaching (NCC) principles. NCC is one of many coaching approaches (e.g. career coaching, life coaching, executive coaching). For Stelter (2014), it stands out from the importance placed on narratives that people (HP coach and PLC in our case) share when exploring the world (HP sport coaching) together (collaborative). Stelter (2014) defines NCC as:

> a developmental conversation and dialogue, a co-creative process between coach and coachee with the purpose of giving (especially) the coachee a space and an opportunity for immersing him/her in reflection on and new understanding of (a) his or her own experiences in the specific context and (b) his or her interactions, relations and negotiations with others in specific contexts and situations. This coaching conversation should enable new possible ways of acting in the contexts that are the topic of the conversation.
>
> *(p. 8)*

Following, we present some of the essential components of NCC and link these to the high-performance sport coaching context.

The specific context

HP coaching is a complex profession, requiring the coach to continuously strive toward maintaining a competitive advantage. HP coaches experience loneliness and high levels of stress because of the constant pressure to win (e.g. Mallett & Lara-Bercial 2016). HP coaches cannot be good enough; they are expected to go beyond the basic standards to meet HP expectations. In other words, they must innovate by exploring new ways of addressing recurrent and emerging challenges to regularly elevate their team's performance. This creative reflective process can be stifled if HP coaches must follow a predetermined curriculum designed by their peers and based on the coaching practice of an "ideal coach".

Safe learning space

HP coaches should feel safe to discuss their fears and aspirations, and to question their coaching philosophy and the sport culture that prevails in their sport federation. In this safe learning environment, learning should not be perceived as an addition to the coach's work. The freedom that HP coaches have to explore any aspects of their professional work and even personal life will be, for many of them, a new learning experience (Stelter 2014).

Narrative

In NCC, narratives are essential because they link events and actions together and reveal a HP coach's interpretation of the way things unfolded. In other words, narratives are a representation of the meaning that an HP coach has given to recent events that occurred in his/her coaching practice. The PLC works around those narratives to help the HP coach reflect on his/her coaching practice by:

(a) suggesting other interpretations; (b) encouraging the exploration of alternate perspectives; (c) inviting the coach to re-author the story; and (d) identifying key moments.

Collaborative

If conducted adequately, NCC contributes to the co-creation of knowledge. As equals, the HP coach and the PLC bring their own expertise to the co-creative dialogue and are equally competent in negotiating what it means to coach at HP levels. Therefore, each learning activity is viewed as a co-creative process, rather than as a problem to solve.

Coaching

The HP coach and the PLC will have ongoing dialogues called "coaching conversations". These coaching conversations may happen at any time, for varying durations, and through various mediums (e.g. face to face, phone calls, e-mails, web conferences). Other people will be invited to participate into the dialogues when the dyad feels the need to explore additional perspectives.

Considering these key components, PLCs are not playing the same role as traditional coach developers or mentors, who often work with coaches during their certification process. HP coaching is becoming more complex and the workload tends to increase along the overwhelming flow of information that globalization and new technologies bring. Thus, HP coaches, like many other professionals, find it difficult to stop, step back, find time to reflect on what is relevant, and dare to innovate. The role of PLCs is to accompany HP coaches in a reflective process about their actual coaching practice. We believe this fellow human companion (e.g. PLC) needs to be knowledgeable about three interconnected aspects: (a) sport coaching practice, to understand the HP coach's context; (b) sport coaching science, to bring new perspectives into the dialogue; and (c) the NCC approach, to be a valuable learning companion and to be able to explain what they do.

A guide to the NCC approach

Stelter (2014) mentioned that NCC is not a coaching approach composed of a series of steps that must be strictly followed. Nonetheless, a guide can be used to set up a valuable and sustainable process. Appreciative inquiry can help do that, because it reaches a healthy balance between the learners' strengths and weaknesses. It also fosters an uplifting exploration of possibilities, because it focuses on positive topics as the starting point. Although strengths are the starting point, weaknesses will appear as the learners work toward their optimal self and realize the limiting factors of their performance. Hence, appreciative inquiry (Whitney & Trosten-Bloom 2010) serves as the guiding structure for organizing

A "personal learning coach" for HPCs **145**

the NCC relationship in our approach (Milistetd, Peniza, Trudel, & Paquette 2018; Stelter 2014). The four phases of an appreciative inquiry are discovery, dream, design, and destiny. In the discovery phase, participants are invited to reflect on, understand, and appreciate their strengths. Then, in the dream phase, they imagine an optimal version of themselves through a series of questions that challenge their perspective. In the design phase, the participants target avenues to achieve their optimal version. Finally, the destiny phase is when the PLC and the HP coach participate in ongoing coaching conversations and take concrete actions to improve the HP coach's coaching practice.

Examples of narrative-collaborative coaching with university sport coaches

This section provides a general description of a PLC's use of NCC with five university sport coaches. Table 11.1 presents an overview of the activities performed and the coaching topics discussed during each phase of these five coaches' personal learning journeys, which was supported by a PLC.

Phases one and two: discovery and dream

The first two phases (discovery and dream) are grouped together for convenience and logistical reasons. The goal of these phases is for the PLC and the HP coach to develop a better understanding of the coach's biography and interests in ongoing learning. The first activity is an autobiographical exercise that invites HP coaches to examine their past and envision their future.

Autobiographical exercise

1   The PLC sends a document to the HP coach one week prior to the meeting. The document contains instructions for creating a hypothetical table of contents of an autobiography describing the coach's journey to becoming the coach that he/she is today. In this exercise, coaches choose and summarize key events from their life that affected their coaching career. Each event then becomes the topic of an independent chapter, about which coaches must write a meaningful title and a few lines describing that event.
2   The HP coach returns a completed version one day before the in-person meeting with the PLC.
3   The PLC and the HP coach meet to discuss the main story points of the autobiography.
4   Subsequently, they schedule a video self-presentation session (described next).

Table 11.1 indicates some of the main events of each autobiography. Most HP coaches discussed the impact of their athletic backgrounds on their coaching practice. They also emphasized their academic education's influence, regardless

TABLE 11.1 Activities performed and coaching topics discussed during each phase of the coaches' learning journey

Phase	Activity	Gary	Jennifer	Eric	Francis	Brian
Discovery and dream (inception)	Autobiography	Professional athlete Teaching education	National team athlete Personal relationships	University athlete Academic pathway	Coaching experiences Building a program	Multisport athlete Kinesiology education
	Video self-presentation	Drill organization Communication	Assistant coaches Learning objectives	Drill success rate Time management	Challenge zone Feedback strategies	Drill instructions Learning objectives
Design (preparation)	List of coaching topics	Productivity Personnel management Program management Communication Teaching in practice	Technology Mental preparation Physical preparation Program management Nutrition	Leadership Productivity Recruiting Technology Periodization	Analytical skills Leadership Technical preparation Productivity Annual planning	Leadership Mental preparation Nutrition Technology Video analysis
Destiny (coaching conversation)	Session #1	Productivity Mentoring relationship	Program management	Tactical preparation NCCP certification	Technical preparation Pedagogy Reflective practice	Leadership theories Annual planning Reflective practice
	Session #2	Reflective practice Recruiting Program management	Mental preparation Reflective practice Coaching philosophy	Reflective practice	Tactical preparation Productivity Program management	Leadership system Reflective practice Productivity
	Session #3	Tactical preparation Recruiting Personnel management	Program management Reflective practice	Tactical preparation Reflective practice Leadership	Leadership Reflective practice	Reflective cards
	Session #4	Program management Annual planning Recruiting	Video analysis Player development	Reflective practice Game model	Team cohesion Recruiting	Team cohesion
	Session #5	Technical preparation Reflective practice	Mock interview	Tactical preparation Leadership		
	Session #6	Player development Leadership system Game–day operations	Reflective practice			
	Session #7					

of their major's subject. Some of them completed majors directly relevant to coaching (kinesiology, teaching), while others had less relevant majors (science, law).

To complement the autobiography, the next step is to conduct a video self-presentation session led by the HP coach. Video self-presentation invites HP coaches to review their coaching practice and imagine how they could become an optimal coach. It also helps the PLC to support the HP coach because it enhances his understanding of the HP coach's practice, style, and challenges.

Video self-presentation

5   The PLC meets with the HP coach before the training session to discuss the session's plan and objectives.
6   During the training session, the PLC video records the HP coach in various coaching roles such as teaching techniques, introducing tactics, leading a physical drill, working on mental preparation, and giving out instructions.
7   The PLC and the HP coach meet immediately after the training session.
8   In that meeting, they review the video recordings. The PLC reviews the elements that the HP coach appreciates about his/her coaching practice and those he/she would like to improve.
9   The PLC and the HP coach then schedule the upcoming session.

The video self-presentation session highlighted varying aspects of the HP coaches' practices. The PLC led this activity by asking the coach about what he/she liked about his/her coaching practice, what the most prominent challenges were, and what he/she would like to improve. Table 11.1 presents the two most prominent aspects covered during these conversations. Although the center of attention changed from coach to coach, the self-presentation focused on similar coaching topics for these five HP coaches (learning objectives and drill delivery). Four of them expressed a desire to improve the effectiveness of their drills (organization, explanations, or level of difficulty). Two believed that they employed effective communication strategies with their athletes. HP coaches also discussed other topics, such as their ability to achieve the learning objectives, their desire to involve their assistant coaches more effectively, and the challenges faced in optimizing practice time. At the end of this phase, PLCs should have a reasonable awareness of the HP coach's practice and knowledge that will then help them find material, stories, and perspectives to use in the upcoming coaching conversations.

Phase three: design

The goal of the third phase is to build a preliminary list of prioritized coaching topics. These coaching topics will initiate the learning journey, with an understanding that they may change as the journey progresses.

148 Rodrigue and Trudel

List of coaching topics

10 Before the meeting, the HP coach is asked to create a preliminary list of five coaching topics to send to the PLC.
11 The PLC and the HP coach discuss the list.

    a First, the PLC invites the HP coach to present the five coaching topics.
    b Second, the PLC leads the discussion by asking for further explanations or by making suggestions based from the two earlier meetings.
    c Third, they agree on a list of the five most urgent coaching topics, ranked based on priority.
    d Fourth, they develop propositions together for each of those five topics. Propositions are inspiring statements that illustrate what the HP coach envisions as a target for each of those five topics.

12 The dyad selects the coaching topics to examine in the next three coaching conversations of the destiny phase.

Each HP coach identified a unique set of five coaching topics that they wanted to work on and learn about (see Table 11.1). Certain themes were a recurring priority, such as leadership or productivity, although they were ranked differently within their respective lists. These five coaching topics were not all covered during the destiny phase, as the HP coaches' practice made other coaching issues more urgent, or other topics became apparent through the flow of the coaching conversations. Such modifications are accepted in NCC. Our research and consulting experience have shown us that it is important to adapt the learning journey to the HP coach's just-in-time needs and challenges.

Although the personal learning journey must remain open to change and bound for an unknown destination, this first list of the HP coach's priority topics is important. In doing so, participants create an outline of their desired direction and learning content. This outline helps the HP coach to progress toward some positive and short-term change that will contribute to achieving the successful long-term implementation of NCC.

Phase four: destiny

In the final phase, the PLC and HP coach engage in a series of coaching conversations (see Table 11.1). For these HP coaches, it was agreed beforehand to have one 90-minute coaching conversation every month with their PLC. The frequency of these conversations was specific to each dyad, as the occurrence, or lack thereof, was primarily driven by explicit requests from the HP coach and only occasionally facilitated by reminders from the PLC. Personal preferences and needs thus explain why Gary participated in seven coaching conversations and Brian participated in four, for instance. Between these face-to-face sessions, the coaching conversation continued as the PLC and the HP coach frequently exchanged e-mails and phone calls.

A "personal learning coach" for HPCs **149**

Typically, before the conversation starts, the PLC should review the notes from the previous conversation and send a reminder of the date, time, and topic of the upcoming conversation to the HP coach, as well as review any relevant material. To demonstrate the climate of this safe reflective space and their relationship, here is a fictional, but lifelike, coaching conversation between François (PLC) and Thomas (HP coach):

Thomas walks in the room and is greeted by François. A few minutes later, François gently asks, "How is your coaching going?"

THOMAS: "Well, there is never a dull day in this profession. The athletes have been quite challenging lately".

FRANÇOIS: "Oh, yeah? How so?"

THOMAS: "Every time I demonstrate a new tactic, they ask question after question. It is almost as if they are trying to find holes! They even did that in the exit meetings last week".

FRANÇOIS: "I understand, it feels like they are challenging you. Could there be another explanation behind this questioning?"

THOMAS: "I really feel like they are challenging me, but it could be that they are simply trying to understand".

FRANÇOIS: "Maybe. Do you want to discuss that issue today? We can also move on to the tactical progression of your yearly training plan as we had originally planned. . .".

THOMAS: "I would rather move on to annual planning. I have to deliver something to my high-performance director in two weeks".

François moved the conversation forward by revising the exercise completed during the design phase. He then probed Thomas by uttering the proposition created during that phase.

THOMAS: "I still want to improve my annual planning. Even though we won it all three years ago, and still reached the national championship tournament the last two years, I feel like I could optimize our athletes' collective performance even more".

FRANÇOIS: "What did you do that made your team perform well collectively over the last three years?"

THOMAS: "I think there are a few things that made a difference. First, I always decrease the length of our practices five to six weeks before the end of the season. Three years ago, I also asked my players how comfortable and how confident they felt with the tactics we had used so far. From there, we practiced four offensive tactics more often and it turned out to be very good for us".

FRANÇOIS: "Interesting. In the past few years, you have decreased the workload and you have engaged in tactical conversations with your athletes. Did you still do that this year?"

THOMAS: "I cut down practice time, but I haven't talked tactics with my players this year. I don't know why I stopped doing that".

150 Rodrigue and Trudel

FRANÇOIS: "Considering that, what needs to change to make things even better?"

THOMAS: "I need to discuss tactics with my players again".

FRANÇOIS: "OK. What else do you need to change?"

THOMAS: "Hmm, it's hard to say. Sometimes it feels like I am missing some things. I probably need to be more systematic".

FRANÇOIS: "I remember working with a coach that had one sheet that charted the strengths and weaknesses of each of his tactics. Do you have that? Did you ever take the time to chart these out explicitly?"

THOMAS: "I don't have that, but I know my tactics very well. If you want, I can talk to you about them for hours! But . . . I can't say that I can point out to each of them in a succinct way, if that's what you mean".

FRANÇOIS: "That could be a good starting point. It would perhaps streamline your thinking process down the stretch".

THOMAS: "I guess so. If I address it in advance, I could have a clearer vision of my progression during the season. Also, I would probably make better decisions in the first games of the season".

FRANÇOIS: "Most likely, what else do you need to change to make things even better?"

THOMAS: "Come to think of it, I cut down practice time two weeks before the playoffs every year. I should probably not be doing the same thing every year. Some years, players are more fit. Some years, they are more tired".

FRANÇOIS: "Indeed! To make these changes happen, what needs to be done, and by whom?"

THOMAS: "First and foremost, I need to choose a specific week when I will be meeting with my players to discuss tactics and strategies. In that same meeting, we could discuss our fitness level. I also think the strength and conditioning coach would need to conduct an evaluation workout a few days before that. My assistant coaches could also pass out a form to evaluate the athletes' rate of perceived effort".

FRANÇOIS: "OK, but let's get more specific. What microcycle would that be?"

THOMAS: "Hmm . . . Conference playoffs begin in microcycle #44, I would feel comfortable doing that at least two weeks before the playoffs. Microcycle #41 would be perfect. I would have time to digest their feedback for the playoffs, and I could potentially use it to make a game plan for our last two regular season weeks".

FRANÇOIS: "Great. I like that this is operational. So, how are you going to ensure that this happens?"

THOMAS: "I will include it in my yearly training plan report by adding a section that describes our activities, that focuses on developing our tactical progression for the playoffs. I will call our strength and conditioning coach today to schedule a meeting and ask him to brainstorm until then. I will mandate my lead assistant coach to generate a survey".

François brings the coaching conversation to its conclusion phase by summarizing the discussion. He then sets the stage for the upcoming coaching conversation.

FRANÇOIS: "We had planned to discuss your ability to manage your coaching staff during the next coaching conversation, does that still work?"

THOMAS: "I would rather work on leadership. I feel the athletes don't fully trust my abilities because we have lost in the national championship tournament two years in a row".

FRANÇOIS: "That works. I suggest that I call you next week to act as a sounding board for your planning and discuss how we will work on leadership moving on. Does that work?"

THOMAS: "Yes, sir! That's perfect".

François and Thomas then conclude the session with the usual formalities and by scheduling the date of the next coaching conversation.

In this exchange, it is important to note several prompts that were used to guide the conversation: (a) an open question at the beginning of the session to get the HP coach talking; (b) checking with the HP coach to determine what topic he wanted to discuss (planned or unplanned); (c) empathizing with the coach by summarizing his feelings and asking further questions; (d) specifically asking questions that help guide the coach to come up with an action plan; and (e) summarizing that plan and determining the next meeting time. After the coaching conversation, it is important that the PLC finalizes the notes of the coaching conversation and sends a summary e-mail to the HP coach.

In the destiny phase, each HP coach engaged in coaching conversations at different rhythms and for a different number of times over 12 months. This is to be expected considering that HP coaches should be drivers of their own development, and the occurrence of coaching conversations relies on their initiative. Other events, such as job changes, phases of the season (in-season versus off-season), and personal life obligations, also lead to idiosyncratic participation. These variations may generate additional time constraints, which can result in coaches downgrading the priority they assign to learning. In sum, all HP coaches experienced unique and non-linear learning journeys, particularly due to changes in coaching topics and the frequency of coaching conversations from the pre-established priorities to meet the HP coaches' needs in a timely fashion.

Adjournment of the PLC-HP coach relationship

This companionship is evidently not eternal. It will end. The goal is not to have HP coaches dependent on the PLC. When the HP coach considers the companionship unnecessary, the PLC and the HP coach move on. At this juncture, the PLC and HP coach may perform a debriefing interview to review the value that was created during the partnership. We recommend using the Value Creation Framework created by Wenger, Trayner and de Laat (2011). This framework has been used recently in studies on sport coaches' development (e.g. Bertram, Culver & Gilbert 2016). It examines five types of value created in learning relationships from the participant's perspective: (a) immediate – value of the experience; (b) potential – learning gained from the activities; (c) applied – ideas and methods generated for practice; (d) realized – impact on outcomes and goals; and (e) transformative – changes in beliefs and philosophies.

When coaches work to improve their coaching practice, it is important that they know the changes they have made, so they are able to repeat or adjust those modifications. Most coaches we have worked with do not remember the learning activities they participated in 12 months later, even though they changed their coaching practice based on those activities. This examination may also motivate coaches to complete the learning cycle of these activities by intentionally working to create specific types of value (e.g. applied). Overall, our experience suggest that this examination should be done by reviewing the narrative of each learning activity and performing an interview to assess the value that was created, if any, for each of the types of value.

The end of the relationship might also be a good opportunity to deliver a summative report to the administration, with the HP coach's consent. This report should be limited to broad coaching topics and the number of interactions that took place during the partnership. It should not detail anything related to the coaching conversations or strengths and weaknesses, as this could compromise the safety of the learning space.

Personal reflections and wishful thinking

We currently continue to employ this approach with 17 sport coaches who work at various levels: High school, junior college, university, and national.

First, it would be great if organizations would provide personal support or place graduate student PLCs on site to work with their sport coaches while they are being supported by their professors.

Second, coach development administrators should start by initiating an introductory meeting to explain the principles and methods of this approach. Being aware of this learning opportunity, interested coaches could then express their interest to the PLC in a non-coercive way.

Third, we still debate the level of involvement of PLCs in sport. There are obvious constraints in terms of financial and human resources (funding priorities, competent PLCs). How should this role be funded? Who should perform this role? We think that postgraduate coaching programs and coach development researchers might be key in developing PLCs and helping further integrate them in the sport system.

Activities for coach education

Familiarize yourself with the principles of narrative-collaborative coaching by reading Stelter's (2014) book and by reviewing scientific articles that describe its application in the high-performance context (Milistetd, Peniza, Trudel, & Paquette 2018).

Offer some coaches in your network the opportunity to participate in a pilot project whereby they will be supported by a personal learning coach. In doing so, coach developers could practice employing narrative-collaborative coaching with other coaches, while being supervised by an experienced personal learning coach. Participate in a community of practice of personal coaches to share knowledge of personal coaching theories and on-the-job experiences to perhaps co-create knowledge and best practices for themselves.

Additional resources

1   TED talk by Atul Gawande, MD, who discusses the role of coaching in medicine. www.ted.com/talks/atul_gawande_want_to_get_great_at_something_ get_a_coach?language=fr#t-64945
2   Institute of Coaching – MacLean Hospital and Harvard Medical School Affiliate: This organization offers conferences and resources for coaches of professionals. https://instituteofcoaching.org/
3   Reinhard Stelter's website offers a plethora of resources specific to narrative-collaborative coaching: https://rstelter.dk/?lang=en

Bibliography

Bertram, R., Culver, D. and Gilbert, W. (2016) 'Creating value in a sport coach community of practice: A collaborative inquiry', *International Sport Coaching Journal*, 3: 2–16.

Mallett, C.J. and Lara-Bercial, S. (2016) 'Serial winning coaches: People, vision, and environment', in M. Raab, P. Wylleman, R. Seiler, A.M. Elbe and A. Hatzigeorgiadis (eds.) *Sport and Exercise Psychology Research: From Theory to Practice*, pp. 289–322, London: Academic Press.

Milistetd, M., Peniza, L., Trudel, P. and Paquette, K. (2018) 'Nurturing high-performance sport coaches' learning and development using a narrative-collaborative coaching approach', *LASE Journal of Sport Science*, 9: 6–38.

Rodrigue, F., He., C. and Trudel, P. (2015) 'Concept mapping: Its use for high performance sport coach development', in P. Davis (ed.) *The Psychology of Effective Coaching and Management*, pp. 71–90, Hauppauge: Nova Science Publishers.

Stelter, R. (2014) *A Guide to Third Generation Coaching: Narrative-Collaborative Theory and Practice*, New York and London: Springer.

Wenger, E., Trayner, B. and de Laat, M. (2011) 'Promoting and assessing value creation in communities and networks: A conceptual framework'. Online. Available HTTP: <www.leerarchitectuur.nl/wp-content/uploads/2013/03/Value-creation-Wenger-De-Laat-Trayner.pdf> (accessed 6 December 2018).

Whitney, D.D. and Trosten-Bloom, A. (2010) *The Power of Appreciative Inquiry: A Practical Guide to Positive Change*, San Francisco: Berrett-Koehler Publishers.

12

A COMPETENCY-BASED APPROACH TO COACH LEARNING

The Sport New Zealand Coach Developer program

Simon Walters, Andy Rogers, and Anthony R.H. Oldham

Chapter objectives

By the end of this chapter, the reader should be able to:

1   Articulate and demonstrate an understanding of competence-based coaching by way of coach developer training to model such an approach.
2   Appreciate that coach development can move away from telling coaches what to think and how to behave, and can focus more on helping coaches know who they are and recognize their own skills and strengths (competencies).
3   Apply some essential adult learning principles to the design and delivery of a competency-based coach developer program.

Brief chapter overview

In this chapter, we focus on Sport New Zealand's (Sport NZ) Coach Developer program with the intent of describing how coach developers can model a competency-based approach for coaches by learning this way themselves. We provide insight into how "knowledge" is integrated throughout the Coach Developer course, but it is not the course "driver". Andy provides

Competency-based approach to coach learning **155**

> insights into the program's evolution, design and implementation. We provide examples of some key instructional strategies adopted in the course, and conclude with ideas to promote reader reflection on their own coach developer practice.

Why and when I use a competency-based approach to coach development

A *competency-based approach* is a strategy used in coach education whereby coaches have opportunities to acquire and improve on particular competencies, knowledge, and skills through building interpersonal relationships and reflecting on real coaching experiences. In the Sport NZ Coach Developer program, trainers model the competency-based approach, helping the coach developers gain the ability to effectively apply this approach when developing coaches. A competency-based approach supports a purposeful shift in thinking from content-driven to context-driven delivery, and advocates that a key role of a coach developer is to focus holistically on coaches as human beings. Although this competency-based approach aims to help coach developers develop a range of skills, Sport NZ wants each coach developer to have their own philosophy which will underpin how they have conversations and deliver sessions with their coaches. In NZ, we have openly embraced this approach as we believe it reflects a learner-centered approach and more effectively meets the needs of our coaching communities.

The essentials of the competency-based approach to coach development

Definitions, essential components and goals of Sport NZ

It is important to provide some background to the evolution of the Sport NZ Coach Developer program. Eade and Reid (2015) noted that for many years, like other countries, NZ adopted a formalized, tiered accreditation approach to coach development. However, in 2004, the national sporting agency (then SPARC, now Sport NZ) introduced a nationwide coaching strategy and adopted the "NZ Coach Approach". This initiative acknowledged that learning was an ongoing process, rather than a simple accreditation system. Many sports subsequently developed more competency-based coach development frameworks, providing a range of learning opportunities at all levels. Although there had been recognition that a competency-based approach was desirable in coach education, coach developers did not necessarily have the knowledge and skills to facilitate coach learning with this approach. Thus, some coach developers had trouble facilitating and modeling a competency-based approach. It became clear that the majority of coach education programs ignored the development of "arguably the most important link in the chain – the people who develop the coaches" (Eade &

Reid 2015: 350). In 2012, Sport NZ refreshed the national coaching strategy. At the same time, the focus by the International Council of Coaching Excellence (ICCE) on coach developer training influenced thinking in NZ and resulted in the 2014 launch of the Sport NZ Coach Developer training program.

The major challenge identified with implementing a competency-based approach was that coach education/developer courses in NZ, as in many countries, still relied on a content-driven approach which focused primarily on the technical and tactical aspects of coaching. The practice of content delivery was replicated by coach developers in their interactions with their coaches. Côté and Gilbert (2009) suggest that "effective coaching" can be broadly defined within three domains of knowledge: *Professional, interpersonal,* and *intrapersonal*. Professional knowledge/behavior predominantly relates to technical and tactical skills; interpersonal knowledge/behavior focuses, for example, on effective communication and leadership; and intrapersonal knowledge/behavior focuses on reflection and self-regulation. Although it is now recognized that effective coaching requires competence in all three domains, coach development (or education) programs to date have focused primarily on the content-driven professional knowledge domain. A recent comprehensive review of coach development programs which included academic programs (interventions, etc.) and applied programs (available in the public domain), found that of 285 coach education programs eligible for review, 261 focused on professional knowledge, 18 on interpersonal, and only six on intrapersonal (Lefebvre et al. 2016). A competency-based approach needs to focus more on the development of interpersonal and intrapersonal skills, and move away from this dominant professional knowledge model.

Côté and Gilbert (2009: 310) point to risks associated with exposing coaches to professional knowledge out of context, arguing that such knowledge loses relevance and "minimizes the importance of the reflective and complex interactional nature of effective coaching". A similar argument may be put to the training of coach developers, specifically with respect to the resulting skills developed and the sort of goals the knowledge-based competencies promote. In the first case, content related skills are likely to emphasize presentation and transmission of knowledge in so far as the outcome becomes the acquisition and demonstration of knowledge. Having acquired knowledge, the resulting goal for a developer can be argued to be the demonstration of that knowledge to others. This approach suffers problems of congruence (does it fit with the existing knowledge of the coach?) and timing (is the coach receptive to new knowledge?). From this perspective, it can be seen how coach development often ends in a debate around the legitimacy and usefulness of professional knowledge, which drives the devaluation that Côté and Gilbert describe. This problem is mitigated by a focus on interpersonal and intrapersonal skills. Interpersonal skills, by their nature, oblige developers to acknowledge coaches in the process and to interrogate the context within which they work. Thus, a shift may be made from demonstrating knowledge to seeking relevant, applicable knowledge. Intrapersonal skills, by their nature, are grounded in the ability to know and regulate oneself. These skills allow developers at the highest level to reflect on their ability to capture and facilitate experiences for the benefit of the coach. The focus here becomes not on the "what" of professional knowledge but on "how" that knowledge may be delivered. Equipped with these tools, coach developers can deal with problems of congruence and timing when using professional knowledge. The coach developer team in NZ acknowledged that the origin of interpersonal and intrapersonal competencies lay with self-regulation, consequently seeking a framework that focused on this outcome when planning a developer program.

To effectively utilize a competency-based approach, it is especially important that coach developers explore interpersonal and intrapersonal knowledge formation, reflecting on how they have experienced their learning, as well as how they will help coaches reflect and communicate more effectively with their athletes. The effectiveness of this approach in a coach developer course also relies heavily on course designers' understanding of key adult learning principles. As noted by Crisfield (2014), a coach developer course should heighten awareness of the benefits of developing skills in a variety of facilitative approaches, including learner-centered methods, problem-based strategies, and experiential learning techniques.

The NZ Coach Developer program owes a great deal to Self-Determination Theory (SDT) (Deci & Ryan 1985), in that it focuses on the development of competencies through supported autonomous learning experiences. This was, to some extent, the product of a 15-year dialogue between coach development bodies in New Zealand and academia which focused on the practicalities and benefits of SDT. In the course of explaining what underpins the distinction between intrinsic and extrinsically motivated behaviors, Deci and Ryan (2000) argue for three psychological needs: Autonomy, competence, and relatedness. The need for autonomy is met when learners are free to engage in activities of value to them; competence is addressed when experiences add to perceptions of ability; relatedness is fulfilled when learners feel secure and enjoy the unconditional attention of others in the course of their pursuits. When needs are met, learners experience greater self-regulation and higher levels of intrinsic motivation, which should bring about greater professional engagement. The Basic Psychological Needs framework is reflected in the activities undertaken, and behaviors modeled during the NZ Coach Developer program discussed later. The Basic Psychological Needs framework is reflected in the activities undertaken during the NZ Coach Developer program, including pre-course activities that promote relatedness, the LEARNS model that encourages autonomy supported learning, and the use of informational feedback via the REVIEW framework, all discussed later in this chapter.

Competency-based coaching in practice

This section draws upon selected examples of key approaches and strategies that underpin the Sport NZ Coach Development program to illustrate how

158 Walters, Rogers, and Oldham

coach developers learn to model a competency-based approach when delivering coach education programming. The program consists of a three-day residential introduction course, and other components including follow-up forums and a 12-month trainers' development program including ongoing mentoring support. The three-day residential program is a busy course containing a vast range of activities. In the course I reviewed (Simon), there were six trainers delivering the course; two "lead trainers" (one of them the second author to this chapter, Andy) and four "trainers" supporting 16 participants, ensuring that each trainer works closely with no more than four participants. The role of the "lead trainers" is to oversee the course delivery while mentoring the four trainers. Participants are drawn from national and regional sporting networks responsible for the development of coaches in their sport or region.

Selected activities in the course are outlined in the following sections, focusing on how coach developers develop their competencies in: (a) building relationships to nurture a safe learning environment; (b) delivering effective sessions (practical and classroom-based); (c) reflection on self and others; (d) providing feedback; and (e) the use of questioning.

Building relationships: pre-course activities

Working in the Intrapersonal and Interpersonal Domains: Before the course, participants are asked to complete a short e-survey, answer questions designed to promote self-reflection, and provide a photograph of themselves. This provides trainers with an awareness of individual needs, develops knowledge of how participants view their role as coach developers, and indicates participant understanding of the concept of "adult learning". The pre-course information gathering starts the process of encouraging participants to engage in reflection, and it also acknowledges the significance of educators getting to know their learners. On arrival at the course, Andy notes, "even if we haven't met them before, name tags enable us to put a face to a name, to use their name when we greet them, and start to build a relationship from the onset". This forms an important part of the whakatau (welcome) process, which includes building the respect and dignity of each participant. This welcoming approach has intent and is aimed at building an autonomy-supportive environment for the learners, supporting their need for relatedness and autonomy. A sense of feeling safe is important, because during the course, participants move straight into activities which can be challenging in new environments. The importance of relationship building to enable more effective learning is discussed with the participants to help them understand how and why this can be implemented in delivering coach education programs, and is subsequently revisited throughout the course.

Delivering effective sessions

Knowledge does not have to be the driver of a course. In practice, this means that instead of focusing on the content (e.g. on technical and tactical aspects of coaching), the program focuses on processes that develop competencies in the interpersonal (e.g. giving effective feedback) and intrapersonal (e.g. self-reflection) domains of coach development. One of the challenges facing the trainers is for participants to understand what exactly a *coach developers'* role entails. Many participants come to the course believing that their role when working with their coaches is to be an "expert" and to model sessions that their coaches can copy and use in their own practice. Within the program, the coach developers are challenged to reflect on how they might create environments where their coaches can explore and develop their competencies. This ensures that all participants understand the role of a coach developer and the various contexts they operate in, and is a prerequisite to effectively developing their competency to deliver effective learning sessions for their coaches. At the higher level, this eventuates in coach developers who are able to structure environments for coaches that lead to unique, personal learning experiences.

The coaching hats

A strategy used in the course is the use of "coaching hats" to help participants understand the role of a coach developer. Prior to attending the course, participants are asked to plan a 12-minute practical coach development session that they will deliver to a small group of "coaches" (other coach developers) on day one. When I (Simon) reviewed the residential course, I was somewhat surprised given the pre-course "brief" and the nature of a "coach developer" course that nearly every session was delivered like a traditional skill-based coaching session, with the coach developers predominantly modeling or explaining an activity as if they were the coach, and then getting their participants to play it out as if they were the athletes. This is interesting, as when we ask participants to identify the competencies that define a "good" coach, they commonly identify qualities such as being caring, empathetic, an excellent communicator, supportive, positive, motivating, etc. But when asked to "develop" a coach, they reverted to demonstrations of technical and tactical aspects of coaching. Thus, to clarify how they could develop coaching competencies, a series of reflective activities encouraged the participants to put on a colored hat that reflected the role they adopted in their session. A red hat reflected a "coach developer", a blue hat reflected a "coach", and a green hat reflected an "athlete". Ideally, the person who led the session would wear the "coach developer" hat, and the participants in that session would wear the "coach" hats. However, the majority of groups found that the "leader" identified as a "coach" hat, and the participants as "athletes".

The "hats" approach, broadly inspired by de Bono's (1985) concept of six thinking hats, was an extremely effective tool for promoting reflection and shifting thought in this regard. Coach developers reflected on how they can focus more on developing the competencies of the coaches they work with, rather than treating them as athletes. Critically, this deepens an appreciation of the other in relation to oneself. Although it takes some participants longer than others to fully come to terms with this idea, it seemed clear in the course I observed, that they all had a good understanding by day two. There was a clear shift in thinking that the role of a coach developer is not solely to transmit knowledge, but to focus more on their coaches' needs as learners, and to develop coaches' *interpersonal* skills.

To summarize, the pre-course activities and the activities on day one are basically designed to help participants understand the role of a coach developer in taking a competency-based approach, and what that could mean for them in their working environment. We suggest that the "hats" approach works because it encourages people to look at what they currently do and think differently about what they could do.

The LEARNS framework

Once all participants understand the role of a coach developer, it is then possible to move onto how to develop their competency to deliver effective learning sessions. The course provides a range of tools that are used as prompts to help coach developers reflect on the conversations, sessions and workshops they have with their coaches. One of these tools is the LEARNS framework (reproduced here and adapted by Sport NZ from courses they attended with the International Council for Coaching Excellence [ICCE], 2017), which is designed to promote deeper thinking about the activities coach developers design. During the three-day course, coach developers deliver multiple sessions, developing interpersonal (e.g. effective communication) and intrapersonal (e.g. self-reflection) competencies, receiving ongoing feedback from their trainers. Aspects of the framework are then used as a reflective tool before, during and after delivery. The framework is a tool that coach developers can use to add substance to what they do, ensuring that the focus of every session they deliver is designed to maximize coach learning. The LEARNS framework, as presented to the coach developers to use in their coach education programs, is as follows:

> L – *Learner-centered*: Put the *learner* at the center of everything you do. Self-reflective questions you should ask of yourself include: What is the impact of what I am doing on the coach? How will the coach experience this activity? What do I want the coach to feel at the end of this session?
>
> E – *Engagement*: People need to be *engaged* to learn. Is the experience you are designing interesting, exciting, and/or inspiring? Engagement can be influenced by the learning climate and physical environment, so pay attention to these aspects. Is your delivery engaging the coach?
>
> A – *Application*: Give people the opportunity to *apply* their knowledge and skills. For example, get coaches coaching – maximize their practical "coaching" time so you can begin to answer the question: "How do they coach?" Do not let people sit and listen for too long!

Competency-based approach to coach learning **161**

R – Reflection: Promote learning through *reflection*. Give coaches time and space to reflect on what they have experienced and then let them construct their own meaning from that experience.

N – New knowledge: Construct knowledge from the room. People will bring their own *personal practical knowledge* to the room. Let everyone find out what that is by "pulling" through questions or activities which promote the sharing of ideas. This process will also "stretch" and "challenge" coaches as their ideas are reflected on and discussed with others.

S – Stretch: For people to "grow" and "develop" we believe we need to *stretch* them (but not break them!). We want to create a "safe to fail" environment where coaches feel comfortable being challenged, or to challenge themselves, to try new skills or extend the skills they have.

The LEARNS model is a tool introduced to provide a framework for coach developers to develop a range of key competencies including: (a) the ability to design and deliver sessions that are engaging and promote real learning; (b) the self-awareness and confidence to step back and give their coaches the space and time to practice; (c) the ability to self-reflect and to promote reflection in others; (d) the confidence to draw out new knowledge from "in the room"; and finally (e) to recognize the importance of individual needs in order to stretch and challenge each coach they work with.

A key emphasis of the NZ Coach Developer Program is on creating opportunities for all participants to "*stretch*" their learning. To achieve this, it is important for facilitators to understand each individual's needs and current skill level in order to set realistic learning challenges. Csikszentmihalyi's (1990) concept of *flow* proposes that real learning, or *advancement* in creativity and thinking, can only take place when learners are "stretched" slightly beyond their skill level by the challenge set. This concept can be applied practically in coaching sessions, as well as adult learning situations, but is a hard task for leaders (coach developers) to get right (Walters, Hallas, Phelps & Ikeda 2015). Thus, coach developers need to practice both being stretched themselves and learning how to stretch coaches' learning. The problem set by the task needs to be challenging but ultimately achievable. Too hard, and the result is anxiety or demotivation. Too easy, and no learning takes place and boredom quickly sets in. It is important that any activity designed to take the learner out of their "comfort zone" needs to be conducted in a safe and supportive environment. The program does this through the trainers getting to know the participants, establishing individual needs and goals, and offering ongoing support and encouragement when they try something new. A key component of this is regular one-to-one discussions between trainers and coach developers. At these meetings trainers challenge participants about how they will stretch themselves, during their practical delivery session or during group activities and small-group work. It is important that the environment created feels safe (meeting participants' needs for relatedness) and the "stretch" is driven by personal goals (satisfying the need for autonomy).

Reflection on self and others

Reflection is a key competency located within the *intrapersonal* domain. Ongoing reflection is promoted in the one-on-one sessions trainers hold with members of their groups. We feel the ratio of trainers to participants is ideal (1:4) and enables trainers to build relationships with their participants, encouraging participants to reflect on their learning, set their own goals, get feedback, and stretch themselves. The *intrapersonal domain* has been largely ignored in coach developer courses worldwide (Lefebvre et al. 2016), so it is important that coach developer courses acknowledge the significance of reflection to the adult learning process, both for their own learning and coaches' learning under their charge. Coach developers were introduced to and practiced several self-reflective strategies (e.g. walk and talk in pairs, reflect on a video of themselves working as a coach developer). After an activity or practical session, it is helpful to "close the loop" on the learning. People will experience things in different ways, so it is useful to help them create personal meaning from what has just happened. This helps them to consider how what they have experienced might be applied to facilitating coach learning (supporting their need for autonomy).

This course was held in Aotearoa/New Zealand, and the concept of Tikanga Māori is introduced into the course by one of the trainers on day one. This is a Māori concept, and generally means the Māori "way of doing things". As a bicultural country, the significance of Tikanga Māori concepts is threaded throughout the course. For example, acknowledgment of this concept enables reflection on one's practice as a coach developer and encourages coach developers to practice their competencies in a culturally appropriate manner. The competency of reflection is reinforced throughout the course and participants are given multiple opportunities to reflect on self and others. A further example of Tikanga Māori is related to the principles of "Ako", whereby teaching and learning is acknowledged as a two-way process as teachers and learners learn from each other. Building relationships through acknowledging shared beliefs is an important way to build trust, which further supports an autonomy-supportive learning climate (Mageau & Vallerand 2003). This facilitates a safe environment, suitable for developing and practicing competencies, which allows trainers to "stretch" their learners, and to model this by actively demonstrating how they "stretch" and challenge themselves.

The course closes with a final opportunity for self-reflection and sharing. During the course, participants have had multiple opportunities to practice self-reflection. To "close the loop", they are required to consider how they can now incorporate some of these reflective activities into the day-to-day practices of the coaches they work with. Reflection has been identified as a key coaching competency, and as a result of the course, coach developers now have some strategies and tools they can use to develop that competency for their coaches. A support network is also put in place, offering coach developers ongoing opportunities for professional development in their regions.

Competency-based approach to coach learning **163**

Providing feedback

To assist coach developers with building their competency, as well as coaches' competencies in the key skill of providing quality feedback, Sport NZ has developed a REVIEW tool, an acronym standing for:

R – Reassure and Re-integrate.
E – Establish focus.
V – Visit through questions.
I – Invite feedback.
E – Emphasize key points.
W – What was learned?

The framework provides a useful tool to help coach developers to reflect on their practice and generate an action plan for future learning and growth. Coach developers are given multiple opportunities during the course to practice, reflect and plan how to give feedback to their coaches. The review tool is also modeled to coach developers during the course, with trainers using it to provide feedback to other trainers. Likewise, the coach developers can then use this tool with coaches.

Questioning

Facilitative questioning is another tool used in the course to help a person take a deeper look at their beliefs, values, and assumptions – it is almost impossible for a coach to do this on their own, and this is where a coach developer can assist. Facilitative questioning is one way to help a coach reflect, and reflection is a central skill for learning. Like any skill, a coach needs to practice it to get better.

The key elements of facilitative questioning as introduced to the coach developers are:

1   Focus all your attention on the person being questioned.
2   Try to be aware of your own agendas and keep them out of the questioning.
3   Your role is to help the other person explore their own issues in their own ways.
4   It is NOT your role to lead them to a solution.
5   Genuinely try to understand the other person.
6   Ask questions to clarify what is being said.
7   Have total respect for the other person and their ability to find their own solutions to their own questions.
8   Establish trust and respect by being open and honest.

Coach developers then practice this competency and are given feedback by other coach developers using the REVIEW tool identified above. To help develop this competency, coach developers are provided with a Kete (toolkit) of open questions such as:

"Tell me about . . .".
"Can you tell me more about that?"
"Can you elaborate a bit on . . .?"
"Could you give me an example of that?"
"How has that changed?"
"What do you want to happen?"
"So, what I hear you saying is . . . have I got that right?"
"Can you think of other situations where that has happened?"
"So, what things seem to be getting in the way?"
"What assumptions might you be making here?"

Coach developers are encouraged to practice listening and attention skills, and are encouraged to develop an attitude of really seeking to listen and understand.

Personal reflections and wishful thinking

We feel it is important that those interested in developing effective coach developer courses understand the importance of creating an environment in which the coach developer understands how to implement a competency-based approach when working with coaches. It is also important to acknowledge that "one size does not fit all". Although this course in NZ has drawn upon coach developer thinking initiated by the ICCE, the course has been very much tailored to meet the needs of learners in our bicultural country. As stated earlier in the chapter, the concept of Tikanga Māori is introduced early and threaded throughout the NZ course. When designing their own courses, other course developers need to reflect on and consider the unique needs of their own environment and context.

Activities for coach education

1 Reflection: Consider a recent coach education course you have either facilitated or attended.

   a Thinking of the three domains of effective coaching, reflect on how that course drew upon the professional knowledge, interpersonal, and intrapersonal domains. Did the course develop coach competencies in any way? If so, how? If not, why not, and what could you do, based on a competency approach, to address this omission?

   b Reflect on how that course drew upon adult learning principles to motivate learning. It may help you to consider the following questions: How safe did participants feel to try skills or openly voice their opinions? Were there opportunities for individualized learning to take place? Were participants "stretched"? Were there moments and opportunities for participants to reflect?

2   Facilitate a discussion with a group of coach developers from different sports. Ask them what they think are the key competencies required by a coach. In the discussion, consider ways in which coach developer or education courses could become less focused on, for example, accreditation processes, and focus more on developing those key competencies that were identified.

Additional resources

1   Sport NZ has a range of coach developer related information on their website: https://sportnz.org.nz/managing-sport/search-for-a-resource/guides/people-who-develop-coaches
2   The International Council for Coaching Excellence: Sport Developer Framework: www.icce.ws/_assets/files/documents/PC_ICDF_Booklet_Amended%20Sept%2014.pdf

Bibliography

Côté, J. and Gilbert, W. (2009) 'An integrative definition of coaching effectiveness and expertise', *International Journal of Sports Science & Coaching*, 4: 307–23.
Crisfield, P. (2014) *International Coach Developer Framework: International Council for Coaching Excellence*, Leeds: Leeds Metropolitan University. Online. Available HTTP: <www.icce.ws/_assets/files/documents/PC_ICDF_Booklet_Amended%20Sept%2014.pdf> (accessed 11 April 2019).
Csikszentmihalyi, M. (1990) *Flow: The Psychology of Optimal Experience*, New York: Harper and Row.
de Bono, E. (1985) *Six Thinking Hats: An Essential Approach to Business Management*, New York: Little, Brown, & Company.
Deci, E.L. and Ryan, R.M. (1985) *Intrinsic Motivation and Self-Determination in Human Behavior*, New York: Plenum.
Deci, E.L. and Ryan, R.M. (2000) 'The "what" and "why" of goal pursuits: Human needs and the self-determination of behavior', *Psychological Inquiry*, 11: 227–68.
Eade, A. and Reid, B. (2015) 'The role of the coach developer in supporting and guiding coach learning: A commentary', *International Sport Coaching Journal*, 2: 350–51.
International Council for Coaching Excellence. (2017). *NSSU-ICCE Coach Developer Programme: Facilitation Skills Handbook*. Tokyo: NSSU Coach Developer Academy.
Lefebvre, J.S., Evans, M.B., Turnnidge, J., Gainforth, H.L. and Côté, J. (2016) 'Describing and classifying coach development programmes: A synthesis of empirical research and applied practice', *International Journal of Sports Science & Coaching*, 11: 887–99.
Mageau, G.A. and Vallerand, R.J. (2003) 'The coach athlete relationship: A motivational model', *Journal of Sports Sciences*, 21: 883–904.
Walters, S.R., Hallas, J., Phelps, S. and Ikeda, E. (2015) 'Enhancing the ability of students to engage with theoretical concepts through the creation of learner-generated video assessment', *Sport Management Education Journal*, 9: 102–12.

13

SELF-PACED ONLINE LEARNING TO DEVELOP NOVICE, ENTRY-LEVEL, AND VOLUNTEER COACHES

Andrew P. Driska and Jennifer Nalepa

Chapter objectives

By the end of this chapter, the reader should be able to:

1 Understand how usability and appropriate learning technologies can shape the learning experience.
2 Understand how objectives-based assessment and backwards design principles can be used to match learning activities and appropriate assessments.
3 Create meaningful learning activities and assessments based upon two guiding theoretical frameworks (TPaCK; KSA assessment).

Brief chapter overview

In this chapter, we introduce self-paced online learning as a form of coach education. The benefits of self-paced online courses include their extensive reach and fidelity, low cost, and low burden to the coach, and contextualized learning activities. We advance theoretical frameworks that guide online course design, and we share our experience with online learning, including several practical strategies.

Why and when I use self-paced online learning

Over the past 15 years, faculty, staff, and students at our university have been immersed in online learning as a means of reaching large, diverse, and dispersed populations of coaches and sport leaders. We have developed two self-paced online courses for collegiate and high school wrestling coaches through a partnership with the National Wrestling Coaches Association (NWCA), a captains' leadership course through a partnership with the Michigan High School Athletic Association (MHSAA) and National Federation of High Schools (NFHS), and a mentorship course for emerging tennis coaches through a partnership with the United States Tennis Association (USTA). We have conducted program evaluations of USA Swimming's Foundations of Coaching course (Driska 2018) and the captains' leadership course (Walker & Gould 2017), which have broadened our understanding of how these courses work. Our expertise has been informed by the intersection of coach development and online learning theory, and also our extensive practical work on these courses.

The primary impact of self-paced online courses has been their extensive reach relative to face-to-face in-person workshops. For instance, our face-to-face captains' leadership course has reached approximately 3,000 student-athletes in the state of Michigan over a 10-year period. Comparatively, the online version of the course has reached more than 14,000 users across the United States in a two-year period (Walker & Gould 2017). A secondary impact has been the fidelity of a self-paced online course relative to in-person workshops, which require extensive training of presenters. These courses also benefit from the contextual validity of learning videos that feature expert coaches. These impacts have led coach developers working for sport governing bodies, scholastic athletic associations, coaching associations, athlete safety organizations, and sport advocacy organizations to employ self-paced online courses to reach a broad audience of coaches and other sport stakeholders.

The essentials of self-paced online learning (s-pol)

Definitions, essential components, and goals of s-pol

As defined by the Online Learning Consortium (onlinelearningconsortium.org), self-paced online learning consists of a learning situation that involves interaction between the learner, learning activities delivered through an internet-based program, and an instructor. Notably, many self-paced online courses resemble online trainings, whereby interaction with an instructor is minimal or zero, relying almost entirely on automated assessments. Learning activities include mediated video/audio lectures, interviews, structured readings, internet searches, interactive assessments, and discussion with other students. Instructor involvement varies, but where involvement is higher, learners may discuss items, have their work assessed, and interact with an instructor.

Online learning's extensive reach, paired with decreased financial costs, has allowed coach development programming to reach a larger population of youth sport coaches, bringing us closer to the reality of widespread compulsory coach education. However, a deeper examination of the potential for online learning shows that its benefits extend beyond its convenience. Online learning can leverage the benefits of modeling (Bandura 1986) through extensive video libraries of expert coaches performing specific coaching activities that are contextualized to very specific coaching situations. For instance, a novice swimming coach can watch (and re-watch) a demonstration video of an experienced coach conducting a lesson for a group of early adolescent swimmers (Driska 2018). Compelling online media can shape coach attitudes, challenging them to adopt contemporary practices (Driska 2018). Online learning keeps coaches in their native contexts, whereas location-based coach development programs may pull successful grassroots coaches toward more elite-serving high-performance coaching positions (i.e. "brain drain" effect).

With a move to online learning, the coach developer must shift into the role of learning designer, and efforts turn from delivering compelling lectures and facilitating meaningful discussions to the development of rich media to deliver learning activities. We have found this move rewarding. It has caused us to question the assumptions of classroom-based face-to-face learning, and to design clear objectives, learning activities, and assessments. It has led to our development of media production skills (e.g. graphic design, audio/visual recording and production) that ultimately aid all our teaching and scholarship.

Doing self-paced online learning

Our work designing and evaluating self-paced online courses has been informed and shaped by the Technological, Pedagogical, and Content Knowledge framework (TPaCK; Mishra & Koehler 2006), an adaptation of Shulman's (1987) pedagogical content knowledge framework to account for the constraints of technology. TPaCK thus frames this section, as we present technological aspects (usability and accessibility considerations), followed by pedagogical and content knowledge considerations (developing learning outcomes, learning activities, and choosing assessments).

Technology and usability

Online course designers need to be aware of how the design and inclusion of technology influences the user's experience and learning (Koehler & Mishra 2009). Usability refers to whether and how easily students can accomplish their goals for the course (David & Glore 2010). Maximizing usability should be a primary goal for a course designer. Cognitive load, or the amount of information working memory can hold at a given time, is of foremost concern. If the learner is focused on navigating the course and finding learning materials, then fewer cognitive resources will be devoted to learning and reflection. Use of more elaborate technologies in a course requires more organization for learning designers and course administrators. Often, there is a trade-off between a novel, hard-to-use technology and the inclusion of important content and assessment objects.

Coaches should be able to find information and navigate the course without a steep learning curve, allowing them to focus on the content and course objectives. To improve navigability, we use modules (units) to organize course content into smaller, topically focused chunks. The familiar structure decreases cognitive load devoted to navigation, and increases cognitive resources devoted to learning course content. We also use logical and self-describing menus to enhance navigation. For example, coaches should be able to use the menu to return to the course homepage easily from anywhere in the course. For sequential courses, links to material outside of the sequence should be used only when they satisfy specific learning outcomes, as taking a user outside of the course environment increases the likelihood of distraction. Limit the amount of scrolling or clicking, which can shift the cognitive burden toward navigation and away from learning. Orientation videos are essential to help students master technology quickly; they consist of a screencast of an instructor modeling how to find, navigate, and use the technology employed in the course. Orientation videos are also related to lower rates of withdrawal, an important outcome for self-paced online courses that are taken only once (Taylor, Dunn & Winn 2015).

Visual design of the course, including font, color, and images, will influence user opinion of the course and its completion rate (David & Glore 2010). The visual design must appear legitimate and professional, with appropriate color schemes, organization, and imagery to make the course accessible. High contrast is preferred, as bright background color combinations make content difficult to read, and certain colors impact readability for colorblind people. Course designers are referred to the Nielsen/Norman Group website (www.nngroup.com/articles) for extensive guidelines to promote usability through visual design. In addition, the Web Content Accessibility Guidelines (WCAG; www.w3.org/TR/WCAG21) provide recommendations for the use of color, contrast, visual presentation, and other design elements to make course content accessible.

Online courses offer the opportunity to integrate technologies into the course, but the reality is that technology often fails. User testing is a crucial step to ensuring a successful online course. Pilot testing a website with five users has been shown to give suitable feedback to the website's function (Nielson 2000) and using an iterative design process (whereby the course is revised in response to user feedback) will help ensure course functionality. It is a given that coach developers will have issues with course functionality and technology, and pilot testing is the best strategy to develop troubleshooting strategies for when issues arise later.

Pedagogical and content knowledge

Clarifying learning outcomes

In our work consulting with coach developers, we have found that stakeholders hold different goals for how a coach should be "developed" by a program, and thus getting consensus on learning priorities early in the course development process will contribute to a better online course. The evaluation of USA Swimming's Foundations of Coaching course (Driska 2018) outlines a process of using a participatory focus group to clarify learning goals among seven key individuals who implemented the program. In this focus group, these individuals responded to the following prompts: (a) How will a coach think differently when they complete this program? and (b) What will a coach do differently when they complete this program? Discussion of these prompts generated a list of learning outcomes that were classified as either knowledge-based, skill-based, or attitude-based using the training outcomes framework of Kraiger, Ford and Salas (1993).

Skill-based outcomes are largely informed by modeling principles from social learning theory (Bandura 1986). For instance, if a learning outcome includes coaches learning to use video analysis, then the program should feature training videos in which real coaches model how they use video analysis in a realistic coaching situation. The most reliable way to deliver knowledge-based outcomes in self-paced online learning is through a compelling, well-produced didactic lecture, though some attention to style and delivery will help to create a compelling video for coaches. A documentary-style video in which an array of experienced coaches present facts, concepts, and meaningful narratives will be much more compelling than a voice-over slideshow that features a noted university researcher. Attitude-based outcomes – which are subjective and affective by nature – need to be clearly identified, and require constant and deliberate attention from learning activities in the course. For instance, evaluation of the Foundations of Coaching course (Driska 2018) determined that for attitudes on which program developers agreed (e.g. developmentally appropriate coaching, importance of fun), learning activities delivered a clear, compelling message, and the attitude-based learning outcomes were largely met. For attitude-based outcomes on which program developers had less consensus (e.g. coach as a role model), learning activities were equivocal – and thus, learning outcomes were mixed. Furthermore, knowledge-, skill-, and attitude-based learning activities that coalesced around a common theme (e.g. developmentally appropriate coaching) delivered the most consistent learning outcomes.

Developing knowledge

It is critical to identify the learning habits of coaches, and some researchers find that coaches learn best through reflective practice, problem-solving approaches, and discussions with peers (Camiré, Trudel & Forneris 2014; Lemyre, Trudel &

Durand-Bush 2007). However, peer discussions can be difficult to facilitate in a self-paced online course, as the instructor is not present to organize the discussion around the problems and situations that coaches routinely encounter. Thus, presenting expert knowledge followed by reflective prompts is more appropriate. In previous asynchronous courses, we found that the degree of reflection varied based upon the student's own level of "reflectiveness" and was not influenced much by specific reflective learning prompts (Driska & Gould 2014). Thus, in subsequent practice with credit-based online students taking an asynchronous course, we have found usefulness in specific learning activities and artifacts that can drive reflection, including reflection papers or journals as primary course assessments, specifications grading (Nilsson 2009) that requires revision of writing, and videos that explain both the reflective learning process (Schön 1987) and the writing style for a reflection paper. Therefore, it is essential for instructors to spend time teaching the process of reflection and clarifying expectations for the course to increase the quality of the students' work.

Another common method for teaching is the video lecture, which includes a narrator explaining concepts over video, still images, or text. While efficient, it can lead to learner fatigue if videos are too long, and we have found it useful to segment videos into small time frames. For example, we may break 30 minutes of video into multiple segments of five to seven minutes in length, allowing learners to pause and reflect on the content. Structured reflective prompts or formative quizzes may appear between videos to keep the learner focused. Scripting should be used so that video is dense and narration concise, with the goal of reducing total video time to the essential points of the lesson. Though many teachers are accustomed to talking "off the cuff" during face-to-face learning situations, the effect often fails in online videos, making them too long and unfocused. Additionally, we have found that using a variety of speakers or presenters within the lecture videos helps keep learners engaged through the different styles and presentations.

Written information can also serve as a strategy for teaching when it attends to the preferred reading style of the audience, and it can break up the monotony of using lecture videos. Unlike in-person workshops, an online course can link multiple resources into the course. For example, within the written text, the instructor can provide a link to an article, blog, or video that may add to the information being shared. This approach could also help connect a coach to existing internet sites where coaching is discussed, thus helping to promote more independent efforts at continual learning after the course has been completed.

Teaching skills

We define a skill as a goal-oriented psychomotor process that can be learned, consciously controlled, and usually has observable outcomes of performance. Skills are generally guided by knowledge, but what separates them is that they almost always have some form of sensorimotor component (e.g. observation, listening, speaking). For example, a swimming coach seeking to refine a swimmer's front-crawl motion would need to observe an errant motion, identify a suitable task constraint to modify the motion, and implement the task constraint. To teach this sequence in a self-paced online course, an ideal approach would feature a sequence of three videos to address the learning outcomes. The first video would model what a coach needs to observe in a swimmer's stroke. The second video would present an array of task constraints available to the coach to modify the swimmer's stroke and what the coach might expect from implementing a given constraint. The third video would show a coach implementing a chosen task constraint. This sequence is rooted in observational learning (Bandura 1986; Hodges & Ste-Marie 2013), and demonstration videos are nothing new, given the long history of training films. However, in a self-paced online course, a coach gets full control over the pace, as they may watch, re-watch, and pause the video at any point. Additionally, the course may serve as a repository for numerous skill-instruction videos that can apply to a wide range of coaching contexts. Notably, such videos widely populate free online video platforms (e.g. YouTube), thus forming an informal source of learning for many coaches.

A trickier matter is facilitating and ensuring that skills are practiced, learned, and deployed correctly. Although online video modeling can provide targeted demonstrations, a limitation of a self-paced course is that an instructor cannot provide immediate feedback. In some cases, automated assessments might work to challenge a coach's depth of skill learning (e.g. a video-based quiz that asks the coach to identify a biomechanical error that could cause an overuse injury). For more nuanced skills (e.g. instructing, questioning, listening), automated assessments do not have the capability of providing meaningful feedback to the learner (at least at an affordable and widespread level). Furthermore, if a national governing body has a duty of care to the athlete that might be compromised by a coach who cannot perform a skill correctly (e.g. spotting in gymnastics), that organization should make some consideration into how those skills should be assessed. One practical solution would be delivering knowledge and skill demonstration through an online course, but a physical performance of those skills might be assessed in-person later.

We also pose a question to coach educators about two competing strategies for online videos that use modeling and observation of coach behaviors as the guiding pedagogy. Strategy A shows the video model first and asks the learner to identify relevant information (e.g. specific coach or athlete behaviors) before scientific concepts and principles are elucidated in a follow-up video. For example, a novice coach watches a video of a zone defense and a man-to-man defense, then is asked to identify differences between the two videos through an assessment. A follow-up video then explains the differences over a slow-motion recap of the two videos, explaining the principle distinctions. Strategy B is the reverse, whereby theoretical knowledge is taught before an example showing its application, a common sequence in many undergraduate lecture courses. Constructivist learning theories (Jonassen 1991, 1997) support Strategy A, noting how the

Self-paced online learning **173**

strategy taps the learner's existing knowledge structures before new information is presented. However, we are not aware of studies that have tested these two strategies in a coach development context.

Teaching attitudes

Sport is a site for socialization and the development of social and moral values, and the values learned in sport have a strong likelihood of following us throughout life. Thus, part of developing coaches is conveying particular attitudes about athletes, parents, referees, fairness, and even the purpose of sport itself. Many of sport's biggest problems have attitudinal roots in ethics and moral behavior inclusion, mental health, racism, and discrimination. Clarifying attitudes and developing persuasive techniques matters, because for many complicated issues, imposing more knowledge will not tip the scales of attitude change or attitude formation (e.g. attitudes on climate change). Social persuasion adopts a different approach, typically relying on the underlying social psychological factors that persuade humans to adopt beliefs and engage in particular behaviors. Though research on this topic is plentiful, few sources explain the techniques of social persuasion as applied to educational training videos (Simonson & Maushak 1996). These authors present six guidelines for attitude change using instructional media (see Table 13.1), noting that attitude change is more likely when content is unique, contextually relevant and authentic, when it strikes an emotional appeal to the learner, and when it prompts dialogue.

We offer the proviso that the persuasive, emotional elements that make for successful television shows and motion pictures are required when attitude change or formation is a learning objective. If awareness, persuasion, and social pressure are critical, then creating a compelling awareness video might be an effective strategy, as this could make coaches more receptive to learning. In such cases, it would be wise to consult with a production company that has a successful record of online awareness campaigns.

In some cases, the attitudinal component of learning should not be handled through an online video or course. Intosh and Martin (2018) note that when teaching coaches how to navigate issues of race and racism with their players, an important first step uses expert facilitation to help coaches examine their racial attitudes, which in many cases are deeply implicit. In the views of Intosh and Martin, attempting this process through a self-paced online video would not have the same effects, but worse, could be misinterpreted or off-putting, having the opposite effect and isolating the coach from the effects of the intervention.

Assessment

Objectives-based assessment and backwards design (Kraiger, Ford & Salas 1993; Wiggins & McTighe 1998) provide a strong framework for aligning assessments with learning outcomes in self-paced online coach development courses.

TABLE 13.1 Guidelines for shaping attitudes with instructional technology in coach development settings

Guideline	Contextualization to coach development
Guideline 1: Learners are persuaded, and react favorably, when mediated situations include the discovery of useful new information about a topic.	Information should be set in the specific context of coaching. Makes a better case for sport-specific and age-specific programming; it will be more contextualized, and therefore perceived as more useful.
Guideline 2: Attitude change is likely because of, and learners react favorably to, mediated situations involving the use of instructional technologies that are authentic, relevant to them, and technically stimulating.	Use real coaches to deliver important messages, to explain nuance and detail of coaching situations, and to lend credibility to the attitude being advanced by the course.
Guideline 3: Learners are positively affected when persuasive messages are encountered in mediated situations that are authentic and credible as possible.	Expert coaches may have appeal, but might also be seen as detached from a specific coaching context. For instance, expert college-level or elite-level coaches may have credibility from their achievements but may lack credibility in that they do not understand the recreational sport environment. Consider the use of successful but "everyday" coaches.
Guideline 4: Learners who are involved in a situation requiring their participation in the planning, production, or delivery of media-based instruction are likely to react favorably to the situation and to the message delivered by the media.	Interactivity of an online video, such as a scenario-based decision tree, is one way of increasing participation. More involved courses that requested students to produce a video for critique could extend the potential for attitude adoption.
Guideline 5: Learners who experience purposeful emotional involvement or arousal during media-rich instructional situations are likely to change their attitudes in the direction advocated in the situation.	Emotional arousal is a critical feature of attitude change; emotional appeals for awareness and subsequent action are more likely to hold the learner's attention. Arousing fears without providing remedies can diminish likelihood of attitude adoption, as fears are downplayed to diminish tension.
Guideline 6: Learners who participate in situations whereby technology-based instructional situations are openly critiqued in an attitudinally appropriate way are likely to develop favorable attitudes toward the situations and toward the message.	Plan for post-video discussion, through a live videoconference discussion or a mediated discussion forum, providing an opportunity for learners to process their reactions and opinions. Prompt and encourage learners to critique and analyze as they watch an educational video.

Self-paced online learning **175**

However, it should be acknowledged that assessment in most self-paced online courses is automated and lacks the depth of authentic assessment that a devoted instructor provides.

Assessing knowledge, skills, and attitudes requires different approaches and measures. Assessment of knowledge can be accomplished through formative quizzes and comprehensive tests. If the purpose of a test is to gain certification or reach another level of membership, we suggest that instructors use firm psychometric and assessment guidelines in the delivery of the test (e.g. randomizing questions, question banks with multiple items). The use of quizzes and comprehensive tests is especially effective on self-paced online courses, as they can be assessed automatically without instructor intervention. The downside of such assessments is that their limited predictive validity for overall coaching performance.

Skill assessments may be limited in the online arena, but skills such as observation and identification of critical performance factors can be assessed with video-based quizzes and decision-tree activities. In decision-tree activities, student-coaches are presented with a contextualized vignette (typically a short video or reading) and then must react with a series of decisions. They are useful for coaches, as they are problem-based and challenge the student to use different strategies for finding solutions. We have found this strategy to be the most effective and meaningful assessment in a self-paced course. Another strategy, rooted in the principles of reflective practice, is the use of workbooks whereby coaches create action plans for executing the skills they have learned in the course. In our experience, workbooks have not been assessed by a coach developer, and they are purely for the use of the student; however, when a coach developer is able to assess workbook activities, they do provide a window for meaningful, critical feedback.

Attitudes may be assessed through validated survey instruments embedded into an online course, although much care should be given to selecting instruments that measure the appropriate attitudinal constructs. Pre-test/post-test designs are a simple way of measuring attitude change, and provide quick evidence on the course's effect, but longitudinal follow-up designs would show better evidence of attitude retention. As with all data collection efforts, care should be given to confidentiality, timing, and length of surveys, as well as ownership and future use of the data (i.e. for internal use or external publication).

The self-paced courses that we designed or evaluated typically relied on quizzes to assess knowledge and skills, decision trees to assess decision-making, and limited use of surveys to assess attitude change. Providing the depth of assessment customarily provided in credit-based courses (i.e. graduate-level coaching science courses) may be unrealistic, given the time commitment required, and thus assessment has been through automated elements or questions that prompt independent, unassessed reflection.

Personal reflections and wishful thinking

As we see it, a problem that has dogged the field of coach development since its foundation is the limited capacity of coach developers to provide assessment, especially at a national scale. Rather than viewing a one-time self-paced online course as the comprehensive solution of educating coaches at scale, our wish is for coach developers to reframe their expectations for what a self-paced online course can achieve. Self-paced online courses should be seen as a first step in a series of coach development exercises, which could include a range of advanced certifications, communities of practice, or formal mentorship. While they provide foundational information for coaches, they also begin a dialogue between coach and coach developer about the importance of professionalism and lifelong learning. Given that such a course could be the only mandated contact between coach developer and coach, we challenge coach developers to rethink and reframe what they want from this limited contact.

Activities for coach education

1   Examine the Web Content Accessibility Guidelines 2.1 (WCAG 2.1) and the Usability Standards from the Nielsen/Norman Group, and determine how these principles and standards could shape an online course you might design.
2   Identify critical learning outcomes for coaches in your course/program, separating them into knowledge-based, skill-based, and attitude-based outcomes. Identify assessment tools that could measure these outcomes in the context of a self-paced online course. Identify essential learning activities that could deliver on these learning outcomes.
3   If you could build a resource library of expert coaches for your sport, what topics would you want them to address? What questions would you want them to answer? And how would these relate to the course's learning objectives?

Additional resources

1   Web Content Accessibility Guidelines (WCAG) – www.w3.org/TR/WCAG21/
2   Nielson/Norman Group – www.nngroup.com/

Bibliography

Bandura, A. (1986) *Social Foundations of Thought and Action: A Social Cognitive Theory*, Englewood Cliffs: Prentice-Hall.
Camiré, M., Trudel, P. and Forneris, T. (2014) 'Examining how model youth sport coaches learn to facilitate positive youth development', *Physical Education and Sport Pedagogy*, 19: 1–17.
David, A. and Glore, P. (2010) 'The impact of design and aesthetics on usability, credibility, and learning in an online environment', *Online Journal of Distance Learning Administration*, 13.
Driska, A.P. (2018) 'A formative, utilization-focused evaluation of USA swimming's nationwide online coach education program', *International Sport Coaching Journal*, 5: 261–72.

Driska, A.P. and Gould, D.R. (2014) 'Evaluating a problem-based group learning strategy for online, graduate-level coach education', *Kinesiology Review*, 3: 227–34.

Hodges, N.J. and Ste-Marie, D. (2013) 'Observation as an instructional method', in D. Farrow, J. Baker and C. MacMahon (eds.) *Developing Sport Expertise: Researchers and Coaches put Theory into Practice*, 2nd edn, New York: Routledge.

Intosh, A. and Martin, E.M. (2018) 'Creating athlete activists: Using sport as a vehicle to combat racism', *Journal of Sport Psychology in Action*, 9: 1–13.

Jonassen, D.H. (1991) 'Objectivism versus constructivism: Do we need a new philosophical paradigm?', *Educational Technology Research and Development*, 39: 5–14.

Jonassen, D.H. (1997) 'Instructional design models for well-structured and ill-structured problem-solving learning outcomes', *Educational Technology Research and Development*, 45: 65–94.

Kaner, S. (2014) *Facilitator's Guide to Participatory Decision-Making*, Hoboken: John Wiley & Sons.

Koehler, M. and Mishra, P. (2009) 'What is technological pedagogical content knowledge (TPACK)?', *Contemporary Issues in Technology and Teacher Education*, 9: 60–70.

Kolb, D. (1984) *Experiential Learning: Experience as the Science of Learning and Development*, Englewood Cliffs: Prentice-Hall.

Kraiger, K., Ford, J.K. and Salas, E. (1993) 'Application of cognitive, skill-based, and affective theories of learning outcomes to new methods of training evaluation', *Journal of Applied Psychology*, 78: 311–28.

Lemyre, F., Trudel, P. and Durand-Bush, N. (2007) 'How youth-sport coaches learn to coach', *The Sport Psychologist*, 21: 191–209.

Mishra, P. and Koehler, M.J. (2006) 'Technological pedagogical content knowledge: A framework for teacher knowledge', *Teachers College Record*, 108: 1017–54.

Nielson, J. (2000) 'Why you only need to test with 5 users', *Nielsen Norman Group*. Online. Available HTTP: <www.nngroup.com/articles/why-you-only-need-to-test-with-5-users/> (accessed 4 January 2019).

Nilsson, P. (2009) 'From lesson plan to new comprehension: Exploring student teachers' pedagogical reasoning in learning about teaching', *European Journal of Teacher Education*, 32: 239–58.

Schön, D.A. (1987) *Educating the Reflective Practitioner*, San Francisco: Jossey-Bass.

Shulman, L.S. (1987) 'Knowledge and teaching: Foundations of the new reform', *Harvard Educational Review*, 57: 1–22.

Simonson, M. and Maushak, N. (1996) 'Situated learning, instructional technology, and attitude change', in H. McLellan (ed.) *Situated Learning Perspectives*, Englewood Cliffs: Educational Technology Publications.

Taylor, J.M., Dunn, M. and Winn, S.K. (2015) 'Innovative orientation leads to improved success in online courses', *Online Learning*, 19: 1–9.

Walker, L. and Gould, D.R. (2017) 'An evaluation of a national online captain's leadership training course', *Journal of Sport & Exercise Psychology*, 39: S330–1.

Wiggins, G. and McTighe, J. (1998) 'What is backward design', *Understanding by Design*, 1: 7–19.

14

AUTHENTIC E-LEARNING

Using an educational design research approach to develop a hybrid coach education program

Bob Crudgington

Chapter objectives

By the end of this chapter, the reader should be able to:

1   Articulate the benefits of using an educational design research (EDR) approach to a hybrid (online/in-person) coach development program (CDP).
2   Employ an EDR approach to build an authentic learning experience for sports coaches.
3   Incorporate an authentic e-learning framework into hybrid coach education and use it to create a course evaluation framework.
4   Develop hybrid learning tasks that provide coaches with opportunities to apply their learning within their practice.

Brief chapter overview

Hybrid coach development programs (CDP) provide a mix of online and in-person learning strategies. They are useful in coach education because they provide flexibility for the learners and opportunities for coach developers to apply various instructional strategies for coach learning. In this chapter, I focus on using an educational design research (EDR) approach to design a hybrid course, with an emphasis on developing authentic learning experiences for the coaches. EDR refers to a group of design-oriented approaches

Authentic e-learning **179**

> to conduct educational research (Kopcha, Schmidt & McKenney 2015), and can be used to improve learning interventions in coach education programs, especially when paired with an authentic learning framework.

Why and when I use the EDR approach for authentic learning in hybrid CDP

I have been working in online and in-person coach education for over ten years, creating and delivering courses in sports coaching at the postgraduate level. During this time, I also served as a coach developer consultant to several national sporting organizations (NSOs). Due to these experiences, I was motivated by research conducted in higher education and the potential use of an educational design research (EDR) approach to apply empirically grounded theories in creating engaging and collaborative hybrid learning experiences for coaches. Using an EDR approach included collaborating with an NSO coach development administrator in order to identify and mitigate current problems by implementing a blended (or hybrid) model of learning for coaches. An authentic e-learning framework (Herrington, Reeves & Oliver, 2010) underpinned the design and implementation of the course in order to construct an appropriate learning framework with suitable learning activities and methods of evaluating participants' contributions and coaching competencies during the workshop.

A well-designed online learning environment can incorporate a variety of technologies for creating content, curation, and distribution, as well as provide a vehicle for communication and collaboration (Johnson, Becker, Estrada & Freeman 2015). Given the complexity of coaching and coach development and the emergence of technology-enhanced learning (TEL), there has been a recent emergence of research focusing on coach learning in digital contexts. Despite the potential to engage learners, the efficacy of TEL is weak (Cushion & Townsend 2018). Therefore, I investigated the use of an EDR approach to underpin a coach development course that incorporated online and in-person components.

In order to design a more engaging hybrid learning experience, authentic learning activities – predominantly based on social constructivism – may be used to underpin the design process. Authentic learning is an instructional strategy designed to engage participants by allowing them to explore and discuss complex, real-world problems in order to find solutions. In this case, authentic learning experiences provide coaches with learning activities that reflect the dynamic world of sports coaching, thus providing them with opportunities to apply or solve problems within their own coaching context. The opportunity to engage in authentic learning may include, for example, a community of practice (CoP), whereby coaches learn and generate meaning from each other through interaction (Lave & Wenger 1991; Culver & Trudel 2008). From the coach developer's perspective, designing an authentic learning environment may require a greater investment in time and effort than designing traditional instructor-centered teaching strategies, particularly for online courses in which the learners do not necessarily interact synchronously (Herrington, Reeves & Oliver 2010). However, this investment in design and providing authentic learning activities can lead to greater engagement from the learners and provide a chance to evaluate the quality of a CDP and its impact on coaching practice using an authentic e-learning framework (Herrington, Reeves & Oliver 2010).

There are nine principles of authentic e-learning outlined by Herrington, Reeves and Oliver (2010), and their application to the CDP is outlined as follows:

1   Provide an authentic context that reflects the way the knowledge will be used within the coaching context.
2   Provide authentic activities, which are coaching specific and represent a complex task to be completed over a period of time.
3   Provide access to expert performances and modeling, including presentations and narratives from experienced coaches.
4   Present multiple roles and perspectives and provide opportunities to gather different points of view such as role plays with players, officials, and parents.
5   Collaborative construction of knowledge through group work and problem-based learning tasks.
6   Encourage opportunities for reflection on course work and learning activities particularly in relation to the learner's own coaching practice.
7   Provide opportunities for articulation through designing tasks that give opportunities for participants and groups to express points of view and to defend their position through debate or public position in order to reach a consensus.
8   Provide appropriate levels of coaching and scaffolding whereby the course facilitator acts more as a partner than an instructor.
9   Provide authentic assessment by ensuring any assessment aligns with the learning activities for coaching.

A strong connection between the curriculum, the pedagogy, the assessment, and the subsequent coaching practice can lead to a more meaningful experience for the learner, especially if the learning activities are authentic or relevant to the context in which the skills and knowledge are used (Hay, Dickens, Crudgington & Engstrom 2012). In many online and hybrid CDPs, there is extensive investment in the sport-specific content that needs to be taught. Topics often include technical and tactical components, as well as coaching methods and sports science. Oftentimes, a training manual is simply transferred into an online format, creating a "ready-made" course. This type of resource is usually didactic and heavy with text, and often has multiple-choice questions or short answers that test comprehension rather than application of the knowledge. While it is important to make this knowledge available, hybrid CDPs can extend meaningfulness of the content by also creating assessment and using the aforementioned authentic e-learning framework to develop coach learning activities that link theory to practice.

The essentials of hybrid coach development

Definitions, essential components, and goals of HCD

In this section, I outline the design of a CPD for a group of 20 softball coaches, invited by their NSO to participate in the course as a component of their coach accreditation program. The hybrid course involved online activities and an in-person workshop. In this section, I will outline the design process and its implementation in terms of the EDR process, which adhered to an authentic learning instructional strategy.

EDR comprises three progressive stages, including: (a) analysis and exploration; (b) design and construction; and (c) a review and reflection of the process in order to improve the learning intervention for future participants (McKenney & Reeves 2012). These three stages are described in detail following.

Step one: analysis and exploration

Analysis: identifying any problems

The first stage of this process was to review previous CDPs and identify any issues with their implementation. In this case, the previous instructional strategies included an in-person workshop whereby content was delivered by coach developers and content experts, and participants were provided with a workbook, as well as post-course work associated with their coaching practice. Coaches were also required to seek the endorsement of their practice via a coaching mentor, who was obligated to complete documentation around observing the coach in action. Apart from lack of availability for many coaches to attend these workshops, other issues identified through discussions with other coach developer administrators included the numerous coaches who did not complete their post-course work and thus failed to complete their accreditation and receive their certification. An informal survey of previous participants highlighted further difficulties in securing a suitable mentor and a lack of support in completing the post-course work. We recognized that the CDP needed to be redesigned to solve these problems.

Exploration: the search for potential solutions

In terms of the course delivery, we proposed to adopt a flipped classroom to enable content to be delivered and for coaches to engage in authentic learning activities. The use of the flipped classroom is common in educational programs and has emerged as a useful instructional strategy in CDP (e.g. Cronin & Lowes 2016). We recognized that the use of online learning methods could be a vital component, in addition to the in-person workshop, as coaches are busy people and hence require a level of flexibility. Other advantages of a well-designed online environment include the ability to create self-paced learning, reduced costs (learn anytime anywhere), and the fact that coursework can be accessed in many places through the use of mobile devices. Exploration around possible technical solutions for creating online content included vetting of social media and online platforms and digital learning tools such as blogs, discussion boards, and wikis.

Flipped classroom

In the flipped classroom, the coach developer provides the content beforehand, either as a technical manual or via an online platform or portal. This allows the coach developer to take on a greater role of facilitating learning during the in-person component, focusing on interpreting the content and its application to the learner's coaching practice, thus creating authentic learning opportunities. It also provides an opportunity to use a problem-solving approach, whereby coaches can interact with their peers and apply their recently acquired knowledge. The flipped classroom can work well for competency-based programs, provided that the attendees have completed the preliminary work before attending the workshop. The advantages of providing the content before the in-person workshop includes flexibility for the learner, as they can work at their own pace (Cronin & Lowe 2016).

Application of Technology-Enhanced Learning (TEL)

An informal survey e-mailed to the participating coaches revealed they all used digital resources such as YouTube video clips, streaming of games, blogs, and websites as sources of information to enhance their coaching practice. They also valued working with or observing the work of other – in many cases, more experienced – coaches. In this case, the potential use of a social media platform such as Facebook was explored, as well as other collaborative tools such as Trello, Slack, and several wiki platforms. The use of a wiki to support courses has been demonstrated as a valuable collaborative tool within educational settings and, if designed well, has the capacity to link collaborative and personal learning (Chen, Jang & Chen 2015). At the time of the course development, there were a number of free wiki platforms available for use in classroom settings, and they represented a potential online environment to support the learning of developing coaches.

Step two: design and construction

Pre-course work

The curriculum component of the course could have been delivered via an online platform, but costs were a limiting factor, especially considering the

Authentic e-learning **183**

relatively low number of coaches participating at the performance level compared to participation or recreational coaching. In preparation for the in-person workshop, we provided coaches with curriculum content via a digital coaching manual. The content focused on technical, tactical, and physical components of the sport. A complementary workbook was developed, containing a series of learning activities based on the content provided in the manual. Closed-ended and open-ended questions were used so that participants could articulate their interpretation for each case, find potential solutions, and critically reflect on their practice.

Instead of an online shared platform, the pre-course documents were provided to each coach via e-mail. Given the difficulties that we knew coaches had had in finding and working with mentors, we decided that requiring them to complete the workbook of learning activities with their mentors prior to the start of the course was too challenging, and so this former requirement was abandoned, along with any other post-course activities. Instead, the coaches were simply asked to read the content of the manual and try to complete the workbook, but the method of documenting each coach's knowledge of the material was in giving them the chance to articulate and interpret the technical components of the course in the workshop. The workshop thus became the vehicle for determining the competency for each participant. If deemed competent, each coach would receive accreditation as a performance coach.

In-person workshop

This workshop, while bringing the coaches together into the same room, also took a hybrid approach because we used a group wiki to allow coaches to document and articulate their practical solutions to authentic tasks online, while also reflecting on the solutions provided by the entire group. A wiki is a collaborative web page authoring system for multiple users. It allows people to create and edit web content at their fingertips with fast publishing, which supports sharing of information and collaborative editing. Thus, the wiki provided a peer-reviewed approach to coursework and generated in-person discussions among the coaches and the coach developer. A wiki also has the capacity to meet many drivers of a sustainable CoP through the generation of activities, conversations, and reflections, and through reification via the generation of resources, processes, and methods enabling participants to make meaning (Lave & Wenger 1991).

The designated wiki was preloaded with various learning activities and extra pages were set up for group work. To enhance the learning environment, the content pages contained a number of media resources, including sport-specific images and videos. Participants were invited to join the wiki, and a "how to use the wiki" section was included in the introduction for the workshop so that coaches felt competent using the wiki.

Designing authentic learning activities

As outlined earlier, the development of authentic learning activities can have a positive impact on learning and engagement for coaches. In order to incorporate the authentic e-learning framework into the CDP, a matrix was created to ensure the curriculum, pedagogy, and assessment aligned with practice associated with coaching performance athletes. An example of this matrix is presented in Table 14.1.

The objective of the workshop was to provide coaches with opportunities to collaborate with their peers and the coach developer to find practical solutions to their own coaching context. To facilitate an authentic learning setting, the workshop was conducted at a high-performance softball tournament so that learners could observe and reflect on the demands of coaching at a high-performance competition. Thus, the learning activities were based on tasks associated with coaching at this level.

The following is an example of an authentic learning activity at the workshop. The coaches were divided into groups of four coaches, and each group observed and worked with one softball team that was performing at the competition. The task was to design a scouting process and prepare a report on the strengths and weaknesses of each player within the designated team, as well as outline both teams' offensive and defensive strategies. Each group had a project page

TABLE 14.1 Design matrix for course structure

Message system	Design elements
Program goal	Provide coaches with the knowledge and skills to act as agents for developing athletes with high level technical and tactical skills in individual player and team settings.
Curriculum	Learning objectives or goals.
	Subject matter (course content).
	Competencies or standards.
Pedagogy (flipped classroom)	Self-paced learning (pre-course work)
	• Workbook with quizzes and short-answer questions targeting reflection of coaching practice.
	• Ongoing communication via coach developer administrator (e-mail).
	Face-to-face workshop
	• Collaborative problem solving.
	• Micro-coaching activities.
	• Articulation through reports and presentations.
	• Construction via a wiki website platform.
Assessment (summative)	Completion of pre-course workbook.
	Observation of coaching practice during learning activities.
	Reflective work on workshop activities.

Note: Table is adapted from Bernstein (1971).

allocated on the wiki site where they were required to document the design of their scouting process, identifying what components of the game they were assessing and criteria for their evaluation. They were then tasked with observing the performance of their designated team in competition and compiling a report of their observations for presentation to the other groups of peer coaches. The in-person presentation was in the format of a team performance meeting in preparation for an upcoming game against the designated team. To ensure each learner contributed to the presentation, each participant needed to explain the recommendations for the game, provide supporting evidence and check for understanding with the audience. The coaches had to provide a summary of the strengths and weaknesses of the opposing team and outline strategies and recommendations they could use to counter them. Each group also uploaded the final report to the wiki so that all of the coaches and the coach developer could access it immediately to follow along in the presentation, make notes, and have multiple examples of the work that they were learning. The design matrix for this learning activity is summarized in Table 14.2.

Authenticity for learning activity

This task aligns with the coaching practice used in competition. It requires the coaches to design a template incorporating technical, physical, mental, and tactical criteria during performance. For example, a batter can be analyzed for their technique, including swing plane, bat speed, and feet placement; physical attributes, such as baserunning speed; mental criteria, such as decision-making and performing under pressure; and tactical attributes, such as pitch selection. The task is complex and requires coaches to recall and apply elements of the

TABLE 14.2 Design matrix for learning activity, "evaluating team performance" using authentic e-learning framework

Task: evaluating team performance/ authentic framework	Design template	Observe and document game	Written report	Presentation	Reflect on process	Recommendations to improve process
Authentic context	✔	✔				
Authentic activity	✔	✔	✔	✔		
Access to experts	✔			✔	✔	
Roles and perspectives	✔	✔	✔	✔		
Collaboration	✔	✔	✔	✔	✔	✔
Reflection	✔				✔	✔
Articulation			✔	✔		✔
Coaching	✔			✔	✔	✔
Authentic assessment			✔	✔		✔

Note: Table adapted from Herrington, Reeves and Oliver (2010).

186 Crudgington

information presented digitally in the pre-course work, as well as problem solve by finding solutions to counter the strengths, and take advantage of perceived weaknesses, of a designated team. Importantly, the use of an online platform for group work allows each learner to instantly share their experience while also being drawn into the experience and observations of their peers. Collaboration is further enhanced during the presentation process when coaches from other teams and the coach developer can provide feedback to the coaches, both in person and through the wiki site.

Furthermore, the task had relevance and applications beyond the original activity of documenting and preparing a report for competition. For example, observations of elite performance can be incorporated into coaching practice and other scaffolded activities can emerge, such as designing training activities to improve both defensive and offensive plays, as well as considering technical modifications to individual players.

Role of the coach developer

Underpinning the role of the coach developer is the understanding of authentic learning and in particular, ensuring tasks are not over-prescribed. Learning tasks should be relevant to their coaching context, but relatively ill-defined to allow coaches the opportunity to develop their own tasks and sub-tasks, identify relevant information, and take time to explore potential solutions (Herrington, Reeves & Oliver 2010).

For the in-person workshop, the role of the coach developer was to support the learners by communicating and, if necessary, clarifying any components of the task. In this case, a valid approach was to use questioning techniques and references to the learning material rather than providing ready-made solutions. By using the wiki platform, the coach developer could also check the templates and written reports from each group in order to check progress and, where necessary, provide guidance on good practice. In terms of the group presentations, the coach developer acted as an observer and – when appropriate – asked questions about the groups' findings for consideration by all participants. Finally, their role was to evaluate the performance of each group and individual coach via the set criteria determined for each assessment item, including the written report, contributions to presentations, and finally, the reflective piece.

Step three: review and reflection

The final component of the design process is for the coach developer to review the course activities and seek feedback from participants. This information can be used to improve the next iteration of the coaching course. An anonymous feedback survey was provided to the coaches at the completion of the workshop. The survey comprised of open-ended and closed-ended questions, including the applicability of the learning material, quality of resources and teaching, as well as administrative matters including communication and logistics. A section of the survey also gathered feedback on the design of the course and the workshop learning activities.

Overall, the participant survey responses indicated that the workshop was well received, and the course met expectations in terms of content and teaching. A number of coaches highlighted the value of group work and networking, identifying the chance to work and learn from other coaches, as well as the quality of the presentations and learning activities, as aspects most helpful. However, some noted that the schedule for observing games made it difficult to complete all of the work within the workshop timetable.

From the feedback, one-third of the coaches noted that they disagreed that the pre-workshop provided them with enough information to have the knowledge and confidence needed to complete the workshop activities. Some coaches noted that the topics in the manual were difficult to comprehend, with too much text. Less experienced coaches found the material regarding international games difficult to apply within their current coaching practice. To improve the pre-course work, the subject matter needs to be better aligned with the workshop learning activities and provide content in a more engaging format for course participants. The technical and tactical skills should be presented with a greater proportion of visual learning aids, including diagrams, images, and videos of selected skills and methods of coaching. The workbook as a text file e-mailed to coaches had limited capacity to engage coaches. Coach developers should consider using a digital platform such as a website, blog, or a collaborative social media platform (e.g. Facebook, Padlet, Trello, Slack) to create and facilitate a more engaging authentic learning experience for coaches before they attend the workshop.

The wiki component of the workshop was well appreciated, and participants took pride in developing their own spaces (e.g. each group added a name and logo for its team and included short profiles on each member. They also enhanced their work by uploading images, diagrams, and videos to support their work). Some coaches commented on the value of being able to refer to the course wiki after the completion of the course. There was Wi-Fi available in the classroom, although it was noted that many coaches used their own "hotspots" with their mobile devices to get faster broadband service. When coach developers consider using digital tools within a classroom setting, they need to consider availability and quality of Wi-Fi services.

Personal reflections and wishful thinking

While the flipped classroom approach enabled a mix of digital and in-person learning opportunities, in the future, it might be worthwhile to include the course content (manual and workbook) within the wiki platform, thus creating one online working space. This could be rather complex, as it would mean creating a series of project pages for each learner (ensuring confidentiality), as well as providing team project pages and general content pages. Access to a learning portal to store content, and perhaps using a different type of collaborative tool such as Trello or Slack, might be a solution. Further, while relying on access to the competition enabled an authentic learning environment, it was also somewhat problematic because it was difficult to predict the length of the games and the subsequent delays in scheduling, and this had an impact on the CDP schedule. I wish that I could use pre-set video footage of games, although the editing and production would be time-consuming and expensive. This would alleviate any potential scheduling issues, as well as enable the course to be conducted with rich learning activities at other venues and at times of the year when access to elite competition isn't possible.

Activities for coach education

1   Collect stories and case studies from experienced coaches in order to create content for authentic learning activities. Can you think of creating questions and tasks that involve providing potential solutions to these case studies and scenarios?
2   Develop an evaluation process for the course by using the authentic e-learning framework. Develop questions around the context and activities such as:

   a   The workshop represented the kind of setting and activities whereby the skills and knowledge could be applied to my own coaching practice.
   b   The learning activities represented the kind of activities performed in the real world of coaching my sport.
   c   I was able to hear and share stories about coaching practice.
   d   I was able to explore issues from different viewpoints.

3   Explore wiki sites and other online platforms that could be used in hybrid CDP to create innovative and engaging, authentic e-learning opportunities.

Additional resources

For coach developers working in online settings and developing coaching communities of practice, I can recommend the following two resources:

1   Bond, A.M. and Lockee, B.B. (2014) *Building Virtual Communities of Practice for Distance Educators*, Basel: Springer International Publishing.
2   Wenger, E., White, N. and Smith, J.D. (2009) *Digital Habitats: Stewarding Technology for Communities*, Portland: CPsquare.

Bibliography

Bernstein, B. (1971) *Class Codes and Control*, London: Routledge.
Chen, Y.-H., Jang, S.-J. and Chen, P.-J. (2015) 'Using wikis and collaborative learning for science teachers' professional development', *Journal of Computer Assisted Learning*, 31: 330–44.

Cronin, C.J. and Lowes, J.L. (2016) 'Embedding experiential learning in HE sport coaching courses: An action research study', *Journal of Hospitality, Leisure, Sport & Tourism Education*, 18: 1–8.

Culver, D. and Trudel, P. (2008) 'Clarifying the concept of communities of practice in sport', *International Journal of Sports Science & Coaching*, 3: 1–10.

Cushion, C.J. and Townsend, R.C. (2018) 'Technology-enhanced learning in coaching: A review of the literature', *Educational Review*. DOI: 10.1080/00131911.2018.1457010.

Hay, P., Dickens, S., Crudgington, B. and Engstrom, C. (2012) 'Exploring the potential of assessment efficacy in sports coaching', *International Journal of Sports Science and Coaching*, 7: 187–98.

Herrington, J., Reeves, T.C. and Oliver, R. (2010) *A Guide to Authentic E-Learning*, New York: Routledge.

Johnson, L., Becker, A., Estrada, V. and Freeman, A. (2015) *NMC Horizon Report: 2015 Higher Education*, Austin: The New Media Consortium.

Koocha, T.J., Schmidt, M.M. and McKenney, S. (2015) 'Editorial: Special issue on educational design search (EDR) in post-secondary learning environments', *Australian Journal of Educational Technology*, 31: i–ix.

Lave, J. and Wenger, E. (1991) *Situated Learning: Legitimate Peripheral Participation*, Cambridge: Cambridge University Press.

McKenney, S. and Reeves, T.C. (2012) *Conducting Educational Design Research*, London: Routledge.

15

DIFFERENTIATED INSTRUCTION THROUGH ENGAGED LECTURING FOR COACH DEVELOPMENT

Kathryn L. Russell

Chapter objectives

By the end of this chapter, the reader should be able to:

1. Identify the primary concepts of differentiated instruction.
2. Discuss factors that support the need for differentiated instruction.
3. Understand the use of engaged lecturing in support of differentiated instruction.
4. Design a class session that lends to and supports differentiated instruction through engaged lecturing.

Brief chapter overview

Differentiated Instruction (DI) recognizes the diversity of learners (coaches) taking a coach development course and sees to their understanding of the required knowledge, skills, and abilities, while engaging each in a manner to facilitate their learning and enhance their desire to learn. Engaged lecturing within DI means that the presentational skills with which the lecture is given, and what is included in the lecture, keeps participants interested throughout the session, which results in improved learning. In this chapter, I present an overview of the primary concept upon which DI is based, an overview of the research supporting DI, how engaged lecturing supports DI, and how I use this instructional strategy for coach education. In today's large-scale coach education initiatives provided by national sport governing

Differentiated instruction and engaged lecturing **191**

> bodies, the coach developer is responsible for creating a learning-centered environment from which the coach can walk away with not only content knowledge, but the skills and abilities to apply that knowledge, following their evaluation of a given situation. Given the short time period in which coach developers work with coaches in these courses, a suitable instructional strategy is differentiated instruction through engaged lecturing.

Why and when I use differentiated instruction

Through my experience as a strength and conditioning coach, presenter, instructor, and course developer, I have had the opportunity to explore, examine, and apply a wide variety of instructional strategies in coach development. I've had discussions with coaches about the "sage on the stage", and from the opposing perspective, coach developers who identify coaches who don't participate in their classrooms. No longer is it acceptable to provide content with the expectation that the coaches will learn the information in a manner allowing for eventual application. For example, since 2013, I have been tasked with overseeing the provision of clinics for the National Strength and Conditioning Association (NSCA) that prepare coaches for entry-level practice. My task is not only to ensure they have the foundational knowledge for coaching, but that they can apply that knowledge in practice. I develop and oversee the instruction of exam preparation live clinics (EPLCs) for individuals seeking to become an NSCA certified strength and conditioning coach (CSCS). Participants in these clinics bring with them a wide range of experiences in education (i.e. some college to graduate degrees, exercise science degrees, and non-exercise science), geography (i.e. all across the United States, Latin America), and identities (i.e. practical experience, gender, race). The key to the success of these clinics is not the provision of the content itself, but the method by which that content is delivered. Clearly for the coach developer who may be presenting to ten coaches or 100, many considerations must be made to meet the instructional objectives, so it is key to examine the process used to achieve those objectives. The method I find most beneficial to my situation is differentiated instruction (DI) through engaged lecturing.

The essentials of differentiated instruction through engaged lecturing

Definitions, essential components, and goals of DI

DI dates to the days in the United States of the one-room schoolhouse, where learners of all ages were in one classroom and consideration was taken by the teacher for their varied knowledge, abilities, and skills. As the educational system grew, and grade levels were developed, there came the assumption that individuals within the same grade learned similarly, and DI was cast aside for more teacher-centered and teacher-directed approaches, including lecturing information without much student engagement or consideration of the students' knowledge. A re-emergence of DI in the American educational system principally occurred as a result of the introduction of achievement tests, the passing of the Individuals with Disabilities Education Act, and other requirements showing that there were gaps in learning (Weselby 2014).

Carol Ann Tomlinson, a leader in the field of educational leadership, identified planning as a key area in which instructors could organize DI, considering a student's individual learning styles and levels of readiness prior to designing a lesson. Researchers suggested that differences that should be considered include coaches' backgrounds, readiness levels, languages, interests, and learning profiles (Santangelo & Tomlinson 2009; McCarty et al. 2016; Dosch & Zidon 2014). However, Parsons, Dodman and Burrowbridge (2013) identified that the early focus on planning was too narrow a view of the complex work of instruction necessary to meet students' diverse needs. They suggested that adaptations made in the midst of instruction should also be an important aspect of differentiation. In their broader view of DI, they suggested that effective differentiation is not only carefully planned, but also that moment-by-moment adaptations should occur to meet specific needs that become clear during instruction – needs that were not or could not be anticipated.

Fundamentally, DI provides a learning experience that is social and collaborative, with the tenet that instructors must engage each learner. Nonetheless, lecturing is an instructional strategy that is often used as a means to provide information to coaches succinctly in a short time frame. Thus, employing DI within engaged lecturing can allow for a directed approach while also accounting for coaches' differences. DI results in higher intellectual growth and interest in the subject, and assessment revealed that most learners in a DI classroom demonstrated sound understanding of major concepts taught in the course (Joseph, Thomas, Simonette & Ramsook 2013). DI allows coaches to be valued for what they bring to the learning environment, a situation that is encountered with every EPLC offered by the NSCA. At any given clinic, coaches vary in age, educational background, athletic exposure, and strength and conditioning experience. Coach developers must not only engage coaches to identify these differences, but thoughtfully adapt instruction in the moment to account for these differences.

The essential components of DI are variation in: (a) the complexity of the content; (b) the method of presentation; (c) the methods by which a coach demonstrates what they've learned; and (d) the learning environment. The following is a description of how I use these components in the EPLCs.

Content

In any given topic presented within a lesson or course, I expect coaches to have some foundational knowledge from which their learning can progress. As the

CSCS is responsible for the physical development of an athlete over time, as demonstrated by improvements in performance, this means a working knowledge of the exercise sciences (i.e. anatomy and physiology, exercise physiology, biomechanics, etc.). But, because the CSCS does not require a degree specifically related to exercise science, coaches may or may not have mastery of the different subjects. Through the identification or provision of specific tasks for those less familiar with the information, and discussions requiring higher-order thinking, the needs of the different coaches can be met.

For example, within an engaged lecture, a PowerPoint slide identifying the components of a muscle cell contains asterisks after certain words. This is a cue to the instructor to ask if someone can define or identify the substance. Those with mastery are easily able to do so, and those without can begin to identify gaps in their knowledge for later development.

Method of presentation

Coaches at the clinics differ in the methods by which they prefer to learn (visual, auditory and kinesthetic, or verbal), the support they need for learning (one-on-one discussions with the coach developer vs. group discussion), and the strategies they use for exam preparation. The time within which the EPLC is conducted is limited, so while attempts are made to provide variation, as part of the engaged lecture, I discuss the methods they have used and present other options they should use when they leave the course to support and encourage self-responsibility for learning. Many coaches still believe they learn better when they use one of their preferred learning styles, yet there remains insufficient evidence to support learning styles as an instructionally useful concept when planning and delivering appropriately individualized and differentiated instruction (Landrum & McDuffie 2010). An example of variance in the method of presentation occurs with the lesson on resistance training techniques. Coaches are shown images or videos (visual) of given resistance training techniques while the coach developer discusses potential errors (auditory). Following this, the coaches participate by observing (visual) each other demonstrating (kinesthetic) the various resistance training techniques, and then discuss (verbal) the potential issues or concerns.

Demonstration of learning

Demonstration of learning is typically accomplished through a test, project, presentation, or other activity that supports the different learning styles. As the EPLC is limited in time, it is not possible for all these options to occur, and ultimately, the goal of an EPLC is to assist coaches in identifying their individual gaps in knowledge, skills, or abilities as needed to practice as a CSCS. Instead, two sets of multiple-choice practice questions are provided with the first being reviewed and discussed at the beginning of day two. Additionally, I conduct a hands-on resistance training session where each coach participates in role play as athlete or coach. When acting as athlete, the coach performs a specific lift intentionally creating errors, or sometimes presenting with errors due to their own lack of skill in performing the lift. When acting as the coach, individuals observe the athlete and if necessary, identify possible issues and suggesting corrections. As the instructor, I observe the groups as they role play and provide feedback or answer questions when needed. This session ends with a group discussion allowing the coaches to share and discuss what they learned.

Learning environment

In a DI approach, the learning environment is inclusive not only of the physical elements, but also the psychological elements. Physical elements include the arrangement of the classroom and subsequent management techniques used by the coach developer, and can vary from lesson to lesson, dependent on the goal for the session. For example, a lecture-only session will have the tables and chairs facing forward, but when group interaction is needed, the tables and chairs should be arranged in a square or circular fashion, allowing coaches to face each other and interact comfortably. Management of the classroom is accomplished when coaches are involved and focused on the instructor each session, which requires more than just standing at the front of a room and regurgitating information. In the EPLC, I move about the room, observing the coaches as I talk, and I make eye contact to not only let them know I am attending to them, but to see if what I am presenting is making sense. Essentially, I am looking to see if the "light" is on. A psychologically supportive learning environment is provided when coaches are encouraged to stand and move about as needed. Care is taken to screen the EPLC locations to ensure that the instructional environment is conducive to learning. Facilities are required to include a lecture room that will reduce disruptions and allow for all to view the PowerPoint presentations easily, and during practical sessions in the weight room, the facility managers are asked to restrict the area to coaches only. When disruptions such as noise in adjacent rooms or others observing a session occur, it can affect a coach's ability to focus and be open to learning. Additionally, as the individual in charge of the EPLC for the organization, I observe and evaluate all coach developers to ensure that they are providing differentiated instruction through engaged lecture.

In the next section, I draw upon Dr. Robert Gagné's work to show how I've integrated his Nine Events of Instruction, which aptly bring together pieces of DI and engaged lecturing within EPLCs (Gagné, Briggs & Wager 1992).

Developing a course that provides differentiated instruction through engaged lecturing

I will use my experience from the classroom and the EPLCs as a guide to coach developers seeking to provide a course that supports the diversity of today's coaches. Much of this can be replicated, with modification as necessary, when

Differentiated instruction and engaged lecturing **195**

instruction and engaged lecturing are beneficial. It should be noted that Gagné's nine events do not need to occur in a specified order, only that they should occur during the course of instruction, and sometimes more than once.

Gain attention

It is important to ensure that coaches are ready to learn and participate in the lesson. This can be done by presenting a stimulus such as posing a thought-provoking question, utilizing ice-breaker activities, conducting a brief survey, or with body language, eye contact, and use of room in the first ten minutes.

At the beginning of the EPLC, I gain the attention of the coaches by conducting a brief survey, presenting a thought-provoking activity, and making eye contact. After a brief introduction of myself, I ask the coaches to introduce themselves and provide their educational background and practical experience in strength and conditioning. By exposing the variety of backgrounds in the group, I can thoughtfully adapt instruction as suggested when using DI. Throughout the clinic, rather than using my own experiences as examples, I can engage the coaches by using their experiences as the examples.

I then ask the coaches to write their name on their workbook while I walk around and loudly encourage them to "hurry up" with the task. This activity may seem disjointed; however, it is purposefully done and debriefed to allow the coaches to understand the depth of knowledge expected of them for success on the exam. I explain that the ability to write one's name without thought for each letter while under stress is knowledge. Knowing the alphabet and that letters can be put together to form their name would be familiarity, but doing so is knowledge – and this knowledge came from practice. I explain further that just like learning a specific skill for a sport requires practice, so too does intellectual knowledge. For intellectual knowledge, the coaches will need to practice writing and verbalizing the information they are expected to know and apply on the exam.

This process sets the stage for the clinic. I've identified the need for differentiation, provided myself the tools to differentiate my instruction, provided a thought-provoking activity that sets a level of expectation for learning that, when met, results in success, and walked around the classroom making eye contact with each coach.

Inform learners of the objective

Coaches should be aware of the objectives or outcomes of a course to help them understand what they are expected to do or take away. Within the first hour of the EPLC, I identify the objectives of the clinic, as well as the responsibilities of myself as the coach developer and theirs as the learner. I explain to the coaches that as adults, learning is their responsibility, and that I expect them to seek clarification of information when needed or if the information being discussed is unknown and an explanation will take longer than one to two minutes, then we have just identified a gap in their knowledge. This expectation, to seek clarification or additional knowledge, requires coaches to be engaged in the clinic. These objectives are provided in writing on the PowerPoints and within their workbooks to emphasize the importance of this information. In engaged lecturing, important information should be reiterated (e.g. orally, written).

Stimulating recall of prior learning

Coaches come with prior experiences and knowledge. While they may not initially see how this experience is useful to the course, through my use of questions and guidance, they begin to understand this connection.

An example of this occurs when discussing biomechanics of lever arms and mechanical advantage. A discussion centered on the use of math to determine the mechanical advantage of a lever arm is often met with a large number of blank stares. But a discussion that centers on the height and weight of different athletes and the sports they participate in, which is commonly an experience from which they can draw knowledge, can be guided in a manner that allows the coaches to recognize the physical components that support mechanical advantage relative to speed as compared to strength.

Presenting the content

Information in lectures should be organized and grouped in a manner that is meaningful and enhances the effectiveness and efficiency of the instruction. For example, the EPLC is organized to provide the foundation from which a coach will draw information to practice the profession. And, while presented using PowerPoint inclusive of images and videos, the EPLC is designed with the intent that the coach developer will also utilize demonstrations as needed and incorporate real-life examples to connect knowledge to practice.

Providing learning guidance

Coaches should be provided strategies to aid them in learning inclusive of available resources. The identification of instructional support, modeling of various learning strategies, and the provision of case studies, analogies, or metaphors are different methods that can be utilized. During the first hour of the EPLC, I provide coaches an overview of how to prepare for the CSCS exam. I identify that while most of them have heard of or believed in the use of a learning style (visual, auditory and kinesthetic, and verbal), it would be better for them to approach their preparation at the same level as required for the exam. I share how the exam is developed and that it is not based on rote memorization, but on their ability to analyze and apply the knowledge, skills, and abilities that they should have as a competent coach. I then explain to the coaches the difference between

Differentiated instruction and engaged lecturing **197**

surface, strategic, and deep approaches to learning. To keep the coaches engaged in the lecture, I survey them to identify how many use flash cards or cringe at the thought of essay questions.

Eliciting performance

Coaches should be encouraged to process new information over time and allow for the internalization of new skills and knowledge. Coach developers can ask deep learning questions, ask coaches to recall information, or guide coaches to process information when they question. The last is a method I commonly use. When a coach asks a question, rather than providing them with an answer, I work on asking a series of questions that will develop the ability to think using information they know and/or have recently learned to come up with an answer. This can otherwise be identified as teaching thinking. All too often in today's world, I find that individuals have developed a pattern of finding an answer to a question without seeking to know why a given answer is what it is. The "why" is deep learning, and as previously identified, is necessary when responding to analysis or application questions on the exam and in the real world. Many situations a coach will face may be different on the surface, but deeper understanding and the ability to tap into processing information will allow them to determine the correct response.

Providing feedback

Feedback of coaches' performance should be immediate to assess and facilitate learning. This can be done in several ways, from immediate confirmation of a correct answer to remedial feedback, informative feedback, or analytical feedback. Remedial feedback will direct coaches in a manner to find the correct answer, but does not provide the correct answer; informative feedback will provide new or different information and confirms that the coach has been actively listening; and analytical feedback provides suggestions or recommendations for correction. In line with DI, I instruct the coaches to have dinner and then answer a set of multiple-choice questions for review in class the next morning. It is imperative that this activity be combined with learning guidance from the coach developer. Each multiple-choice question is aligned with three columns. The first column identifies that the coach felt they knew the answer, the second identifies that they are pretty sure of their answer but might have had a slight hesitation, and the third column identifies that they did not know the answer. I ask the coaches to check the column that identifies their level of knowledge relative to the answer, and to also write out why the answer selected is correct. I explain to the coaches that the work will not only allow them to identify their level of knowledge, but provide us with opportunities to examine their thinking. When individuals self-assess using multiple-choice questions, they only look for the errors, but when faced with information that requires deep learning, I find that it is easier to identify the gaps when self-assessment includes an identification of the comfort level the coach has with a question and what they are thinking when a review is provided. At the beginning of day two, I provide the answers to the questions and the appropriate feedback.

Assessing performance

To assess if the expected learning outcomes were achieved, an assessment should be conducted. In a normal classroom setting, the coach developer can choose any number of methods from a pre-test and a post-test to a post-test only, as well as embedding questions throughout the instruction. Ultimately, the assessment should clearly identify the level of mastery, whether it is criterion referenced or normative referenced.

As the EPLC is a review of content for the certification exam, I do not identify outcomes prior to the clinic, and I do not conduct a formal assessment of the coaches at the end of the clinic. I do provide coaches two sets of practice questions during the clinic, and as mentioned, utilize one to teach them how to self-assess their own learning. Ultimately, performance of the coach is assessed when they take the CSCS exam. Results show that coaches who attend the clinic perform better on the exam.

Enhancing retention and transfer

New knowledge must be internalized so that coaches can develop expertise. Methods to develop mastery include paraphrasing content, using metaphors, creating outlines, and generating examples. At the end of the EPLC, I provide coaches with recommendations for retention, such as writing out tables and charts repeatedly by hand, writing out why they choose an answer when using multiple-choice questions, finding others to discuss information with, and questioning each action from program design to running drills when viewing or practicing their profession. Following the EPLC, coaches often join my Facebook group, CSCS Exam Prep (www.facebook.com/groups/273091563080307/). This group allows them to continue their preparation and extends their learning.

Personal reflections and wishful thinking

While engaged lecturing using a DI approach has provided more interaction in the classroom, I wish we could have more interactive tools or capabilities, such as real-time audience response, to use within the EPLC. Real-time audience response would allow me to pose a question on the screen so that coaches would immediately, and confidentially, choose an answer. This should be done with support for all the coaches, and unfortunately, not all locations at which the clinics are held provide internet access, nor do all the coaches have the cell phone

Differentiated instruction and engaged lecturing **199**

functionality required for this. The ability to engage and interact consistently is key not only to DI through engaged lecturing, but also allows me to identify coaches' knowledge gaps. The content knowledge required of a CSCS and assessed on the exam is broad, and it can be difficult for the coach developer to review and evaluate coaches' knowledge of topics, such as sport psychology and endocrinology, by asking coaches to demonstrate physical actions. When practicing resistance training techniques or reviewing different training programs, we draw the coach to think back on what they know of anatomy, physiology, or biomechanics to complete the understanding of "why". This is not so easily done with sport psychology or endocrinology, because they cannot see the interactions; I would like to incorporate activities such as role playing to demonstrate the use of both adaptive and maladaptive experiences in sport practice or competition. I think it would also be beneficial to explore options for activities that involve the endocrine system, which could help coaches better understand the specificity of hormone-receptor interactions.

Activities for coach education

1   Consider the differences (e.g. age, sex, cultural, education, experience, etc.) you will encounter in your coaches.

    a   Can you list methods by which you can connect with them based on these differences?

    b   Can you identify information that you think is "common knowledge", but may not be due to these differences?

2   Facilitate a discussion with your coaches about their learning styles and methods.

    a   What works for them?

    b   What activities and actions encourage and support them through the learning process?

3   Discuss your course and the potential differences you will face with other coach developers and seek new ideas and methods of connecting.

Additional resources

1   McCarty, W., Crow, S.R., Mims, G.A., Potthoff, D.E. and Harvey, J.S. (2016) 'Renewing teaching practices: Differentiated instruction in the college classroom', *Journal of Curriculum, Teaching, Learning and Leadership in Education*, 1: 35–44.

2   Cash, R.M. (2017) *Advancing Differentiation: Thinking and Learning for the 21st Century*, Minneapolis: Free Spirit Publishing. Online. Available HTTP: <www.freespirit.com/files/original/Advancing-Differentiation-preview-1. pdf>.

3 7 Ways to Engage Coach-attendees in Lectures from King's Learning Institute (King's College London, 2000) www.kcl.ac.uk/study/learning-teaching/learning-and-teaching-support/quickguides/kcl-qg/dl/7ways-engage-coach-attendees-lectures.pdf

4 University of Florida's Center for Instructional Technology & Training provides online teaching resources including: Gagné's 9 Events of Instruction at: http://citt.ufl.edu/tools/gagnes-9-events-of-instruction/

Bibliography

Dosch, M. and Zidon, M. (2014) '"The course fit us": Differentiated instruction in the college classroom', *International Journal of Teaching and Learning in Higher Education*, 26: 343–57.

Gagné, R.M., Briggs, L.J. and Wager, W.W. (1992) *Principles of Instructional Design*, 3rd edn, pp. 177–97, Fort Worth: Harcourt Brace Jovanovich College Publishers.

Joseph, S., Thomas, M., Simonette, G. and Ramsook, L. (2013) 'The impact of differentiated instruction in a teacher education setting: Successes and challenges', *International Journal of Higher Education*, 2: 28–40.

Landrum, T.J. and McDuffie, K.A. (2010) 'Learning styles in the age of differentiated instruction', *Exceptionality*, 18: 6–17.

McCarty, W., Crow, S.R., Mims, G.A., Potthoff, D.E. and Harvey, J.S. (2016) 'Renewing teaching practices: Differentiated instruction in the college classroom', *Journal of Curriculum, Teaching, Learning and Leadership in Education*, 1: 35–44.

Parsons, S.A., Dodman, S.L. and Burrowbridge, S.C. (2013) 'Broadening the view of differentiated instruction', *Phi Delta Kappan*, 95: 38–42.

Santangelo, T. and Tomlinson, C.A. (2009) 'The application of differentiated instruction in postsecondary environments: Benefits, challenges, and future directions', *International Journal of Teaching and Learning in Higher Education*, 20: 307–23.

Weselby, C. (2014) 'What is differentiated instruction? Examples of how to differentiate instruction in the classroom', *Teaching Strategies*. Online. Available HTTP: <https://education.cu-portland.edu/blog/classroom-resources/examples-of-differentiated-instruction/> (accessed 10 February 2019).

SECTION 3

Inclusive coach development strategies

16

SPORT COACH DEVELOPMENT

Education and mentorship for women

Nicole M. LaVoi

Chapter objectives

By the end of the chapter, the reader should be able to:

1 Understand the importance of women-focused coach education.
2 Identify why same-sex role models and mentors matter for girls and women.
3 Identify exemplar women-focused coach education and mentorship programs.
4 Reflect on the role of the coach developer in creating an inclusive climate for women.
5 Facilitate women-focused educational and mentorship programming.

Brief chapter overview

In this chapter, I present evidence-based information on why women-focused coach education and mentorship programs are needed. I outline some emerging exemplar programs and organizations which are doing work in this area, and share key learnings that can be used to make future programming more effective.

Why and when I use women-focused coach education and mentorship

I believe that girls and women should have the opportunity to be coached by a woman at some point in their athletic careers, and far too often, that fails to be a reality. Similarly, boys and men rarely get to experience strong female role models or see women in leadership positions, which fails to challenge outdated stereotypes about women leaders. Research shows that women are underrepresented as head coaches in nearly all sports and at all levels of competition around the world, and representation has been stagnant at the collegiate level in the United States for nearly two decades despite concerted efforts by many (LaVoi 2016). Data also demonstrate that as positions become more visible, powerful, desirable, and lucrative, the more those positions are occupied by men (LaVoi 2016). I began to think about how I could help to reverse the current stagnation and increase the number of women coaches at all levels. As a starting point, we asked women who competed in collegiate athletics, who currently did and did not coach, to share strategies to recruit and engage women in coaching. The most clear and prevalent theme that emerged was to develop and hold all-women "single-sex" coaching education and mentorship programs (Leberman & LaVoi 2011).

Essentials of women-focused coach education and mentorship

Definitions, essential components, and goals of WFCEM

Single-sex education refers to programming that has only one sex, defined by a biological classification. The alternative, in which all gender identities are present, is referred to as "coeducation" (Signorella 2015). Until recently, nearly *all* coach education programming across sports was coeducational. Despite evidence which suggests female athletes and coaches desire and often prefer single-sex programming in sport contexts (Thul & LaVoi 2011), the research to support single-sex instruction outside of sport contexts is equivocal (Bigler & Signorella 2011), and nearly non-existent within sport contexts.

Outside of sport, arguments for and against single-sex education are rooted in three perspectives: *Gender essentialism* (biologically-based, inherent differences between men and women), *gender environmentalism* (socializing forces in the environment differentially reinforce or model culturally defined masculine or feminine behaviors), and *gender constructivism* (gender differences are mediated and moderated by the social and cognitive qualities of women themselves, and the meaning given to experiences) (Liben 2015). These three perspectives provide a backdrop for developing, implementing, and evaluating women-focused sport education and mentoring.

Coach development for women **205**

TABLE 16.1 Evidence-based support for importance of female same-sex role models and mentors

---

Reasons why female same-sex role models and mentors matter

- Role models.
- Emulation.
- Valuation and increased self-perceptions.
- Positively affects self-esteem.
- Visibility: "If she can see her, she can be her".
- Proof that women can coach, and that coaching is a viable career pathway.
- Provides insight and advice.
- Understands experiences of other women in the occupational landscape.
- Challenges outdated gender stereotypes about leadership.
- Less likelihood that athletes will experience sexual abuse.
- Females coached by women are more likely to go into coaching and stay in coaching!
- Female athletes should see people like them (i.e. representational leadership).
- Increased percentage of women in workplace reduces negative workplace outcomes for women.

Source: see LaVoi (2016) and LaVoi and Dutove (2012)

In our research, we have uncovered reasons why women desire and appreciate women-focused programming in coaching contexts, which include a dedicated women-focused space to network; build community; to be free from the male gaze; to be heard and valued; to be free from intimidation, harassment, discrimination, and paternalism; to participate in a judgment-free educational context; and to feel safe and supported (Leberman & LaVoi 2011).

Given robust documentation that the percentage of women coaches is stagnant, and women coaches at all levels and in nearly all sports are underrepresented, exist in male-dominated, male-led environments, are isolated, and experience a wide range of barriers compared to male colleagues (see LaVoi & Dutove 2012; LaVoi 2016), a women-focused educational environment and mentorship program is warranted. In addition, evidence suggests that same-sex role models and mentors matter for girls and women, for numerous reasons (see Table 16.1.)

Undertaking women-focused sport education and mentoring programming: exemplars

Attention to the importance and development of women-focused programming has increased within the last decade and gained momentum within the last three to five years. In this section, I outline some emerging exemplar programs and organizations in this area. Note that this list is incomplete, and there are likely many others doing good work. It is my hope that with time, programs not included here can be highlighted and evaluated for effectiveness.

WeCOACH

The forerunner to recent developments began in 2003, when the National College-giate Athletic Association (NCAA) agreed to pilot a program for women coaches across all sports and all NCAA divisions, what is now known as the NCAA Women Coaches Academy. This professional development program exploded into a network of women coaches and eventually, in 2011, led to the birth of the Alliance of Women Coaches (renamed WeCOACH in 2018). WeCOACH is the premiere non-profit organization in the United States dedicated to the recruitment, advancement, and retention of women coaches of all levels and sports (WeCOACHSports.org).

The flagship of WeCOACH is the aforementioned NCAA Women Coaches Academy (WCA), a four-day educational training available to NCAA coaches of all experience levels. The WCA is designed for women coaches who are ready and willing to increase their effectiveness by learning advanced skills and strategies that directly affect their personal and team success. Participants focus on non-sport-specific concepts, beyond the Xs and Os, in an environment that fosters inclusion across the sports community. The curriculum for the WCA, which includes aspects of adult learning and engagement such as lecture, workshops, discussion, activities, pair and share, case studies, and reflection, is constructed in two ways. First, the curriculum encompasses aspects of the Eight Domains of Coaching Competencies (NCACE) that includes philosophy and ethics, teaching and communication, organization and administration, and evaluation. Second, program evaluation data and feedback are utilized to modify and update curriculum topics based on the needs of women coaches and the changing landscape of coaching. This iterative process keeps the curriculum relevant, meaningful, and effective for women coaches. For example, analytics are an increasingly prevalent part of coaching; therefore, a data analytics class was added to the WCA. Another modification based on coach feedback included the addition of more individual reflection and partner discussion times to better integrate and process the immense amount of WCA information. To facilitate partner discussion, each coach is randomly assigned an inquiry pair partner (IPP), and throughout the WCA, the IPPs are given time to connect, discuss, support each other, and process information. The IPPs are an extremely popular component, because support and friendship extend far beyond the WCA. During the WCA, coaches make an action plan as to how and when they will implement what they've learned. After the WCA, one-year and two-year follow-up surveys are sent to coaches to document the ongoing nature or completion of their action plans. The purpose of this is to hold coaches accountable, and to document that the WCA is making a tangible impact on participants.

Since 2003 when the first WCA session was held, there have been 46 academies that have produced approximately 1700 graduates (WeCOACH 2018). The WCA is designed to provide education, professional development, and networking, with the goal of supporting and retaining women in the coaching profession. Unique to the WCA is the research partnership with the Tucker Center for Research on Girls & Women in Sport at the University of Minnesota. Members of the Tucker Team conduct program evaluation and longitudinal tracking of WCA graduates. In this retention tracking research, to document current occupational status and career trajectory trends, data pertaining to occupational position, division, and institution is collected each summer, and then compared to the time that the coach attended the WCA. Since 2014, when we began to keep more complete data on WCA participants, we know that 470 of 540 women coaches (87 percent) in the study are currently coaching, and a large percentage of those still coaching have remained at the same position, level, and institution (LaVoi & Cummings 2018). Current research is underway to examine what supports and factors have helped women survive, thrive, and stay in coaching. The available data suggest that the WCA is an effective catalyst for supporting, developing, and keeping women in coaching.

As a result of the popularity of the WCA and positive experience of WCA graduates, WeCOACH in 2017 offered the first WCA 2.0, a three-day master class for graduates of the initial WCA. WCA 2.0 provides a learning opportunity that progresses the skills, strategies, and knowledge gained from the initial WCA (WeCOACHSports.org). The curriculum for WCA 2.0 is largely constructed based on "what women coaches need" to succeed, develop, and survive. The focus is helping coaches build personal and professional skills, enhance their critical thinking, develop a portfolio, and become a leader for women in the coaching profession. Topics include interviewing and executive presence, moral exemplarity, building your legacy, tackling tough issues, public speaking, and owning your narrative. Instruction techniques include interactive workshops, discussions, lectures, and coach presentations.

For the past six years, WeCOACH has also sponsored a regional one-day Women Coaches Symposium (WCS) and workshop hosted by the Tucker Center and Gopher Athletics which serves more than 350 women each year. The purpose of the WCS is to provide professional development, networking, and community building for women coaches of all sports and all levels of competition. The WCS is a place for women coaches to feel safe, supported, valued, and cared about. Based on the data, we know many women coaches do not feel any of these values, and the WCS is the only place where they do and receive the message they matter. The WCS is evaluated, and almost all participants (96 percent) would recommend that a colleague attend, nearly everyone (98 percent) indicated the WCS is a unique professional development opportunity, and over 95 percent of participants stated they would attend the WCS in future. Given how quickly the WCS has grown – from 80 coaches in 2014 to sold-out capacity of 350 attendees in 2017, 2018 and 2019 – the demand for women-focused coach education is clear. To our knowledge, the WCS is the largest event of its kind in the United States, and perhaps the world. Go to http://wcs.umn.edu for more information, to see past programs, and the full evaluation report.

Due to the work of WeCOACH, the Tucker Center, and others (e.g. LA84 Foundation, Positive Coaching Alliance, Women's Sport Foundation), additional individuals and groups have recently been inspired to develop women-focused professional development and networking groups including, but not limited to, US-based programming such as: United States Olympic Committee Women in Coaching Conference, Women4Women and Pass the Baton (track & field), Women in Soccer Symposium hosted by the Wisconsin Women's Soccer Advisory Council, Women Coaches Advisory Council of United Soccer Coaches, Women in Rugby Conference, and the "So You Want to Be a Coach" program of the Women's Basketball Coaches Association. In addition, many international efforts are underway pertaining to women coaches, including the Japanese Women Coaches Academy, Women in Sport Aotearoa (New Zealand), the Female Coaching Network (UK), and the Canadian Association for the Advancement of Women in Sport (CAAWS). The efforts of CAAWS will be covered in the following section.

In 2017–2018, due to demands of their membership, WeCOACH – after reviewing best practices of existing mentor programs – launched a year-long mentor pilot program for women coaches. It defined mentorship as "A relationship in which a person with useful experience, knowledge, skills, and/or wisdom offers advice, information, guidance, support, or opportunity to another for that individual's professional development" (Berk et al. 2005: 67). The normative structure for mentoring is typically a mentor-mentee dyad. The WeCOACH mentorship program is comprised of a unique "Mentor Trio" design consisting of three individuals. The Mentor Trio program was developed due to WeCOACH membership feedback and the need coaches expressed to stay connected and supported outside of the WCA and WCA 2.0. Another purpose was to leverage the wisdom and expertise of more experienced, veteran women coaches for the benefit of less seasoned coaches.

The Mentor Trio pilot included 48 participants grouped into 16 trios comprising:

1   *Gold Mentor:* The trio leader, more than ten years of coaching experience, with at least five years of head coaching experience.
2   *Silver Mentor/Mentee:* More than five years of coaching experience; less than ten years as assistant, associate, or head coach.
3   *Bronze Mentee:* Less than five years of coaching experience.

While traditional mentor programs consist of a mentor-mentee, the Mentor Trio approach includes Silver coaches who have coached for seven to ten years because based on the data, these women are at a pivotal point in their career and statistically leave the profession at the highest rate (LaVoi 2019). All mentors and mentees were required to participate in a mandatory mentor onboarding training video call to set expectations and "coach" the mentors, and filled out pre-, mid-, and post-program surveys. Mentor Trios were provided monthly conversation prompts and "met" via video conference with the WeCOACH program associate. Conversation prompts included for example: Share your "why" of why you coach. What is your dream job, and why? How do you know when you're ready for your next position? How do you talk to your team after a tough loss? What are the biggest detractors of team culture, and how do you manage them? Due to its success, the WeCOACH mentor program expanded in year two to 66 participants matched to 22 Mentor Trios. Initial results were mostly positive, and "lessons learned" are summarized later in this chapter. One reason why the WCA, WCS, and Mentor Trio approach may be effective is due to the building of meaningful horizontal relationships (with those at equivalent level) *and* vertical relationships (with those above them or with more experience) that help create a greater sense of belongingness or the sense that she (the coach) is not alone (Norman, Rankin-Wright & Allison 2018).

Canadian Association for the Advancement of Women in Sport

The Canadian Association for the Advancement of Women in Sport (CAAWS) was founded in 1981 to advocate for progressive change within Canada's sport system by enhancing the presence of girls and women at all levels and in all areas. Today, CAAWS mission is "dedicated to creating an equitable and inclusive Canadian sport and physical activity system that empowers girls and women – as active participants and leaders – within and through sport" (www. caaws.ca). CAAWS is widely considered to be a worldwide leader pertaining to programs, advocacy, and advancement of girls and women in sport. Through their partnerships, especially with Coaching Association of Canada (CAC), CAAWS is involved in a variety of educational and development programs for women coaches, including the Apprenticeship Program, the Alberta Women in Sport Leadership Impact Program, and the Female Coach Mentorship Model (FCMM). The FCMM will be detailed later because it is, to my knowledge, the only program specifically designed to be women-focused, is theoretically based, and has been implemented and evaluated rigorously. Evaluation was critical so that FCMM findings could be used to create a sustainable, scalable, and exportable female coach mentorship resource. As a result of the FCMM pilot, a mentorship resource was developed that can be used as a guide by future mentors, mentees, and sport administrators to facilitate the mentorship process in a theoretically grounded way.

The Female Coach Mentorship Model was developed by CAAWS, CAC, the University of Toronto, and an external consultant (Banwell, Kerr & Stirling 2017). Zachary's (2009, 2012) four-stage mentoring cycle – *Preparation, Negotiation, Enabling Growth,* and *Coming to Closure* – was used to theoretically ground the mentorship pilot. The Preparation phase involved the mentor and mentee clarifying his or her motivations for participating in the mentorship program and engaging in a self-assessment of the attitudes and skills that each person brought to the mentoring relationship (note: Some mentors were male; all mentees were female). Mentor and mentee workbooks were developed, and pre-participation work was required. In the Negotiation phase, mentor and mentee coaches worked together in a three-day on-site workshop to establish goals, ground rules, and outcomes for the mentorship, and build a foundation for their relationship. During the workshop, research presentations were required of the mentees on the barriers and supports for women coaches, and mentors shared personal stories. The Enabling Growth phase comprised the bulk of the time mentors and mentees devoted over a one-year period and included carrying out their mentoring work plan and achieving the goals they set out in Negotiation. They were expected to communicate at least one time per month, and mentees were also expected to complete reflection exercises in their workbooks. Surveys were sent at four-month intervals to assess the program. Surveys are available upon request from the study authors (Banwell, Kerr & Stirling 2017). The final phase, Coming to Closure, included a final reflection, evaluation, celebration of the relationship, and a concluding meeting to bring the formal relationship to a close. Based on the evaluation report, development of the female mentor program, implementation, evaluation, and resulting curricular materials helped to positively and successfully engage mentor-mentee relationships. Based on the data, a few key changes for the future were garnered. These, along with learnings from the WeCOACH pilot program, are summarized in the following list.

In terms of women-focused coach mentoring programming, from WeCOACH and CAAWS/CAC, the following were learned.

1   Assess readiness: Time must be spent up front to determine mentees' and mentors' readiness for mentorship prior to agreeing to participate.
2   Articulate clear roles, timelines, and expectations for mentee and mentor-coaches.
3   The mentor-mentee matching process is a tricky, moving target!
4   Have coaches volunteer to be mentors and then the mentee coaches apply to be paired with a specific mentor-coach:

   a   There are pros and cons of having same-sport or mixed-sport pairs/trios. Some like mixed sport, but some mentees expressed desire to have mentor in same sport for job networking purposes.
   b   Pair mentees and mentors who are in close geographical proximity.
   c   Pair mentees and mentors who are in the same time zone.

5   Provide support materials online.
6   Mandate onboarding training. If the individual doesn't do the initial onboarding training, she cannot be allowed to participate. Participants must commit to the tenets and processes of the mentorship program, or it will not be meaningful or effective. Expectations must be clear at the outset.
7   The mentors often need training and mentoring.
8   The mentor/mentee meetings matter most: When coaches were asked what they found most valuable about the relationship, many coaches reported "meetings with my mentor(s)/mentee(s)". To make the mentoring program

Coach development for women **211**

effective, it is important for coach developers to provide tools and tips for discussion topics, be open to having coaches ask for what they need, initiate conversation, hold each other accountable, deal with conflict, and receive feedback.

9 Support is needed for the mentor program facilitator: The person(s) in charge of running the program must have tools to help hold people accountable and repair mentor-mentee relationships when someone isn't pulling their weight or fulfilling their role.

Personal reflections and wishful thinking

In terms of women-focused coach education and mentorship programming, the following key ideas have emerged:

1 Male allies want to participate: I never dreamed that men would be calling to ask if they could attend the Women Coaches Symposium, but to my surprise, they did. Lengthy and in-depth discussions between and among the Tucker Team and WeCOACH staff have resulted in how, or if, to include male allies as participants or speakers. Currently, men who genuinely want to participate and learn how to be more effective as a male ally or as someone who supports, recruits, and hires women coaches are welcomed. However, we try to balance this practice with maintaining the integrity and spirit of women-focused professional development. Emerging research highlights the importance of gender allies and the role of men in helping push for individual coach development, social change, and gender equality for women in sport (Elling, Hovden & Knoppers 2018; Heffernan 2018; Taylor 2015). More research and evaluation are needed on how to recruit more male allies and engage them productively to improve the occupational landscape for women coaches. For men reading this: We need you!

2 Use evaluation data to modify and develop future programming: Data, in the form of participant feedback and program evaluation, aid in keeping programming engaging, cutting edge, and meeting the needs of women coaches.

3 Include ample time for non-mandated, optional, and informal networking: To meet the needs of all personalities, coach developers should include unstructured times to allow coaches to process information at various speeds and in different ways. Introverts have told us they need down time to process and recover from being "on", while extroverts want more people time, as they draw energy from others. Women have told us some of the most meaningful discussions happen during unstructured time, alone and with others.

4 Women as coach developers matter, but are scarce: As stated earlier in this chapter, women coaches matter – and so do women coach developers. The culture of sport is known to uphold masculine ideals, and the work expectations and values are structured on the image of men as both coaches and

coach developers, which disadvantages women, devalues their competencies and fails to support women's development and progression (Norman in press). The underrepresentation of women coaches and coach developers is a symptom of the sport culture, not the problem (Norman, Rankin-Wright & Allison 2018). Sport leaders who value inclusivity would do well to stop blaming women for the lack of women in sport roles (LaVoi 2016), provide visible career pathways and support at each stage, and ensure staff is diverse (Norman, Rankin-Wright & Allison 2018).

5   The coach developer is responsible for the educational culture: An inclusive culture created by the coach developer should be flexible, process driven, and positive. Coach developers who listen to, support, value, and champion women, are key to women coaches' retention, development and progression (LaVoi & Wasend 2018; Norman, Rankin-Wright & Allison 2018).

6   Women appreciate and enjoy the unique women-focused experience; for some, it is transformative: As a coach developer, I know that women-focused coach education and mentorship matters to women. I wish that *all* women coaches had the opportunity to participate in and experience the programming I've written about in this chapter. Personally, I am transformed and grow with every WCA, WCS, or women-focused coach event I participate in. Often, I am moved to tears due to the impact and transformation I see in the women participants at the conclusion of the programming. Education, networking, and community building for women coaches is meaningful work!

Following are some testimonies from participating women coaches:

> I loved seeing other female coaches. So often we feel like we're alone or the "only ones" because we get so dispersed throughout the community and different sports, but it was so fun to be in a place where we could network and acknowledge that there are many of us working with athletes as a female.
> *(2018 Women Coaches Symposium coach attendee)*

> The Academy was life-changing for me.
> *(2018 NCAA Women Coaches Academy graduate)*

Activities for coach education

1   Everyone has bias; it is part of being human. Take time to reflect on your own biases that may affect how you perceive, value, and evaluate women coaches. How can you minimize the effect of bias when you teach and develop women coaches?

2   What are the barriers that women coaches face in sport that their male colleagues do not? Try to take the perspective of women coaches from different intersectional (i.e. overlapping, unique axes of oppression) identities. How might a White, married, heterosexual woman experience coaching

differently than a (un)married, woman of color, lesbian, queer, or gender-fluid coach? To prepare for this discussion, read:

> LaVoi, N.M. and Dutove, J.K. (2012) 'Barriers and supports for female coaches: An ecological model', *Sports Coaching Review*, 1: 17–37 or LaVoi, N.M. (ed.) (2016) *Women in Sports Coaching*, New York: Routledge.

3 What can you "do", specifically, as a coach developer to ensure that you are creating a positive, inclusive, and safe educational culture for women? To prepare for this discussion, read Norman's work listed in the bibliography.
4 Personal reflection or small-group discussion: Identify mentors you have had in the past or currently have. What made the mentor (in)effective, and why? What role did gender play in this (in)effectiveness? What changed with respect to your coaching skills as a result of the mentorship? Did you as a coach change (e.g. thoughts, feelings, behaviors including coaching skills) because of the mentorship?

Additional resources

1 Canadian Association for the Advancement of Women in Sport: www. caaws.ca
2 The CAC Female Coach Mentorship Model resources for mentors, mentees, and sport administrators: https://bit.ly/2PSFr6T
3 Chambers, F.C. (ed.). (2018) *Learning to Mentor in Sports Coaching: A Design Thinking Approach*, New York: Routledge.
4 The Tucker Center for Research on Girls & Women in Sport: www.cehd. umn.edu/tuckercenter/
5 Zachary, L.J. (2009) *The Mentee's Guide: Making Mentoring Work for You*, San Francisco: Jossey-Bass.
6 Zachary, L.J. (2012) *The Mentor's Guide: Facilitating Effective Learning Relationships*, 2nd edn, San Francisco: John Wiley & Sons.
7 WeCOACH: https://wecoachsports.org

Bibliography

Banwell, J., Kerr, G. and Stirling, A. (2017) 'An evaluation of the AWWS/CAC Female Coaching Mentorship Pilot Project', pilot project, University of Toronto.
Berk, R.A., Berg, J., Mortimer, R., Walton-Moss, B. and Yeo, T.P. (2005) 'Measuring the effectiveness of faculty mentoring relationships', *Academic Medicine*, 80: 66–71.
Bigler, R.S. and Signorella, M.L. (2011) 'Single-sex education: New perspectives and evidence on a continuing controversy', *Sex roles*, 65: 659.
Elling, A., Hovden, J. and Knoppers, A. (eds.). (2018) *Gender Diversity in European Sport Governance*, London: Routledge.
Heffernan, C. (2018) 'Gender allyship: Considering the role of men in addressing the gender-leadership gap in sport organizations', doctoral dissertation, University of Minnesota, Minnesota.

LaVoi, N.M. (2016) *Women in Sports Coaching*, London: Routledge.

LaVoi, N.M. (2019) 'Head coaches of women's collegiate teams: A report on seven select NCAA Division-I institutions 2018–19', Minneapolis: The Tucker Center for Research on Girls & Women in Sport.

LaVoi, N.M. and Cumming, S. (2018) 'NCAA women coaches academy graduate tracking report: Year 2', Minneapolis: Tucker Center for Research on Girls & Women in Sport.

LaVoi, N.M. and Dutove, J.K. (2012) 'Barriers and supports for female coaches: An ecological model', *Sports Coaching Review*, 1: 17–37.

LaVoi, N.M. and Wasend, M. (2018) 'Athletic administration best practices of recruitment, hiring and retention of female collegiate coaches', Minneapolis: Tucker Center for Research on Girls & Women in Sport.

Leberman, S.I. and LaVoi, N.M. (2011) 'Juggling balls and roles, working mother-coaches in youth sport: Beyond the dualistic worker-mother identity', *Journal of Sport Management*, 25: 474–88.

Liben, L.S. (2015) 'Probability values and human values in evaluating single-sex education', *Sex Roles*, 72: 401–26.

Norman, L. (in press), 'I don't really know what the magic want is to get yourself there: Women's sense of organizational fit as coach developers', *Women in Sport and Physical Activity Journal*.

Norman, L., Rankin-Wright, A.J. and Allison, W. (2018) '"It's a concrete ceiling; It's not even glass": Understanding tenets of organizational culture that supports the progression of women as coaches and coach developers', *Journal of Sport and Social Issues*, 42: 393–414.

Signorella, M. (2015) 'Challenges in evaluating single-sex education', *Sex Roles*, 72: 397–400.

Taylor, H. (2015) 'Activating change through allyship', *Journal of Intercollegiate Sport*, 8: 37–42.

Thul, C.M. and LaVoi, N.M. (2011) 'Reducing physical inactivity and promoting active living: From the voices of East African immigrant adolescent girls', *Qualitative Research in Sport, Exercise and Health*, 3: 211–37.

WeCOACH (2018). *NCAA Women Coaches Academy*. Online. Available https://wecoach sports.org/programs-events/wca/ (Accessed 25 September 2019).

Zachary, L.J. (2009) *The Mentee's Guide: Making Mentoring Work for You*, San Francisco: Jossey-Bass.

Zachary, L.J. (2012) *The Mentor's Guide: Facilitating Effective Learning Relationships*, 2nd edn, San Francisco: John Wiley & Sons.

17

WHAT'S GOOD FOR THE GOOSE IS GOOD FOR THE GANDER

Using adult learning principles to synergize coach education and coaching practices in Masters sport

Bettina Callary and Bradley W. Young

Chapter objectives

By the end of this chapter, the reader should be able to:

1 Understand how adult learning principles are useful in coaching adult sportspersons (Masters athletes).
2 Employ these principles as instructional strategies for coach education among coaches of Masters athletes.
3 Develop coaches' understanding of using these strategies with their Masters athletes.

Brief chapter overview

In this chapter, we engage the reader in acquiring new understandings of how to effectively use adult learning principles. More specifically, we elaborate upon a critical idea: The learning principles we advocate for coaches to employ in learning situations among their adult athletes are the *same* principles that coach developers can use to enrich the coach education process. Adult athletes are commonly known as Masters athletes (MAs), a broad cohort of adults who are typically aged 35 and older, registered for organized sport, and who prepare in order to participate in sport, often with a coach. In a line of research exploring the nuances of coaching MAs, we have found that coaches who frequently apply adult learning principles are highly effective in meeting the needs and interests of this cohort (for more

> information, see Callary, Rathwell & Young 2015, 2017, 2018a). Outside of sport, these same principles for adult learning have proven effective when applied by learning facilitators to students in adult education (Knowles, Holton & Swanson 2012).

Why and when I use Andragogy

As professors of coaching research, we have had the opportunity to act as coach developers for coaches of Masters athletes (MAs), who we will refer to hereafter as Masters coaches, in a number of different ways, via in-person workshops, online courses, and conference presentations. Within these coach education situations, we facilitated Masters coaches' learning by using adult learning principles, and we discussed how the coaches could also use these learning principles with their athletes. We have also employed adult learning principles with a high degree of success in supervising many young adult graduate students in the coaching science and sport psychology domains (Callary, Young & Rathwell 2014). In our work, we observed enhanced learning that has heightened our confidence in employing adult learning principles as foundational strategies for addressing coach education, especially those who coach MAs.

The essentials of Andragogy

Definitions, essential components, and goals of Andragogy

From our research, we note that many coaches are ill-equipped to coach MAs. This can lead to a disconnect between what MAs want and what they get from coaches, and to the rewards of coaching MAs not meeting coaches' expectations (Callary, Rathwell & Young 2017). Masters sport is one of the fastest-growing cohorts of sport participants, but there exist no formalized coach development programs designed to help coaches understand how to work with this age cohort, and there is no guidance for coach developers to facilitate these coaches' learning. Developing Masters coaches is a neglected and important endeavor.

We start by addressing what we have learned about the utility of adult learning principles when coaching MAs. Throughout the chapter, we refer to adult learning principles within the Andragogy in Practice model (Knowles, Holton & Swanson 2012) that our research has adapted for coaching MAs in sport (Callary, Rathwell & Young 2017; MacLellan, Callary & Young 2018, 2019). This model comprises the following principles:

1 Coaches enable and allow adults' *self-direction*.
2 Coaches explain *why adults are working on particular skills* or activities.
3 Coaches *take into account adults' prior experiences* in and out of sport.
4 Coaches make efforts to include a *problem-oriented approach* to training.

Coaching Masters sport **217**

5   Coaches work within the constraints of each adult's *readiness to train and learn*.
6   Coaches facilitate an *intrinsically motivating environment*.

These principles help to individualize MAs' learning, which is important because the motives that MAs attribute to their pursuits are highly varied, with emphases on competition and performance, achievement striving and personal mastery, social affiliation, and health and fitness (see Young, Callary & Rathwell 2018). MAs are a highly heterogeneous group to coach (aged anywhere between 18–90+, with differing abilities, differing priorities, etc.), and they can be challenging! We suggest that to engage and retain MAs in sport, coaches should be sensitized to the unique realities of working with adult sportspersons (Young & Callary 2017).

In developing effective instructional strategies for coaches within other contexts, several coach development programs appear to have turned to understanding adult learning principles for creating engaging and motivating learning environments. For example, within the Coach Developer Academy, a program through the Nippon Sport Science University in collaboration with the International Council for Coaching Excellence, the *Facilitation Skills Handbook* (2017) suggests that coach developers should be learner centered, relating new knowledge to prior learning. Further, it advocates for teaching to be matched to the learner's abilities, motivation, and readiness to learn. It also promotes an approach that is better suited to self-directed learners. Bottom line: Coaches learn effectively when their learning is facilitated by a coach developer who employs adult learning principles.

Likewise, our research indicates that coaches' varied use of Knowles, Holton and Swanson's (2012) adult learning principles is associated with more positive perceptions of tailored and personalized coaching (Callary, Rathwell & Young 2017), with benefits beyond skill acquisition (e.g. confidence, active lifestyle benefits; see Callary, Rathwell & Young 2015). In understanding how adult learning principles can be adapted overtime, Hogg (1995) advocated that swim coaches adopt a progressive approach whereby they initiate young swimmers (childhood and early teens) in a coach-controlled environment in which they are dependent on the coach for skill acquisition and guidance, indicative of traditional pedagogical approaches to coaching. We note that this may also be an appropriate coaching strategy with MAs who are novices in their sport. Hogg encouraged coaches to progress over time, and in accordance with the increasing maturity of athletes, to adopt more collaborative partnerships with their athletes termed "power sharing". We suggest that this recommendation is an invitation for coaches to increasingly search for and incorporate interdependent learning between coach and athlete, epitomized by shared decision-making and reciprocal (two-way) communication (MacLellan, Callary & Young 2018). Finally, Hogg stressed that emerging adult athletes (18+ years) should be granted increasing opportunities for self-management and self-determination in accordance with their maturity. Our research concurs, suggesting that Masters coaches take opportunities to transition responsibilities to MAs, to empower them to exercise autonomy and personal accountability for matters relating to training intensity, routines, and practice strategies.

Our research also indicated a number of attributes and characteristics that Masters coaches should demonstrate, including the coach showing professionalism, loyalty, commitment, and engaging in ongoing professional development to improve coaching knowledge and competence (Callary, Rathwell & Young 2015, 2017). When MAs recognize these demonstrations by their coaches, they are satisfied because they feel their coaches' efforts are commensurate with their own investment of time and effort in sport. This research also uncovered behaviors that Masters coaches could demonstrate, including holding MAs accountable during training, providing feedback that is in line with MAs' personal preferences, planning structured practices that fit within a coherent program, and framing practice situations in preparation for upcoming aspects of competition. All of these attributes and characteristics motivated and validated MAs' investment of time in their own learning and practice.

Now that we have portrayed our understanding of valuable adult learning principles for coaches to use with MAs, it is important to address the analogy in the title of this chapter (what's good for the goose is good for the gander) – how coach developers might use adult learning principles with their adult learners (the coaches). Coach developers should adopt strategies that will encourage coaches to feel their personal investment in bettering their craft is being respected and validated. One point has been clear in our research on Masters coaches: They are tasked with integrating athlete control over many instances (but not all) of learning in adult sport. Although this does not mean coaches should forfeit structure, it does mean they need to plan and organize occasions and activities whereby they progressively move along a learning continuum, away from coach-directed and controlled training, and toward shared coach-athlete control. Thus, coach developers: (a) are tasked with affording and integrating learner control of coach development; and (b) should not neglect aspects of planning and designing activities to enhance the learner's progress – rather, they need to design/plan differently using occasions and activities that utilize adult learning principles.

Facilitating adult learning principles during coach professional development

In this section, we discuss our initial efforts to infuse knowledge from our research described earlier into professional development for Masters coaches. We explore how we designed, planned, delivered, and evaluated the ways in which we, as coach developers, used adult learning principles as instructional strategies to facilitate Masters coaches' understanding of using adult learning principles.

Designing the professional development

In designing coach education for Masters coaches, we started with an exploratory approach. We believed that starting by observing coaches in their natural settings and seeking to understand what they were doing with their MAs was an important first step before initiating any explicit planning of a coach development strategy. For example, I (Bettina) observed ten fitness coaches who work with adults, over a three-month period (each coach was observed in a minimum of four coached sessions, with the head coach being observed the most often, in 11 classes). The head coach and I had discussed what we wanted to observe. This included key behaviors that he was interested in knowing more about, including, for example, the coach showing commitment by refraining from accessing his/her mobile phone. Predominantly, discussion centered on characteristics and behaviors that were connected to the six adult learning principles. These behaviors were written down into a 35-item survey and after each observation of the coaches' practices was complete, I assessed each coach on the items on a scale of 1–5 (1 – inadequate: Failed to coach; 2 – adequate: Did the bare minimum; 3 – good: Did their job; 4 – very good: Was engaged and actively coaching; and 5 – excellent: Went above and beyond what was expected). I also wrote an open-ended reflection on each coach's approach during his/her practices. I asked several MAs to complete this assessment, as well. After three sessions, I typically found that the assessments were relatively stable for each coach and it gave me a good idea of his/her approach. I could see how each coach did or did not use adult learning principles, and what particular areas of their coaching could use improvement. This individualized information then provided the basis for what to design in coach education for these Masters coaches.

Planning the professional development

In planning professional development for Masters coaches, we leaned heavily on our research so that it is clear that we have evidence-based information to share. Predicated upon the finding that MAs like it when their coaches share their knowledge and expertise (Callary, Rathwell & Young 2015), we contend that coach developers need to make efforts to share their expertise and knowledge with coaches, and especially knowledge tailored to the adult sport context. However, just as MAs like to be engaged in their own learning (Callary, Rathwell & Young 2017), the expectation for developer-delivered expert content should be moderated by significant planning that steers professional development toward learner-controlled exercises during coach education. Thus, in planning, we have tried to incorporate various facilitation strategies to give coaches many chances to think through how the information that we are presenting applies to them, and to evaluate whether they use it already or how they might put it into action. For example, an important aspect of planning our professional development was to provide resources through a website (coachingmastersathletes.com). In having this website available, coaches could peruse the site and choose information relevant for their specific needs and interests. In planning, we also sought to bring in the use of technology including PowerPoints with bright and engaging photos and content, and Wi-Fi to enable them to access web links and interactive surveys. Finally, what was organized mostly by facility and site organizers (not the coach developers), but still was an important aspect of planning, was considering the room and/or virtual platform used, timing of the session, breaks and nutrition, and costs. These details should be checked by the coach developer to ensure that they can effectively facilitate coach learning. In online courses, the virtual platform is of particular importance. Coaches may or may not have experience with online courses and technology. Thus, simple platforms, with limited options, colorful displays, videos, and easy-to-navigate windows/pages need to be planned carefully.

Delivering the professional development

In delivering workshops, presentations, and courses, we took the following two steps to help Masters coaches see the value of adult learning principles. First, we talked about our research, which shows our own knowledge and competence, as well as professionalism and commitment to coach development specifically in the Masters sport context. Second, we asked the coaches to reflect on how they might demonstrate these qualities and others presented in the research in their coaching approach with their MAs. Specifically, in applying the adult learning principles to coaches, we asked the coaches about their prior experiences and lessons learned in Masters sport, to know more about them and provide a more learner-centered approach. We explained why they are learning about different content and got them to think about how knowing why they are learning something was important to getting them to "buy in" to the session. We checked their readiness to learn the content by gauging fatigue levels, interest in discussions, and the time they have readily available to participate in workshops.

In a recent presentation, we elected to begin with a segment that was designed to heighten the coaches' readiness to learn by getting them to consider their key roles in facilitating quality adult sport experiences for athletes in their program. Specifically, we asked the coaches to provide their perceptions of the characteristics of a quality adult sport experience, and how these are different from quality sport experiences among youth or younger high-performance athletes. This exercise proved fruitful, as it empowered the coaches to share their perspectives, and it allowed us to gauge their levels of activity in Masters sport, as well as their philosophies and astuteness to their MAs. Importantly, as the coaches described the characteristics of quality adult sport experiences, they developed a scaffolding to initiate discussion on how they see their roles as Masters coaches in facilitating such quality experiences. Thus, there was genuine context in which we could discuss the goals they set to work on with their MAs, why they think they should work on these goals, and how working on these goals could help orient their approaches to features of a quality adult sport experience. Overall, this ensured a greater degree of learner control in the conversation, in a manner that was personally meaningful, drawn from coaches' insights in their past experiences. This activity appeared to be successful, as learners were motivated to engage in activities.

Coaching Masters sport **221**

After using adult learning principles to ready the coaches for activity, we typically proceeded to ask them several questions in relation to the content and discussions. We prompted coaches to think about their MAs' readiness to train, including the various factors that may influence their MAs' readiness and to consider how these factors impact their planning. We questioned them about their goals for learning and whether they set goals with their MAs and why. We made the learning intrinsically motivating by posing questions that pertained to their own experiences, using multiple strategies (i.e. self-assessment, discussion, small-group work, etc.) to get them to personally connect to the work and to consider these strategies in relation to their contexts. We asked them to consider various ways they motivate their MAs through their coaching, then we encouraged them to reflect on their own approach and its effectiveness. We had them consider whether they were motivated to accept and try new adult-oriented coaching strategies after having learned about the research and having had the rationale for new strategies explained and presented to them in a problem-oriented and pertinent manner.

Evaluating the professional development

The evaluation of the coach development sessions is also of utmost importance, especially as the research and practical development opportunities for Masters coaches are still in their infancy. In presentations and workshops, we included paper and pencil assessments and asked coaches to provide feedback on what new insights they had acquired, what content could be most directly applied to their current coaching, something they might still not understand, and something they would like to learn more about. These last two questions help us to understand what we might spend more time on with the coaches. Regarding the application of the content, we asked various specific questions, such as: "What can be most directly applied to your current coaching regarding the information you learned about adult learning?" or: "What can be most directly applied to your current coaching regarding communication with MAs?" In this way, we can gauge what the coaches found most useful and relevant from the particular content of the sessions. This evaluation process was also done online with limited success, perhaps because we did not provide a specific time for the coaches to come together with us for the reflection and assessment to occur. Thus, we recommend that any evaluation collected from Masters coaches be purposefully completed within a given timeframe.

Furthermore, as coach developers, we evaluated the sessions, often reflecting together in less structured ways. These discussions varied between rather open-ended questions: "What did you learn?", to more specific questions: "What did you think about the timing of the session? Would you change anything? What went well?" Alternatively, written reflections are easy to complete. Here is one from our recent workshop debrief:

Instructional strategies: Open dialogue went well. A lot of back-and-forth conversations. Lots of different types of activities from self-assessments, small-group

222 Callary and Young

discussions, etc. Good facilitation as participants started to debate the topic among one another but staying respectful of each other's points. We laid the groundwork early about being vulnerable about learning and respectful of one another and it paid off. We actively listened and affirmed their responses.

In summary, we found it vital to have designed sessions based on coaching needs for this cohort. Our early research on exploring Masters coaches' knowledge and engaging them to better understand their approaches indicated a need for discussions on adult learning principles. In designing and planning these sessions, we sought to help coaches understand how adult learning principles could effectively support their own professional development. Further, we discussed synergies with how specific adult leaning principles could enhance their coaching practices with MAs. In delivering these sessions, we made efforts to link the content to the instruction, and then to have the coaches reflect back on their own approaches and learning. Finally, in engaging in ongoing evaluation, we sought further refinements by thinking about what we perceive we did well and could improve upon, and also about what the coaches perceive is relevant, what they learned, and what they would like to know more about.

Personal reflections and wishful thinking

Apart from the work that we are doing, there is currently no coach education that is designed to help Masters coaches learn the psychosocial needs and interests of their MAs based on empirical research with Masters sport participants. We explored this topic starting from the ground up – researching what MAs want, what Masters coaches are doing, what these coaches are learning and not learning, and how they are learning. It has taken time to develop evidence-based resources for coaches in Masters sport. Others have created coach education tools for Masters coaches that draw on research from younger cohorts and relate it back to adults, or that are based in experience and opinion. While it is admirable that they are thinking of these coaches' needs, there are limits and flaws in resources and education for Masters coaches that are not based on research in the Masters sport context. One participant in our research (Callary, Rathwell & Young 2018a) talked about a pilot program aimed at coaches in Masters swimming:

> It was good. There was some information that I would say was pertinent to any kind of coaching, but also quite specific to Masters. The problem with it was that the instructors tended to be experts in age group [youth] swimmers and not a lot really translates in terms of diversity and goals of the Masters swimmers.
>
> *(p. 55)*

We urge coach developers to consider that the information they share with Masters coaches is evidence-based and grounded in the context of adult sport participation. Context and empirical rigor, using mixed methods (qualitative, quantitative), and voices of both coaches and athletes is critical.

Our current project is creating a diagnostic tool for Masters coaches to perform a 360-degree evaluation of their coaching in order to better understand what they perceive they are doing, and how their athletes perceive their approach. We have received much interest in this tool from Masters coaches and coach developers, but it is in formative stages of rigorous testing for reliability and validity – both statistical (e.g. psychometrics) and practical (i.e. how practitioners describe their use of the tool; Callary, Rathwell & Young 2018b; Rathwell, Callary & Young 2017; Young, Rathwell & Callary 2017). This tool will be critical in debriefs after practice, but also in formal coach education activities. Masters coaches will be able to use it for repeated assessment to gauge improvement and to assess relevant adult-oriented coaching principles and attributes that are associated with outcomes indicating a positive adult sport experience.

In association with the tool, there is a need to spend more time in the process of reflection, providing the space and questions to guide them into understanding how they are learning, what we as coach developers are doing, and how this can translate to their MAs in concrete, relevant, and usable ways. In particular, we have found the online courses to be difficult to engage Masters coaches in the depth of reflection that can be more easily achieved in person. Perhaps this is a function of our lack of experience in online teaching, the asynchronous nature of the course or the platform being used, or the motivations of the coaches. It is likely some combination of all three. Regardless, the online courses require further refinement.

Finally, we urge coach developers to consider how professional development opportunities fit into the scarce time adults have available for coaching. Masters coaching is not professionalized, so individuals wishing to attend workshops or pursue online courses will not do so as a mandated aspect of their profession. Rather, pursuit of these development opportunities will be a voluntary decision to invest in one's Masters coaching role, to better oneself and better one's ability to interact effectively as a coach in the adult sport context. The one thing we have learned as researchers in Masters sport is that all people in this sphere, whether they are athletes or coaches, have had to "jump through hoops" or negotiate other demands in their lives to be in adult sport, such as familial responsibilities, trading leisure time opportunities with a spouse, and demands at work. In our research, we have partly defined one adult learning principle – readiness to train, as adults having or finding the energy and disposable time to devote to practice (Callary, Rathwell & Young 2017). Moreover, governing sport bodies are not generally requiring coaches to prove they have specialized certification to work with this cohort. In fact, we recently had the chairwoman of a large Masters swim club caution us against mandating coach education activities for this cohort because she was already having a difficult time finding Masters coaches, and worried that the requirement of lengthy, or repeated, developmental activities would risk scaring coaches away. All this means that, like MAs who forfeit other leisure time activities to do sport, their coaches will be asked to trade some of their scarce free time to pursue our proposed professional development activities. The implication for coach developers is that we need to convince prospective attendees of the value of learning outcomes derived from these activities, and importantly, we need to strike a balance between effectiveness and efficiency in how we use adults' scarce time for Masters coaching education. These adults are keen to learn, grow, and invest in themselves, which are all benevolent aspects of intrinsic motivation, but they will hold themselves and others accountable to efficient and effective use of time. Thus, it is important as we go forward to refine our coach education activities that we consider how our research meets the needs of the coaches and the Mas, and does not create a burden on them.

Activities for coach education

1 Icebreaker: What is your favorite lesson learned from coaching MAs?
2 Coach developers can generate ideas about the coach's role in quality adult sport: What does quality adult sport mean to you? What is your role in facilitating that as a coach of adults? Use key themes that you characterize as representing a quality adult sport experience to rationalize how you set objectives and adapt your coaching practices with MAs.
3 Coach developers can create small-group discussions to explore reciprocal commitment: In what ways do you show your commitment to coaching? In what ways do you model this commitment to your adult athletes? Do they notice? Do you think this in turn encourages your adult athletes to heighten their own commitment to the program and what you ask them to do?

Additional resources

1 Coaching Masters Athletes: The art of coaching adults in sport, https://coachingmastersathletes.com
2 Baker, J., Horton, S. and Weir, P. (eds.). (2010) *The Masters Athlete: Understanding the Role of Sport and Exercise in Optimizing Aging*, London: Routledge.
3 Dionigi, R.A. (2008) *Competing for Life, Older People, Sport and Ageing*, Verlag: VDM Verlag.

Bibliography

Callary, B., Rathwell, S. and Young, B.W. (2015) 'Masters swimmers' experiences with coaches: What they want, what they need, what they get', *SAGE Open*, 5: 1–14.
Callary, B., Rathwell, S. and Young, B.W. (2017) 'Coaches' report of andragogical approaches with Masters Athletes', *International Sport Coaching Journal*, 4: 177–190.
Callary, B., Rathwell, S. and Young, B.W. (2018a) 'Coach education and learning sources for coaches of Masters Swim Athletes', *International Sport Coaching Journal*, 5: 47–59.

Callary, B., Rathwell, S. and Young, B.W. (2018b) 'Examining the factor structures of a survey of adult-oriented coaching practices', *Journal of Sport and Exercise Psychology*, 40: S81.

Callary, B., Young, B. and Rathwell, S. (2014) 'Beyond the classroom: How might lessons from adult sport experiences inform facilitators' ongoing learning in higher education', paper presented at Annual conference of the Society for Teaching & Learning in Higher Education in Ontario, Kingston, June.

Hogg, J.M. (1995) *Mental Skills for Swim Coaches*, Edmonton: Sport Excel Pub.

Knowles, M.S., Holton, E.F., III and Swanson, R.A. (2012) *The Adult Learner*, 7th edn, New York: Routledge.

MacLellan, J., Callary, B. and Young, B. (2018) 'Same coach, different approach? How Masters and youth athletes perceive learning opportunities in training', *International Journal of Sports Science and Coaching*, 13: 167–78.

MacLellan, J., Callary, B. and Young, B. (2019) 'Adult learning principles in master's sport: A coach's perspective', *Canadian Journal for the Study of Adult Education*, 31: 31–50.

Nippon Sport Science University. (2017) *Facilitation Skills Handbook*, Liverpool: International Council of Coaching Excellence.

Rathwell, S., Callary, B. and Young, B.W. (2017) Preliminary investigation of the validity of the instructional perspective inventory with an international sample of masters coaches. *Journal of Exercise, Movement, & Sport*, 49: 123.

Young, B.W. and Callary, B. (2017) 'Doing "more for adult sport": Promotional and programmatic efforts to offset adults' psychosocial obstacles', in R. Dionigi and M. Gard (eds.) *Sport and Physical Activity Across the Lifespan: Critical Perspectives*, Basingstoke: Palgrave Macmillan.

Young, B., Callary, B. and Rathwell, S. (2018) 'Psychological considerations for the "older" athlete', in *Oxford Research Encyclopedia of Psychology*, New York: Oxford University Press.

Young, B.W., Rathwell, S. and Callary, B. (2017) 'Exploratory factor analyses and initial inspection of coaches' responses to a survey of adult-oriented coaching practices', *Journal of Exercise, Movement, & Sport*, 49: 144.

18

BETTER COACHING, BETTER ATHLETES

Developing quality coaches of athletes with impairments

Scott Douglas

Chapter objectives

By the end of this chapter, the reader should be able to:

1   Recognize effective instructional strategies for developing quality coaches of athletes with impairments of all ages and ability levels (grassroots to high performance).
2   Describe, develop, and implement instruction to provide novice or new coaches[1] with the knowledge, skills, and confidence to coach athletes with impairments.

Brief chapter overview

In this chapter, I will identify unique issues related to coaching athletes with impairments and offer strategies for coach developers to properly inform and implement meaningful coach development programs in adapted sport and parasport. The information presented assumes that the process of developing quality coaching through effective coach education is based on the fundamentals of good coaching for any athlete, impaired or not. The chapter's sections provide an outline of concerns and instructional strategies for coach developers to help cultivate more knowledgeable and effective coaches of athletes with impairments.

Why and when I coach athletes with impairments

I competed for the United States in three Paralympic Games (1992, 1996, and 2000) and was a bronze medalist in the sport of wheelchair tennis at the 2000 Paralympic Games in Sydney, Australia. In 2004, I served as the Assistant Chef de Mission for the United States Paralympic Team in Athens, Greece. I was the first wheelchair tennis player and coach to earn United States Professional Tennis Association (USPTA) teaching certification at the Professional 1 (P1) level (in 1992), and have taught at numerous instructional wheelchair tennis camps and coach development workshops all over the world. I have also taught high school and Amateur Athletic Union (AAU) boys basketball and youth baseball, and I am a professor and program director for a university-based degree in sport coaching.

Why coach development in adapted and parasport is needed

In 1960, the International Stoke Mandeville Games were staged for the first time in Rome, Italy. The Stoke Mandeville Games went down in history as the "First Paralympic Games", attracting 400 athletes from 23 countries. The first Paralympic Winter Games took place in Örnsköldsvik, Sweden, in 1976. Over time, the organization and structure of the Paralympics has become more professional, which is reflected by the continuous improvement of the classification system, an increase in standards of coaching, training, refereeing and umpiring, continual amendments of the *Handbook of Rules* for each sport, and growing number of athletes and countries participating in the Games (see Paralympic.org).

Despite the growth in the Paralympic Games, athletes with impairments have remained marginalized in sporting culture everywhere from societal exclusion or limited acceptance because of culture, gender, ethnicity, class, or disability affiliation (DePauw 1997). It has been a continuous struggle for recognition and acceptance as "athletes". However, the need for developing quality coaches in adapted and Paralympic sport (parasport) has emerged from the rise in the popularity and profile of the Paralympic Games and a corresponding awareness of the need to raise the sport performance standard levels of athletes with impairments. The terms adapted sport and parasport are used in this chapter to describe two different levels of sport for athletes with Paralympic-eligible impairments. Adapted sport describes sport for novice through recreational/club level athletes (of all ages) with impairments, which can serve as a "stepping-stone" to the Paralympic level. Parasport is used to describe high-performance athletes who train and compete at the national and/or international levels, including the Paralympic Games.

Considerations for coaching an athlete with impairment places demands on coaches' knowledge and skills beyond that expected in mainstream sporting contexts (Burkett 2013). According to McMaster, Culver and Werthner (2012), content in formal coaching education has been deemed "rudimentary" and often focused on able-bodied sport settings. Most adapted and parasport coaches

228 Douglas

completed coach education programs that were designed for skills and tactics focused on able-bodied athletes (Cregan, Bloom & Reid 2007; Douglas, Vidic, Smith & Stran 2016). Yet, Paralympic sport is growing in participation and popularity; thus, coaches of athletes with impairments need continuing support and meaningful learning opportunities to enhance their coaching knowledge and skills. Adapted and parasport coaching education programs currently lack sufficient learning opportunities to foster the development of quality coaches in parasport. To address this systemic shortcoming, all coach education programs should explore ways to improve their overall curricula through integration of resources and materials, such as this chapter, that address the development of effective coaching of athletes with impairments.

Addressing expectations and fear of the unknown

Coach developers must be mindful of the uncertainty that novice coaches may bring to the adapted and parasport environments. Perceptions, stereotypes, assumptions, first reactions, terminology and language, and fear of the unknown are all issues that must be considered when coaching individuals with impairments. It's vital for coaches to maintain an "athlete first" mentality when communicating with athletes. Novice or new coaches' initial discussions with athletes should revolve around past experiences, individual strengths and weaknesses, goals, sport knowledge, and, most importantly, the performance implications based on the athlete's impairment. Whenever possible (and appropriate), coaches should communicate at eye level with athletes by kneeling or sitting.

Athletes will fall into a disability category or recognized "classification" for their particular sport (see www.paralympic.org/classification), but each will have different challenges of daily living, including training and competition. Parasport athletes are placed in categories or "sport classes" for competition, based on their impairment. The International Paralympic Committee (IPC) classification system determines which athletes are eligible to compete in a sport and how athletes are grouped together for competition. As each sport requires different skills, the impact of the impairment on that sport differs. Effective coach-athlete communication should avoid assumptions by the coach about the ability level and performance potential of an athlete based on their diagnosed impairment and assigned classification. No one ever imagined that a double-amputee sprinter or blind marathon runner would qualify for and compete for a medal in the Olympic Games, yet it has been done. Coach developers must emphasize the importance of being up front about past experiences coaching athletes with impairments, and always be willing to learn. Seeking out other athletes with similar impairments can also be a valuable source of information about a sport and the athletes who compete in it.

Coach developers should plan application activities for coaches that allow for self-reflection and a safe space to examine their own potential biases (e.g. believing that disability sport is less than able-bodied sport). Many novice or new coaches may make assumptions about what athletes with impairments can or can't do. There is a wide range of abilities, levels, and varied attributes among athletes with impairments. Coach developers must make coaches aware, depending on the impairment, that athletes may not be able to feel a limb or have limited ability to control or regulate internal body temperature (thermoregulation). Other athletes will have limited mobility, uncoordinated and involuntary movements, lesser cognitive abilities, low fitness levels, hearing impairments, lack of spatial awareness, impulsiveness, or difficulties with bowel and bladder control (that may interrupt training sessions), and some are vulnerable to pressure sores, bruising, and urinary tract infections. Athletes become a vital source of knowledge about their impairment and how it influences their training and performance, and coaches must learn to tactfully extract this information from the athlete. Some athletes come to parasport with a lot of experience (e.g. able-bodied athlete, military background), whereas others are "rookies", leading to tremendous diversity in knowledge, skill, and attitude.

Finding ways for the novice or new coach to spend quality time and engage in candid conversations with athletes will enable them to establish clear communication and the beginnings of a trusting and open coach-athlete relationship. A key component is to not ignore the impairment but acknowledge it and see past it. This can help inform the coach of what training methods may need modification. It is important for coach developers to teach coaches to act as they would with any other athlete (e.g. instincts for the game, fitness and skill levels, providing information about proper training techniques). Most adult athletes committed to playing adapted or parasport are at a stage in their life when they have accepted their impairment. This means that they should be open to discussing their personal issues, struggles, motivations, goals, dreams, and fears. Coaches should not be intimidated to ask athletes what they think will help them reach their full potential as an athlete and human. For instance, when I have conversed with an athlete (or coach) with cerebral palsy, it has sometimes been difficult to understand what they are saying. Coach developers can teach coaches to be patient with communication and ask the individual to repeat what they said. If necessary, ask for family, friends, or caregivers to help with dialogue between the athlete and coach, but never pretend to understand.

Expectations of athlete performance should not be lowered because of an athlete's impairment or perception of fragility. A coach must be keenly aware of athletes' capabilities and avoid placing limitations on them. For youth athletes, a parent is the best judge of what their child can or can't do based on their impairment, and coaches are encouraged to discuss these issues with parents. Coaches should be aware of potential overprotective parents and caregivers, yet always consider working together with the parents.

Once these initial conversations have taken place and the fear of the unknown overcome, there are subtle nuances between coaching athletes with or without impairment. Coach developers can encourage coaches to focus on the sport and provide expertise to help athletes reach their full potential while providing an

230 Douglas

appropriate inclusive environment that allows for the psychological and social development of athletes. Coaches should strive to provide accessible sport environments that foster an atmosphere of achievement, acceptance, learning, athlete development, and participation. Gilbert (2017) stated that "athlete motivation and coach-athlete relationships are enhanced when coaches can create sport environments that help athletes meet three basic needs: (a) choice and autonomy; (b) learn and feel competent; and (c) feel connected to others" (p. 155). Social aspects such as frustration, fear of failure, and resistance to change, of athletes with impairments are similar to those of able-bodied athletes.

Inventiveness and creativity

Coach developers can help novice coaches keep an open mind and experiment with new tactics and techniques to overcome obstacles and enhance athlete performance. This is an important stage in the development of coaches, because it allows the coach to focus on sport and performance instead of athletes' impairment. Coach developers should encourage "outside-the-box" thinking when coaches are improving athlete performance. Learning to remain creative will allow coaches to explore and experiment with new technical and tactical strategies that have not been utilized in adapted or parasport environments (Memmert 2015). Wareham, Burkett, Innes and Lovell (2017) reported that coaches permitted to be inventive and creative with athletes with impairments were more effective in achieving desired outcomes, including coaches' fulfillment. Most coaches of athletes with impairments have learned to become particularly resourceful while developing performance levels of their athletes.

Coaches must be problem-solvers and adapt their coaching using prior knowledge, and synthesize it into practical and unique applications in adapted and parasport (Douglas & Hardin 2014). Coach developers must teach coaches to combine current knowledge with experimentation and trial and error. When coach developers promote curiosity in novice coaches, coaches can become comfortable with experimenting through trial and error. For example, 25 years ago, wheelchair basketball players did not "tip" their wheelchairs – at least not on purpose. Tipping is a technique to gain height or position advantage by leaning the wheelchair and body in a lateral direction and lifting one side of the wheelchair off the ground. Through trial and error and improved technology, coaches invented and develop ways for athletes to learn this technique.

Douglas, Falcão and Bloom (2018) noted a lack of formal sources of parasport knowledge, leading parasport coaches to seek alternative sources of knowledge and experiment with modified able-bodied techniques through trial and error. Researchers have also found that coaches of athletes with impairments modified able-bodied techniques and strategies because their formal coach education lacked parasport-specific information (Duarte & Culver 2014; McMaster, Culver & Werthner 2012; Tawse, Bloom, Sabiston & Reid 2012; Taylor, Werthner & Culver 2014). This highlights the need for coach developers and

Coaches of athletes with impairments **231**

existing coach education programs to improve current curricula by providing awareness and strategies for addressing differences in coaching athletes with impairments.

Athletes with impairments have different developmental patterns based on their impairment, past sport experience, and the sport they play. Cregan, Bloom and Reid (2007) reported the importance of coaches accommodating and adapting training needs of athletes with impairments, based on the limitations imposed by each athlete's disability. Coach developers can teach novice coaches to design challenging and distinctive practices to maximize development of athletic potential through effective modification of mental and physical performance tasks specific to the demands of the sport. For example, in a course in which coaches are developing their skills of planning practices, coach developers can ask coaches to consider modifying their practices in relation to athletes' abilities. Appropriate questions and discussions with coaches enable them to establish and discuss realistic and achievable performance goals that do not limit the athlete based on their impairment. These instructional strategies will enable coaches to take risks and not fear failure because the coach and coach developer are working together. This can include creating drills, competition scenarios, and other quality "game-like" training activities unique to each sport.

Acquiring specific sport and technical knowledge

In addition to asking questions and opening dialogue, coach developers should help coaches understand the unique biomechanical differences between coaching able-bodied athletes and athletes with impairments. It is important that coaches learn and understand mechanisms that influence performance and are aware of factors that may predispose athletes to injury, especially injury due to overuse. To become an effective coach of athletes with impairments, novice coaches should be exposed to disability-related simulation (Douglas, Krause & Franks 2019) to gain knowledge of adapted equipment design and fit, repair and maintenance, sports techniques and fitness training (based on impairment), wheelchair pushing mechanics, and amputee running (prostheses and prosthetic adaptations). Coach developers can find ways for novice coaches to experience impairment by pushing a wheelchair, running blindfolded, or by other disability-related simulation. Coach developers should also consider including the use of the classification system and appropriate sport classes during disability-related simulations. As sports require different activities, the impact of the impairment on each sport differs. Therefore, for classification to minimize the impact of impairment on sport performance, an understanding of classification must be sport specific (see Paralympic.org). By coaches getting the opportunity to experience authentic gameplay – for example, playing wheelchair rugby – the coach may become more knowledgeable about, comfortable with, and empathetic of the challenges facing the athlete with an impairment, which can lead to more thoughtful and appropriate athlete developmental plans for training and competition.

Unique issues in adapted and parasport

Coach developers must teach novice coaches ways to coach athletes with impairments, how to develop competency in the skills and tactics of their sport, and to do so while living with the everyday challenges of a permanent impairment. These challenges might include transportation, chronic pain, depression, and other issues related to their impairment. The ultimate purpose of coaching is for athletes to learn about how things work best for them within the challenges of their impairment; thus, novice coaches should understand that the most effective coaches are always learning and seeking improvement, and place athlete development at the core of their coaching practice. The athlete-centered approach is a strategic way to build trusting relationships between coach and athlete, and should be stressed by coach developers to their novice coaches. This is a coaching philosophy that can unleash the full potential of athletes, especially those with intellectual impairments, through a style of coaching that supports player autonomy by implementing strategies to enhance athletes' decision-making during competition and beyond, and promoting learning through athlete ownership, awareness and responsibility. This coaching approach is founded on the belief that people are best at finding their own way, and self-discovery can lead to higher levels of performance. Novice coaches may find this to be challenging when coaching younger athletes with impairments who, because of a fear of physical or emotional injury, may have been coddled and excessively protected by parents and medical professionals (i.e. learned helplessness). While I was the athletic director at the US Olympic & Paralympic Training Site in Birmingham, Alabama, I noticed how nervous and overly cautious parents were about their child playing sport with an impairment – especially the first time. As coach developers, we can help coaches understand the importance of providing an enjoyable initial experience for both the athlete and parent.

To advance their knowledge about different disabilities and the uniqueness of coaching athletes with impairments, mentoring in adapted and parasport can be beneficial for novice coaches. While formalized mentoring programs in parasport are limited, these experiences can be pivotal and meaningful in coach development. These experiences can range from simple observation to "job shadowing" to having the mentee serve as an assistant coach under the guidance of the mentor as head coach. Coach developers should consider formally addressing these opportunities within a supervised internship, practicum, or mentoring experience. Douglas, Falcão and Bloom (2018) highlighted the need for additional parasport coaching education programs and mentoring opportunities to enhance parasport coaching and improve performance of athletes with impairments, and stressed the importance of mentoring as a structured source of education and career development for adapted and parasport coaches.

In summary, these are the strategies that coach developers can use to facilitate coach learning for coaches of athletes with an impairment:

1   Provide knowledge and explore adapted and parasport-specific content, including classification, rules, unique training contexts, competition strategies, and adapted sport equipment and technology.
2   Practice communication skills with novice coaches, including how to talk to athletes (and parents/guardians) to gain trust and learn more about the athlete's prior experiences; disability-related challenges, strengths, and weaknesses; and any medical considerations that may affect training or competition. The more comfortable the athlete is with the coach, the more information the athlete will share.
3   Encourage novice coaches to closely observe how athletes conduct themselves, both on and off the field/court, to gain a holistic understanding of an athlete and their impairment in authentic environments.
4   Be inventive and creative, and explore new techniques and tactics in the course with coaches through modification and trial and error. Coach developers should encourage coaches to take calculated risks, reflect on the experience, and appropriately modify equipment and instruction as dictated by the impairment and sport.
5   Persuade novice coaches to create an atmosphere for achievement by establishing a mindset whereby the athlete is like any other athlete but happens to have an impairment.
6   Encourage novice coaches to build a network with other coaches in their sport and ask to observe one of their practices to gain a sense of how the sport is coached by peers. Creating communities of practice with able-bodied and parasport coaches provides the opportunity to enhance learning.
7   Watch video with coaches to analyze movement of athletes with similar impairments. This can benefit the novice coaches to gain a visual perspective of existing techniques and tactics in their specific adaptive sport or parasport. It is important, however, that coach developers teach caution to novice coaches about imitating another athlete with an impairment, as no two athletes perform skills in the exact same way.

Coach developers should recognize the relevance of formal education, while also understanding that learning to become a parasport coach will benefit from other learning situations, given the myriad of disabilities and various equipment needs (Taylor, Werthner & Culver 2014). Vinson et al. (2015) called for research to understand various ways through which people with impairments engage with, and are excluded by, the structure of coach education, alongside other marginalized groups such as women and ethnic minorities. The reproductive nature of coaching shows that unless new, critical perspectives are offered as a basis for unpacking coaches' beliefs and values, coaching practice in the field of disability will remain unchanged (Townsend, Smith & Cushion 2015).

Personal reflections and wishful thinking

It was the semi-final match of the 2000 Paralympic wheelchair tennis doubles event in Sydney, Australia, and our traditional pre-match warm-up routine never happened – my doubles partner was an hour late to the venue. Our head coach was young and visibly nervous (as was I) about our match, but went forward with an overly casual warm-up without my partner. He tried to play it off as "just Bubba's normal behavior", but in what would be the next to last match of my career, I was upset to my core. I was nearing retirement and competing in the biggest match of my career, and my partner said he overslept. Did he care? I tried to remain cool, but inside, I was chapped. My partner finally showed up in time to stretch and lightly hit a few balls before heading to the stadium. We ultimately lost a hard-fought match to the hometown Aussies, and to this day I am still frustrated by it. I wonder if the result of that match would have been different and we could have played for a gold medal if my coach had been better trained and prepared to guide me at that moment. The lack of formal coaching education opportunities in adapted and parasport continues to be an issue to this day. In order to improve the performance and enjoyment of sport for athletes with impairments, my wish is that all sport coaching education programs include, develop, implement, assess, and research appropriate and meaningful coach development curricula that allow for quality coaching in all adapted and parasport environments.

Activities for coach education

1   To become an effective coach of athletes with an impairment, novice coaches should be exposed to disability-related simulation (Douglas, Krause & Franks 2019). This can be achieved in various ways like having coaches strap into and push a sports wheelchair or ice hockey sledge (if available) and play the game, run blindfolded, or ski behind a guide down a mountain while wearing partially covered goggles, or play flag football while wearing earplugs.

2   Use role playing to have an adapted or parasport athlete "character" simulate having a disability by sitting in a wheelchair, walking on crutches, or similar. Provide the novice coach in the role play scenario with prompts and information that encourage dialogue between coach and athlete. Debrief the lesson with open-ended questions that encourage coaches' critical reflection; for example: "Why is it important for coaches to earn the trust of an athlete with an impairment?"

3   Include opportunities for novice coaches to micro-coach in an authentic environment that includes, as dictated by the sport, the use of adaptive sport equipment. This allows the novice coach to gain valuable experience and increase confidence while coaching in this unique context. I have witnessed undergraduate students in my adapted physical education classes go from hesitant and fearful to assertive and confident after leading, for example, a

one-hour wheelchair basketball practice. If adaptive equipment is not available, consider modifying these sessions using scooters to play wheelchair rugby or setting up pickleball nets to play sitting volleyball. The key is a thorough debrief by the coach developer that allows coaches to both self-reflect and receive feedback from peers.

Additional resources

1   The online International Paralympic Committee Academy program is targeted at qualified coaches looking to transition into training para-athletes: www.paralympic.org/news/ipc-academy-launches-new-online-coaching-programme
2   Coaching Athletes with a Disability is a resource for coaches who are new to coaching athletes with a disability. Many coaches who are already working with athletes with a disability will find useful information and resources in the online module: www.coachesontario.ca/parasport/
3   The purpose of this manual is to provide grassroots coaches who have never worked with athletes with a disability with basic information, guidelines, and tips that will assist in creating conditions for effective participation and inclusion: www.coach.ca/files/Coaching_Athletes_Disability_update2016.pdf
4   I show the critically acclaimed movie *Murderball* to our undergraduate physical education and sport coaching majors at the beginning of my Teaching Diverse Populations class. This movie provides valuable insights into coaching athletes with impairments. It does not get any more real than this movie, and I highly recommend watching it for any coach developer.

Note

1 Throughout this chapter, novice or new coaches refers specifically to newcomers of coaching athletes with disabilities, irrespective of their experience coaching able-bodied athletes.

Bibliography

Burkett, B. (2013) 'Coaching athletes with a disability', in P. Potrac, W. Gilbert and J. Denison (eds.) *Routledge Handbook of Sports Coaching*, pp. 196–209, New York: Routledge.

Cregan, K., Bloom, G.A. and Reid, G. (2007) 'Career evolution and knowledge of elite coaches of swimmers with a physical disability', *Research Quarterly for Exercise and Sport*, 78: 339–50.

DePauw, K.P. (1997) 'The (in)visibility of disability: Cultural contexts and sporting bodies', *Quest*, 49: 416–30.

Douglas, S., Falcão, W.R. and Bloom, G.A. (2018) 'Career development and learning pathways of Paralympic coaches with a disability', *Adapted Physical Activity Quarterly*, 35: 93–110.

Douglas, S. and Hardin, B. (2014) 'Case study of an expert intercollegiate wheelchair basketball coach', *Applied Research in Coaching and Athletics Annual*, 29: 193–212.

Douglas, S., Krause, J. and Franks, H. (2019) 'Shifting preservice teachers' perceptions of impairment through disability-related simulations', *Palaestra*, 33: 45–56.

Douglas, S., Vidic, Z., Smith, M. and Stran, M. (2016) 'Developing coaching expertise: Life histories of wheelchair and standing basketball coaches', *Palaestra*, 30: 31–42.

Duarte, T. and Culver, D.M. (2014) 'Becoming a coach in developmental adaptive sailing: A lifelong learning perspective', *Journal of Applied Sport Psychology*, 26: 441–56.

Gilbert, W. (2017) *Coaching Better Every Season: A Year-Round System for Athlete Development and Program Success*, p. 155, Champaign: Human Kinetics.

International Paralympic Committee. (n.d.) *History of the Paralympic movement*. Online. Available HTTP: <www.paralympic.org/sites/default/files/document/1202091035 36284_2012_02_History%2Bof%2BParalympic%2BMovement.pdf> (accessed 12 December 2018).

McMaster, S., Culver, D. and Werthner, P. (2012) 'Coaches of athletes with a physical disability: A look at their learning experiences', *Qualitative Research in Sport, Exercise & Health*, 4: 226–43.

Memmert, D. (2015) *Teaching Tactical Creativity in Sport: Research and Practice*, New York: Routledge.

Tawse, H., Bloom, G.A., Sabiston, C.M. and Reid, G. (2012) 'The role of coaches of wheelchair rugby in the development of athletes with a spinal cord injury', *Qualitative Research in Sport, Exercise & Health*, 4: 206–25.

Taylor, S., Werthner, P. and Culver, D.M. (2014) 'A case study of a parasport coach and a life of learning', *International Sport Coaching Journal*, 1: 127–38.

Townsend, R.C., Smith, B. and Cushion, C.J. (2015) 'Disability sports coaching: Towards a critical understanding', *Sports Coaching Review*, 4: 80–98.

Vinson, D., Christian, P., Jones, V., Matthews, J., Williams, C. and Peters, D.M. (2015) *Investigating the Culture of Coach Education in the UK: The Supporting and Promoting Inclusive Coach Education (SPICE) Project*, Leeds: Sports Coach.

Wareham, Y., Burkett, B., Innes, P. and Lovell, G.P. (2017) 'Coaching athletes with disability: Preconceptions and reality', *Sport in Society*, 20: 1185–202.

19

STRONGER TOGETHER

Coach education and coaching practices for athletes with intellectual disabilities

Scott Weaver and Annette K. Lynch

Chapter objectives

By the end of this chapter, the reader should be able to:

1 Provide coach developers with effective instructional strategies that they can help coaches use when coaching athletes with intellectual disabilities.
2 Prepare coaches to understand the importance of meeting athletes where they are athletically, and adapting their coaching style to meet the needs of the athlete.
3 Enable coach developers to help coaches produce instructional plans that will continually challenge an athlete to develop sport skills.

Brief chapter overview

While coaches are often said to be role models and character builders, Special Olympics coaches go even further – they help athletes with intellectual disabilities find their own strengths and abilities. They help Unified Sports® partners[1] better understand the similarities they have with Special Olympics athletes, both on and off the field of play. Thus, coach developers can play an important role in fostering these attributes and skills in coaches working with this population. In this chapter, we will provide coach developers with instructional strategies for preparing sport coaches of athletes with intellectual disabilities, with a focus on coaches working with athletes who are training and competing in Special Olympics and Unified Sports.

Why and when we help coaches of Special Olympics

The first International Special Olympics Summer Games took place at Soldier Field in Chicago, Illinois USA in July 1968. The mission was to provide year-round sports training and athletic competition in a variety of Olympics-type sports for children and adults with intellectual disabilities, giving them opportunities to develop physical fitness, demonstrate courage, experience joy, and participate in a sharing of gifts, skills, and friendships with their families, other Special Olympics athletes, and the community. Since then, the Special Olympics Movement has grown to over five million athletes from more than 170 countries, training and competing in 32 Olympic-type sports under the guidance and support of over one million volunteer coaches (Special Olympics 2019). In 1989, Special Olympics became a sports organization for people of all abilities through the introduction of the Special Olympics Unified Sports® program, whereby athletes with and without intellectual disabilities train and compete together as teammates.

As the authors for this chapter, together we have over 50 years of experience teaching coaches effective methods for coaching athletes with intellectual disabilities. Our instructional approach is underpinned by theories and research on positive reinforcement in operant conditioning that focuses on providing positive and corrective feedback to achieve the desired outcomes. For example, if an athlete has trouble with following through on a shot, when they successfully follow through, the coach would provide feedback such as "good job on the follow through" instead of simply saying "good job". Our experience has also shown that it is best to avoid "don't do" language and instead use language on identifying what needs to be changed and how to change. Instead of telling an athlete "don't foul", they should be told to "play at arm's length and move your feet to avoid contact". We have found that positive reinforcement by coaches will typically net the best results in building sports skills and overall athlete performance. When coaching Unified Sports partners, it is important to be consistent in your coaching style – athletes with and without intellectual disabilities need to be coached with respect and shown equitable treatment. They may be at different skill levels, but they are teammates, and a coach can incorporate a consistent style to achieve desired outcomes with all of the athletes. Doing so will help partners better understand inclusion on and off the field of play, and they can help show athletes with intellectual disabilities how to build upon their strengths and improve every day.

The essentials of coaching Special Olympics Unified Sports®

The simple principle of "meaningful involvement" spurred the Special Olympics to optimize participation by all team members (athletes and partners) by acknowledging that every athlete should contribute to the success of the team. Unified Sports coaches should understand that when teams are made up of

Coaching athletes with intellectual disabilities **239**

people of similar age and ability, practices are more fun and games more challenging and exciting for all. As in all sports, the need for most athletes to belong or affiliate with teammates is of critical importance. The process of making friends and developing roles within the team is as much a part of sport as competitions. Unified coaches should be especially alert at the beginning of the season when teammates are getting to know each other and judgments about others are being developed.

A key component of genuine inclusion of athletes with disability in Unified Sports programs is the attitude, knowledge, and subsequent behavior of the coach. Research conducted by Special Olympics in partnership with Dr. Gary Siperstein (for a review, see https://media.specialolympics.org/resources/research/Special-Olympics-Research-Overview.pdf) has shown that genuine inclusion of athletes and partners relies on three key factors, all influenced by the coach:

1 Coaches must encourage interaction among teammates and discourage the formation of partner- or athlete-only cliques.
2 A coach should not create the perception that they are providing special treatment to any individual athlete or partner, or to either of the respective groups.
3 Most importantly, a coach must recognize and accept all athletes as teammates and treat them as equals.

Because of the central role of team cohesion and inclusion on Unified teams, coach developers can emphasize the following practices for coaches to use with their teams:

1 Use small groups (three to six people) for practice drills and tasks such as warm-up and cool down sessions and conditioning drills.
2 Set team goals that team members understand, and the measurement of success can be easily understood.
3 Clarify each team member's role on the team.
4 Encourage all team members to communicate by calling each other by their name.
5 Create opportunities for general communication among athletes before, during, and after practice or competition.
6 Take time to recognize specific athletes for good performance, and encourage teammates to do the same.
7 Use cooperative drills that build respect for each athlete's contribution to the sport.

Effective learning occurs when team members are learning by doing. Instruction designed for small groups and pairs will maximize time on task and aid in providing critical feedback on performance. In designing small groups, the coach can either place Special Olympics athletes and partners with similar ability in the same group, or design groups of mixed abilities.

The following recommendations are useful when making decisions about grouping athletes:

1   When a skill, rule, or strategy is being taught, all teammates need to know to use a single group for instruction, but then allow for small groups of similar abilities to practice the skill.
2   When the activity involves combination drills or team tactics, use multiple groups of mixed abilities for practice. Some teammates will seem to play better with certain teammates, but encourage all to get to know how to perform their best in any group situation.
3   Establish new groups or pairs for practicing different skills. Avoid same teammate pairing for more than one or two activities a practice; instead, mix up the teammate pairings and interaction.

Coach developers can develop micro-coaching opportunities to help coaches practice these recommendations and give coaches the chance to feel competent before working with their athletes. Further, coach developers can help coaches thoughtfully plan how to group or pair teammates for each activity by considering individual's skills and abilities, while avoiding the grouping of the same teammates all the time. Coach developers can also suggest to coaches that athletes occasionally self-select teammates to build a sense of control and competence, but be careful of cliques that tend to devalue less skilled athletes. Successful teams value each team member equally and will improve athlete self-esteem on and off the field.

What coach developers can help coaches understand about Special Olympics athletes

Coach developers play a critical role in helping coaches recognize each athlete's potential, while providing the necessary skills and tools to equip coaches to help each athlete excel. In this section, we cover what coach developers should know about Special Olympics athletes. It is important for coach developers to understand that intellectual disabilities are characterized by significant limitations both in intellectual functioning (e.g. reasoning, learning, problem solving) and adaptive behavior, which can cover a range of everyday social and practical skills (AAIDD 2013). These disabilities originate before age 18 (AAIDD 2013). People with intellectual disabilities are unique, just like everyone else. Disabilities affect each person differently, so it is important for coach developers to emphasize that coaches get to know their athletes individually. Adaptive behaviors, as defined by the AAIDD (2013), include actions and routines performed by people in their daily lives and include three categories of skills:

1   Conceptual: Language and literacy, financial competence and understanding, concepts of time, self-direction.
2   Social: Interpersonal skills, self-esteem, social responsibility, gullibility, naïveté, an ability to follow rules.
3   Practical: Activities of daily living (self-care), occupational skills, schedule/routines, travel/transportation.

Coach developers should also know that some characteristics of people with intellectual disabilities may affect their athletic performance in training and competition, including:

1   Low confidence.
2   Hesitant to try new things.
3   Feeling overwhelmed by a large amount of new information at once (such as multiple steps of a new skill being presented at the same time).
4   Viewing each learning experience as a new one, instead of attaching new experiences to prior-learned knowledge.

Thus, to facilitate a successful Special Olympics athlete and coach experience, it is important for a coach developer to help coaches understand and use appropriate instructional strategies based on the biopsychosocial considerations of these athletes. Next, we explain four psychological considerations related to Special Olympics athletes' ability to learn: Motivation, perception, comprehension, and memory.

Motivation

Coach developers should explore with coaches the following for motivating athletes (Sherlock-Shangraw 2012). In following positive reinforcement, coach developers should note to coaches that they praise successful behaviors, ask them to repeat desired behaviors, and refer to past successes. Coach developers can also help coaches to create competitive scenarios for athletes during drills and other activities. Then, coaches can challenge athletes to think about the competition and what they need to do to prepare themselves for play. Second, coach developers can ask coaches to find and reference local sports teams and well-known athletes when delivering instruction or feedback. Attending a local high school or college game or even watching a game on television can provide a greater awareness of game strategy and create teachable moments for a coach to discuss with their athletes. Third, coach developers should help coaches learn to keep practice drill lines short to maintain athletes' engagement and reduce standing around. Finally, coach developers should talk to coaches about making short-term goals before each practice with their athletes. Goals can be related to sport or behavior performance and be built upon the athlete's current level of performance, so they experience feelings of success and confidence.

Perception

Unlike their non-disabled peers, some athletes with intellectual disabilities may lack background experience in a sport and may also have challenges processing information. For these reasons, it is important that coach developers convey to coaches the role they play in helping athletes process information about the sport, which may be more visual than verbal – more seeing and doing versus listening and doing. During coach education programs, coaches can explore various equipment or other accommodations for athletes with physical impairments that may affect their perception, such as visual or auditory disabilities. A coach developer may need to demonstrate how to properly use adaptive equipment and modifications to drills to ensure that coaches understand how to appropriately incorporate these into practice sessions. Coach developers can also demonstrate to coaches how to intentionally connect new concepts to previously learned ideas to help athletes remember what they already know and correctly organize information. For instance, if a coach teaches her basketball athletes how to do set shots on Monday, she can refer to the hand position and shooting motion of a set shot when she teaches athletes how to make foul shots on Friday.

Comprehension

There are several successful methods that can be taught to coaches to assist an athlete in learning specific sports skills and comprehension. Coach developers can give coaches the opportunity to practice coaching in courses emphasizing the use of trial and error. It is important to note that every athlete will present with their own subset of skills and abilities – even athletes with the same diagnoses or disorder. In these practice sessions, coaches may realize that frequent repetition and reinforcement over time will improve the athlete's skill development. These practice sessions may move to competition-like scenarios via scrimmages or other games that require athletes to feel time pressure, use decision-making skills, or employ newly learned technical skills.

In addition, coaches can practice giving athletes feedback where they ask the athlete to verbally summarize what the coach instructed, and then build on this by having the athlete physically demonstrate what they learned. Importantly, coaches should periodically allow athletes time to rest their bodies and minds. This "settling time" can be provided, for example, via water breaks or permitting the athlete to remove themselves from practice for a few minutes. Finally, coach developers can instruct coaches to "scaffold" their lessons by giving a lot of support to athletes when they first learn a skill, then reduce supports as skill levels improve. A sensible suggestion is for coaches to "chunk" and "chain" content by breaking large concepts into smaller pieces ("chunking") and progressively teaching each "piece" in a progressing sequence ("chaining").

Memory

Coach developers can encourage coaches to repeat and refer to previously learned skills often and in different scenarios or contexts. Coaches must understand that there is no substitution for frequent repetition and reinforcement. This will increase athletes' retention of motor skills, and free up brain power to focus on the next skill.

Essential coaching considerations

Developmental considerations

In our experience, when working with any athlete population, it is important for coaches to ask athletes to perform technical and tactical skills that are developmentally appropriate relative to the athletes' capabilities. Thus, we introduce skills to Special Olympics coaches that are not too advanced for their athletes' intellectual, physical, social, and psychological capabilities, which can lead to an unsafe sport environment and frustration. Conversely, asking Special Olympics athletes to perform skills that are not challenging and do not promote development can lead to boredom and regression of skills. Furthermore, we discuss chronological age versus development with coaches to get them to notice when an athlete's chronological age does not align with his or her developmental age or maturity level, and help a coach identify techniques and games or event strategies that are appropriate for their athletes to perform.

Behavior considerations

We have also guided coaches in understanding an athlete's current ability level and the value of observing specific athlete behaviors in order to determine coaching strategies. We have asked coaches a series of questions to observe an athlete's behavior during training or competition, including:

1 What is the behavior of the athlete when she comes to the training site or competition venue? Is the athlete in control of her body and emotions?
2 Is the athlete in control (attentive, focusing on the task, persistent in completing the task, and handling feedback without incident)?
3 Is the athlete in control and able to inhibit negative impulse behavior?
4 While engaged in a task or immediately following completion of a task, does the athlete exhibit a positive or negative attitude overall?
5 Leaving the site (environmental exit): What is the behavior of the athlete as they leave the training or competition site? Is the athlete in control of their body and mind, especially about reactions to winning or losing?
6 In social interactions with peers or coaches, are the interactions positive or negative?

244 Weaver and Lynch

Essential points for debriefing this line of questioning include informing the coach that athlete control may look different in different scenarios and environments, encouraging coaches to have a plan to keep athletes' bodies and minds engaged throughout drills and activities, reminding coaches that the responses to different competition outcomes should be discussed and rehearsed prior to the competition, and informing coaches that reinforcement needs to connect with athletes' positive behavior, should be slowly withdrawn, and that occasional reinforcement is best.

It is important to teach coaches that the redirection for many of the negative interactions should be consistent. As coach developers, we have reminded coaches that all athletes' behaviors are driven by a need to get something (praise/reward) or avoid something (undesired activity). When a coach understands what drives an athlete's behavior, they can develop a plan for changing it. Change must be slow and steady if it is to be long lasting.

Communication considerations

We have found that the best way for a coach to assess an athlete's enjoyment, fears, and concerns is to speak with them often; check in with each athlete frequently during practice. If possible, coaches should also be encouraged to speak with guardians, parents, or caregivers to assess their perceptions of the athlete's enjoyment. Thus, we take the opportunity to teach communication methods to coaches that they can employ when conveying information to athletes such as verbal communication (providing spoken instruction, praise and constructive feedback), gesture cues (e.g. thumbs up, high-fives, clapping), and visual communication (videos taken on a phone of athletes doing skills, pictures of activities). Additionally, coaches can also practice using appropriate eye contact, respecting personal spaces, giving athletes time to respond fully, and using positive language.

Originally co-developed by one of the authors (Annette) for a coach education course specifically for coaching Special Olympic athletes (see www.asep. com/courseInfo/purchase_courseinfo.cfm?CourseID=233&OrgID=64), coach developers can reinforce the "5 Cs" of communication at practice or competitions:

1 Clear: Words that an athlete can understand or for which an athlete has a point of reference, such as "see the ball" as opposed to "find the target".
2 Concrete: Words that are specific to something physical or real. Concrete communication is important because athletes often have a cognitive delay in processing information (especially words). For example, when coaches are teaching the three-second lane in basketball, instruct the coach to use the physical words of "hot" and "cold" to assist an athlete in learning the concept. "Hot" refers to the lane on offense – the athlete will burn up if he stops in the lane and not move through it; "cold" refers to the lane at the defensive end of the court – a cold lane is the athlete's friend.

Coaching athletes with intellectual disabilities **245**

3   Concise: A few descriptive "key words" or cues. For example: "Reach for the sky". Do not use long sentences or multi-part instructions.
4   Consistent: The same cue words for the same actions.
5   Command-oriented words: Verbal reinforcement of the athlete's behavior immediately after a desired action.

Presenting "c" words can help coaches remember them and easily check in to reflect on their communication. When needed, coaches may have to physically prompt an athlete to look at them to ensure their instructions are being heard and understood.

Level of assistance

We have also found it important that we, as coach developers, assist coaches to assess what an athlete is ready to do and build upon their strengths. Coaches should understand that they can start with verbal instruction and then visual demonstration to see what the athlete understands and can do. If the athlete is not successful, they may add partial physical assistance (e.g. placing the athlete's hand in the proper position and then allowing them to complete the motion) or, if necessary, move to full assistance (e.g. providing hands-on help to an athlete through the entire motion of the skill). The coach developer should practice this progression with coaches to help them understand the importance of when and how to use the appropriate level of instruction – verbal, visual, partial physical assistance, or full physical assistance. If an athlete requires physical assistance, it is the goal of the coach to gradually reduce physical assistance in favor of simple cues – and eventually, no prompting at all.

A coach's *Quick Reference Coaching Guide* (see additional resources) that focuses on behaviors, not labels, was developed to help provide strategies to change behavior and improve athlete performance. We have used this guide as a resource with coaches to discuss information and strategies regarding different functional and learning characteristics of athletes. It is important to note that these are not defaming labels; however, a coach may have unrealistic expectations of an athlete. Thus, an important role of the coach developer is to instruct coaches to talk with parents, providers, teachers, former coaches, etc., about an athlete's characteristics and the successful strategies used to affect performance. As a guideline, coaches can strive to include one or more of the strategies in each practice. The discussion with family members may also bring to light some additional strategies beyond those listed in the guide.

Personal reflections and wishful thinking

Coaching an athlete with an intellectual disability can be complex and daunting, but also one of the most rewarding experiences a coach can have. Looking at the variety of characteristics that a Special Olympics athlete may possibly bring with them to the field of play and adding that to their specific learning challenges is enough to scare away even the most experienced coaches. However, for those coaches who look beyond those challenges and leave behind their preconceived perceptions of what an athlete cannot do, they will enter a world of coaching whereby winning is achieving, and achieving can be something as simple as completing just one bump, set, and spike combination in a volleyball match.

In a perfect world where there is full inclusion, Special Olympics coaches will not be needed, because athletes with intellectual disabilities will be playing on youth sports teams, on their high school teams, and in adult community recreation leagues. However, full inclusion has not yet been achieved, so coach developers are needed to prepare coaches to work with Special Olympics athletes.

Activities for coach education

1 Help coaches take into consideration that disruptive behavior and communication challenges can affect practice sessions and should be addressed accordingly. Ask coaches to think of a time when an athlete disrupted practice. Then, ask them to share their story with another coach. Using the techniques provided in the *Quick Reference Coaching Guide* and the "5 Cs" of communication, ask coaches to come up with ideas that might help them deal with their partner's situation.

2 Consistent enforcement of limits is a *must*. Athletes learn quickly that the coach means what they say. Thus, before the season starts, ask coaches to come up with a clear set of rules, expectations and limits, and designate a specific location for an athlete to regain self-control. Ask coaches to include the following considerations:

   a Consequences should be enforceable and short term.
   b Reinforce acceptable behaviors. Praising positive behaviors may be enough of a motivator for the athlete.
   c Develop a behavior intervention support plan after collecting information about the function of a particular behavior.
   d Help the athlete find a replacement behavior that functions in a similar way as the undesired behavior.

3 Coach developers should model appropriate coaching behaviors to coaches by demonstrating how to communicate through methods other than just telling. As a coach developer, come up with ways that you can ask questions to coaches about what they know about effective communication, without telling or directing them to the answers. Coach developers can point out that questioning is a great way to gauge an athlete's understanding and encourages athlete engagement and inclusion. As mentioned earlier, the "5 Cs" can be used when communicating to the team: Clear, concrete, concise, consistent, and command oriented.

Additional resources

1 www.specialolympics.org
2 Coaching Unified Sports online course hosted by the National Federation of State High School Associations: https://nfhslearn.com/courses/61127/coaching-unified-sports
3 Principles of Coaching for Special Olympics online course hosted by West Virginia University: https://wvu.augusoft.net/index.cfm?method=ClassInfo.ClassInformation&int_class_id=39216
4 Coaching Special Olympics Athletes online course hosted by Human Kinetics: www.asep.com/asep_content/org/SONA.cfm
5 Special Olympics Research: https://resources.specialolympics.org/research/research-overview
6 Special Olympics *Quick Reference Coaching Guide*: https://media.specialolympics.org/resources/sports-essentials/general/Special_Olympics_Quick_Reference_Coaching_Guide_Print.pdf?_ga=2.61072236.1909437174.1564839171-393079243.1557967681

Note

1 Partners is the term used by Special Olympics to describe the athlete without an intellectual disability participating as a teammate on the same team.

Bibliography

American Association on Intellectual and Developmental Disabilities. (2013) *Definition of intellectual disability*. Online. Available HTTP: <www.aaidd.org/intellectual-disability/definition> (accessed 20 June 2019).

Lynch, A., VandenBroek, D. and Fegan, P. (2014) *Special Olympics Athlete-Centered Coaching Guide*, Special Olympics International.

Sherlock-Shangraw, R.A. (2012) 'Identifying instructional practices employed by Massachusetts Special Olympics hall of fame coaches', Doctoral dissertation, Boston University, Boston, MA.

Special Olympics. (2019). *Sports and Games*. Online. Available HTTP: <https://www.specialolympics.org/our-work/sports-and-games> (accessed 25 September 2019).

20

UNDERSTANDING AND ACTING UPON WHITE PRIVILEGE IN COACHING AND COACH EDUCATION

Brian Gearity, Lynett Henderson Metzger, Derrick S. Wong, and Ted Butryn

---

Chapter objectives

By the end of this chapter, the reader should be able to:

1 Articulate an understanding of White privilege.
2 Identify ways sport coaches could implement racially sensitive and antiracist practices at multiple levels (e.g. intrapersonal, interpersonal, group, and organizational).
3 Integrate racially sensitive and antiracist practices throughout coach education programs.

Brief chapter overview

White privilege (WP) is a concept used to explain the "unearned assets" provided to White people (McIntosh 1988) because of their dominance in the Western world, which includes creating social and legal structures for their benefit. WP is a problem because it hurts people – particularly people of color (POC) – physically, psychologically, economically, and socially, and it prevents the realization of democratic ideals such as freedom and justice for all. The purpose of this chapter is to provide coach developers with an understanding of racial privilege and instructional strategies, and tools to use to develop coaches' cultural competence. We focus this chapter on race; however, we acknowledge the importance of intersectionality, a term coined by Crenshaw (1989) as a way of talking about how different identities

> overlap and intersect with systems of power that privilege some and disenfranchise others (Coaston 2019; e.g. White feminism mostly excluded Black women; Black women are nearly non-existent in NCAA administrative and coaching positions). We also contextualize our discussion of Whiteness in coaching within the larger US and global discourses surrounding White racism and White supremacy.

Why and when I integrate race and white privilege throughout coach development

Examples of White privilege (WP) in sport coaching include both the harmful acts of individuals – such as a White coach telling an African-American athlete to cover a wound with a "flesh tone" bandage when the only available color is peach, or penalizing an athlete for wearing a hairstyle not typically associated with traditional White norms – as well as systemic barriers and inequities, such as the disproportionate underrepresentation of people of color (POC) in leadership positions in Division I football, where 94.2 percent of head coaches but only 46.4 percent of athletes identify as White (NCAA 2018), or the widespread use of culturally insensitive examples, language, metaphors, or "humor" to instruct or build rapport. Examples of WP in sport coach education include:

1   Numerous academic books on sport psychology, sociology of coaching, and athlete-centered coaching that overlook or barely mention issues of race or are authored or edited by only White contributors.
2   The lack of POC represented as coach developers or leaders in sport national governing bodies or businesses.
3   Coach education professional development that omits sociocultural issues, including race, that is overwhelmingly delivered by White people who are uncomfortable talking about race and who have been socialized not to see race and ignore its impact in sport and coach education.

(DiAngelo 2011)

We integrate issues of race, privilege, and power into our coach development courses for the same reason we offer this chapter – to address historical and ongoing injustices in order to create a more free, inclusive, and democratic practice of sport and coaching. As succinctly put by the eminent sociologist of sport, Dr. Jay Coakley (2015), "But as long as it [stories about race and ethnicity] remains untold, white privilege in sports will persist without being recognized" (p. 418). Other chapters in this book feature a more straightforward, comprehensive instructional strategy (i.e. case study, Project-Based Learning); however, studying race and related concepts such as ethnicity, diversity, inclusivity, bias, prejudice, discrimination, stereotypes, and racism is fundamentally different. We

250 Gearity, Henderson Metzger, Wong, and Butryn

recommend the issues in this chapter be integrated within the other instructional strategies and content delivered, as well as being taught independently by exploring attitudes, feelings, and perspectives. We focus on three areas in which an understanding of race and WP is critical for coach developers: (a) intrapersonal knowledge; (b) interpersonal and team settings; and (c) organization and societal settings.

The essentials of race and White privilege: three levels for coach developers' action

Developing a coach's intrapersonal knowledge about race

Self-awareness around race and WP has largely been omitted from coach education, but is essential for initiating understanding and change; we as individuals must recognize our individual responsibility to grow if we are to change systemic issues. We often view topics like privilege, racism, xenophobia, and nationalism as too sensitive to talk about, leading to failure to develop a deep understanding and an unchanged status quo. By sharing some of our experiences, we invite coach developers to begin or continue their journey toward understandings of Whiteness and WP, along with implications for each of our personal and professional contexts.

We begin with a personal story to bring to life these issues and to show the value of personal narratives as a tool for intrapersonal knowledge development. While in graduate school studying educational leadership and cultural studies of education, I (Brian, a White male) had an epiphany regarding WP. I was in a philosophy of education class of about ten students, discussing our latest readings on race in schooling, when the professor invited us to share our interpretations of the authors' works. I said something like, "I didn't really understand this point about colorblindness. Isn't that a good thing? America as the melting pot – that's good; that's what we learned (in primary school)". And within that assumption lies the problem: Although often well intended and reflective of progressive liberal ideals (e.g. fairness, meritocracy), the discourse of colorblindness tends to strengthen Whiteness and WP by effectively diverting or even dismissing more critical discussions related to WP in sport and society. The epiphany was this: Because I am White, I see Whiteness as baseline – as the expected or default. For example, I saw myself, not as a White coach, but as a "regular" coach, whereas the Mexican-American, Puerto Rican, and African-American coaches with whom I had worked seemed something other than "the norm".

As a White person, I am not alone in seeing (or failing to see) the world through this lens. Feagin's (2013) analysis of what he calls the "white racial frame" breaks down how White people develop an understanding of race in America. Claiming colorblindness allows people with WP to pretend that they do not "see" race, including their own, and to deny its impact on peoples' lived experiences. For example, I have never expected to be hired or fired from a coaching job because of my race, but through my educational and professional experiences, I've come to understand that this is often not the case for POC, who may face tokenization (e.g. the presumption across all levels of sport that coaching staffs must include at least one POC to be seen as inclusive, without centering the roles of POC to empower genuine change and inclusivity) or have their skills and achievements dismissed (e.g. when I was a coaching intern with the Cleveland Indians – a racially insensitive/racist name – there was a pervasive narrative that the Spanish-speaking coaches got their jobs in part because they could speak Spanish, which diminished the respect they should have been afforded based on their accomplishments). By refusing to see how race affects identity and cultural practices, including coaching and education, we normalize Whiteness at the expense of diversity, difference, and multiculturalism – not only with respect to the prevalence of coaches of color, but in coaching and athletic training ideas and practices. Biases, discrimination, subtle instructions, jokes, etc., used by White athletes, coaches, administrators, and sport business owners work to diminish and marginalize the contributions and experiences of POC, keeping them in a power-down position. By allowing ourselves not to know – or, more accurately, refusing to see – how laws, norms, and practices have been shaped over time and intersect with race, White people who have more power, resources, and cultural capital are implicitly working to keep it – whether we're honest about that or not.

My epiphany in that graduate classroom, that I had been socialized to not see, stoked my curiosity to learn more. Recognition of this sort of racial ignorance hopefully prompts further understanding, not defensive or dismissive reactions. As I became more aware of these dynamics, I began to work to not generalize from my story to others, and to look beyond my interpersonal experiences to systemic, historical understandings that shape groups of people in society. I realized that, if I wanted to be a great coach in any sense of the word, I needed to learn more – to better understand myself and how to coach athletes of all races, and to reduce the historical and systematic effects of WP. Back then, I could find little relevant sport coaching research. I looked to teacher education preparation and found work on culturally sensitive or critical pedagogy and other books on race in the classroom and in physical education (Ladson-Billings 1995). I slowly observed things differently, and in the process, I moved from colorblindness to seeing how race matters, to borrow West's (1994) term. I began to talk with athletes about race, WP, and racist theories of athletic performance (Hoberman 1996), and eventually our research began to fill gaps in the sport coaching literature (Gearity & Henderson Metzger 2017). As a coach developer-professor, I've integrated social issues such as WP and related concepts into new courses, curricula, and professional development presentations for coaches.

It's common for White people to experience denial, anxiety, guilt, or fragility when learning about or discussing race, as well as to engage in various logical fallacies such as begging the question, ad hominem (personal) attacks, "what about"-ism, or blaming the victim. We hope that by sharing a bit of our experiences, and common reactions and responses, coach developers can process this information deeply and respond to others accurately, meaningfully, and with compassion. The use of storytelling and personal narratives can be a powerful tool for coaches to use to understand their own experiences and how these experiences were constructed in society, and to contrast their stories with others, thus enhancing empathy, sympathy, and the responsible use of power. Preparing this chapter once again reminds us that we have much to learn about how we personally understand race. We intentionally began this chapter by identifying the primacy of racial intrapersonal knowledge, because the coach developer will need this for personal growth and as a foundation to prepare coaches for antiracist practices within teams and organizations, to which we now turn.

Interpersonal and team

Sport coaches need to apply their understanding of WP and antiracist practices to one-on-one interactions with athletes, small groups of athletes, and the whole team. Feagin (2013) notes many White people do not want to discuss race for fear of not knowing what to say or being labeled a racist, which unfortunately and ironically strengthens WP. Therefore, in this section, we offer recommendations for coach developers negotiating these situations.

The invisible knapsack

Peggy McIntosh (1988) wrote of White (male) privilege as an invisible knapsack of unearned assets available exclusively based on Whiteness, and without necessarily any conscious awareness on the part of the beneficiary of WP. I (Brian) put the word "male" in parenthesis here because McIntosh talked about the intersecting privileges of race and gender. Privilege as a concept of unearned advantages has been extended to other identities and institutions such as sexual orientation, religion, socioeconomic status, geography, and so forth. WP can exist with or without other forms of privilege. We are born into varying privileges or disadvantages (for a brief example, see Crosley-Corcoran 2014). That is, someone can be said to have WP while being economically disadvantaged or gender advantaged; when we think of voting or reproductive rights, we easily think of women having historically been disadvantaged. Also, people would readily agree that being born into wealth is an unearned privilege, but may find it harder to acknowledge light skin color as a privilege.

As a coach developer, I (Brian) drew upon McIntosh's work to design an undergraduate course titled, Social Foundations and Issues of Sport Coaching. McIntosh created 46 statements that reflect how WP operates, and I used these for an in-class activity whereby we checked off if they were true or not for us, then discussed the results as a class. As a White male, I had never considered many of the items McIntosh brought up, underscoring her point. For example, one item reads, "I can speak in public to a powerful male group without putting my race on trial". As a White male, I would likely be speaking to other White males, and I wouldn't worry about putting my Whiteness on trial. Comments by White people referring to POC as "articulate" or "well-spoken", however – which we and many readers will undoubtedly have heard in and out of class-room settings – underscore the subtle expectation that these are not the default assumptions for POC. Rarely is a White politician described using similar lan-guage, for example. In the example given, the in-class activity resulted in a lively discussion, with many of the White students stating that they never had to deal with these issues, and the students of color speaking somberly about how often they experienced these issues.

In line with McIntosh's work, a coach developer could develop a sport-coaching-specific WP activity or engage coaches in developing a list of state-ments that reflect WP in sport. For example:

1 I've never been accused of getting a coaching job due to my race, or some sort of affirmative action.
2 As an athlete, I could have challenged my coach without being labeled a troublemaker based on my race.
3 When I applied for a sport coach job, I never considered that my race would negatively affect my chances of being hired.
4 I've never been harassed or called names while coaching because of my race.

In debriefing activities like this, coach developers should remember to explore a coach's knowledge, attitudes, and feelings, how others may feel, and consider actions coaches can take to rectify unearned privileges and embody antiracist practices. It's likely less important that coaches know exactly what to do in every situation than developing a deep understanding of race and WP, including racial interpersonal and systemic harm, and acquire an array of practical skills to use in varying contexts to identify and act on these issues.

Frameworks for action

There are several frameworks coach developers can draw upon to act effectively in their own lives or teach to coaches around racial issues including incorporat-ing culturally relevant pedagogy (Ladson-Billings 1995), inviting guest speakers with different racial identities (Wise 2017), and, drawing from Allport's (1954) intergroup contact theory, sustained dialogue (https://sustaineddialogue.org/our-approach/publications/), Sue's (2010) work on microaggressions, Rowe's (2008) work on microaffirmations, and, more recently, Sue et al.'s (2019) work on microintervention strategies, as well as Tuhiwai Smith's (2012) decolonizing methodologies. These frameworks, a few discussed later in this chapter, are not identical, but share a goal of helping individuals understand their own and oth-ers' perspectives; recognize the historical and ongoing causes and effects of racial oppression, domination, supremacy, and privilege; and how to take steps toward more authentic inclusivity while enhancing psychosocial outcomes. The reader

Dialogue then action

Sustained dialogue was originally used for nations to engage in peace talks, and has been extended to foster understanding and relationship building that leads to action or resolution in many settings. Sustained dialogue is facilitated by someone trained in this approach, and focuses on dialogue, not debate or discussion (the latter are more prevalent in society and sport, especially because competition encourages a winner-takes-all mindset). Participants speak about their own lived experiences regarding racism, privilege, and oppression, which makes the dialogue personal, immediate, and concrete. After many meetings, parties would develop shared actions, which in a sport-specific setting might include the creation of an advisory council of athletes on matters of race, an inclusive change toward talent identification and the assignment of positions on the team, or recruitment and selection of team captains or coaches.

Racial put-down and affirmation

Three of the concepts mentioned (microaggressions, microaffirmations, and micro-interventions) can help us understand and act to improve communication, relationships, and psychosocial outcomes among people with different racial identities. Racial microaggressions are essentially communicative put-downs (i.e. invalidations, assaults, insults) related to race, such as attributing a Black athlete's success in sport to genetics, rather than the athlete's hard work, social support, and similar factors.

As these microaggressions cause the receiver to be harmed, and likely damage the interpersonal relationship, coach developers and coaches should learn to appreciate how they might be communicating these hurtful messages and work to change them. For example, rather than taking an approach that omits issues of race, a coach developer teaching about teambuilding or cohesion would specifically integrate issues of race and microaggressions to enhance outcomes and reduce the damage of WP.

Racial microaffirmations are positive messages of inclusion, diversity, and success that can be used to replace microaggressions and counteract WP (Gearity & Henderson Metzger 2017; Rowe 2008). For example, it could be affirming for a coach to have a racially diverse, integrated coaching staff, with POC in positions of leadership at all levels, resources, and authority to provide or be provided meaningful mentoring, and opportunities to contribute feedback that will be heard and acted upon.

Beyond microaffirmations, Sue et al. (2019) describe microinterventions as "interpersonal tools that are intended to counteract, change or stop microaggressions by subtly or overtly confronting and educating the perpetrator" (p. 134). These are words and actions that simultaneously validate the experience of a

Understanding, acting upon White privilege **255**

person being targeted by a microaggression while showing the person is valued, affirming the person's identit(ies), supporting and encouraging the person, and offering reassurance that the person is not alone (p. 134). Strategies depend upon context and can include making the "invisible" visible, disarming the event, educating the offender, and seeking external support (p. 135).

Organizational and societal

Racial injustice includes, but is much bigger than, individual acts of interpersonal harm. Macroaggressions can occur at the institutional and societal level, and include systemic racism impacting "programs, policies, practices and structures of govern-mental agencies, legal and judicial systems, health care organizations, educational institutions, and business and industry" (Sue et al. 2019: 131). Longstanding and pervasive systems of privilege and oppression inform virtually every aspect of life – but, as described earlier, those systems are designed to go unnoticed by those benefiting from them the most.

In a recent workshop, I (Brian) co-delivered with one of my (White) students on racial issues in coaching for (nearly all White) lacrosse coaches, we passed out five lacrosse balls to five coaches seated throughout the room. Some were sitting toward the front of the room, some midway, some to the back, all varying in distance from the center. The coaches were instructed to throw the ball into a trashcan in the front of the room. They all missed, but the coach in the front row had an advantage: His ball bounced back to him. He took another shot and made it. As with WP, this coach benefited from his starting position. We like to think of sport or democracies as meritocracies, but, just like this coach, people often succeed or fail not through merit alone, but through unearned advantages – one of which is skin color. One common theme in these discussions is, "But I worked hard to get where I am today". As this example shows, both things can be true. To make the basket, the coach needed a certain degree of skills; he needed to take aim, think through his shot, and execute the required technique, and not every person sitting in the same seat would have succeeded. However, his success was based on both being skilled and lucky. The point of offering this brief story is to share another activity that coach developers could use to illustrate WP, and to note that this workshop was delivered at a regional conference of a major national sport organizing body. Addressing WP and antiracist practices requires organizational leaders to be committed to these values, enhancing employee understanding on these issues, and changing systemic racism.

Leonardo (2004) eloquently argues that the discourse of WP allows Whites to make minor progress and feel good that they're not racist, but at the peril of not going far enough toward understanding the roots and branches of White supremacy to allow meaningful social change. We must go further. We need our antiracist coaches and coach developers to go beyond themselves and their immediate circles to the larger organizations and social contexts in which they live and work. There are several ways organizations that deliver sport, such as schools, clubs, and businesses, can address WP in powerful ways. Just as individual coaches create the team's practice plans, so too can organizations embrace a racially aware mission statement and enact practices that include diversity training for all (not merely hiring a "Director of Diversity" and giving lip service to "inclusive excellence"); centering multicultural issues within the curriculum or workplace, including hiring practices; creating an advisory board on diversity climate (with real autonomy and influence); and engaging with community partners around useful and welcome programing.

In 2003, the National Football League (NFL) implemented what's referred to as the "Rooney Rule", a policy that requires teams to interview at least one racial minority when a new head coach position opens; however, research continues to show coaches who are members of racial minorities are hired at lower rates than White coaches and are fired, and not re-hired, as head coaches at higher rates than Whites (Cochran & Mehri 2002). Most owners of professional sports teams are White. As Leonardo (2004) notes, POC have been discriminated against in the workplace for years and generally lack the familial, generational wealth to break into professional sport team ownership. Moreover, there's no shortage of racist messages by owners and managers of teams, which sustains White capital (Sanchez 2019). Organizations like the NFL might extend the idea of recruiting racial minority coaches to soliciting minority owners the next time a team is for sale, but WP works to prevent such a consideration (Garcia 2018).

Personal reflections and wishful thinking

Some of my (Brian) fondest memories coaching were talking with athletes about race and WP, attempting to dispel racist myths about athletic performance, and affirming the diverse cultures and social identities around me. As my understanding grew and I could use this knowledge in my everyday coaching, I worked to listen to and support traditionally marginalized groups. My path continues to be bumpy, and alternates between clarity and confusion. I didn't have many sport-coaching-specific examples to draw upon. I'm still trying to see the cultural forces operating through the mental, technical, and tactical aspects of coaching. One recent example is McDonald's (2016) research showing how White coaches and White athletes "other" (i.e. treat as alien, exotic, and "less than") Pacific Islanders, reinforcing Whiteness as both dominant and superior and producing negative outcomes. I wish that the field of sport coaching and coach development would begin to integrate sociocultural awareness (especially related to WP) throughout research, curricula, and professional development opportunities. Through such systematic and ongoing work, we could provide more and better resources for sport coaches committed to their own growth and greater opportunities, freedom, and inclusion for all.

Activities for coach education

1   With a group of coaches, do a critical discourse analysis of a clip from a movie, newspaper or magazine article, or television sports segment. Who

is talking? About what? What messages are they conveying, and to what effect? Then, pose questions that point to racial and other intersecting identities such as: Who wasn't talking? What groups of people did they leave out? What topics do they shy away from or omit? What assumptions did the speakers make? This sort of exercise could be useful to show who and what topics are privileged versus marginalized or misrepresented.

2   Skim the textbook you are holding and look for ways WP may have occurred. Next, alone or with other coach developers, create ways to integrate concepts about WP within the existing instructional strategies. For example, how could race and WP be considered within mentor–mentee relationships? Or, how might we leverage teaching content on purported neutral topics such as genetics, physiology, or biomechanics through a WP lens? From an affirmative perspective, we could highlight the work of scientists (including the African-American sociologist of sport Dr. Harry Edwards) who are POC or show how social forces contribute to athletes' or coaches' success.

3   Physical, mental, technical, and tactical planning is inherent in coaching. Identify what values guide these plans, and then consider where these values come from or whose cultural values they reflect. Next, consider how you might structure these plans with different cultural values, from non-White cultures that place greater emphasis on community, extended families, cooperation, the environment, play, or self-expression.

Additional resources

1   Review and follow organizations that promote equity and provide resources for educators, such as Teaching Tolerance (www.tolerance.org; www.face book.com/TeachingTolerance.org/; https://twitter.com/Tolerance_org).

2   Read from the works of POC such as Moustafa Bayoumi, Ta-Nehisi Coates, W.E.B. DuBois, James Baldwin, Joe Feagin, Paulo Freire, bell hooks, Langston Hughes, Zora Neale Hurston, Gloria Ladson-Billings, Martin Luther King Jr., Toni Morrison, and Cornel West, or the works of Richard Lapchick about racial minority leaders specific to sport. Or, read about the experiences of racial and ethnic minorities in sport; for example, Black athletes' experiences on college campuses, classroom, and sporting fields, particularly at predominantly White institutions (for example, Hawkins 2010).

3   Dr. George Cunningham is a professor of sport management and has extensively studied diversity and inclusivity in sport and authored arguably the most comprehensive textbook in the field on the subject (see Cunningham 2019).

4   Dr. Joe Feagin is an award-winning professor for his work on race and racism, including *The White Racial Frame* (2013).

Bibliography

Allport, G.W. (1954) *The Nature of Prejudice*, Cambridge: Perseus Books.

Coakley, J. (2015) *Sports in Society: Issues and Controversies*, 11th edn, New York: McGraw Hill.

Coaston, J. (2019) *The intersectionality wars*. Online. Available HTTP: <www.vox.com/the-highlight/2019/5/20/18542843/intersectionality-conservatism-law-race-gender-discrimination> (accessed 20 June 2019).

Cochran, J., Jr. and Mehri, C. (2002) *Black coaches in the National Football League: Superior performance, inferior opportunities*. Online. Available HTTP: <http://media.wix.com/ugd/520423_24cb6412ed2758c7204b7864022ebb5d.pdf> (accessed 16 July 2019).

Crenshaw, K. (1989) *Demarginalizing the intersection of race and sex: A Black feminist critique of antidiscrimination doctrine, feminist theory and antiracist politics*, University of Chicago Legal Forum. Online. Available HTTP: <http://chicagounbound.uchicago.edu/uclf/vol1989/iss1/8> (accessed 19 June 2019).

Crosley-Corcoran, G. (2014) *Explaining white privilege to a broke white person*. Online. Available HTTP: <www.huffpost.com/entry/explaining-white-privilege-to-a-broke-white-person_b_5269255> (accessed 19 April 2019).

Cunningham, G.B. (2019) *Diversity and Inclusion in Sport Organizations: A Multilevel Perspective*, 4th edn, New York: Routledge.

DiAngelo, R. (2011) 'White fragility', *International Journal of Critical Pedagogy*, 3: 54–70.

Feagin, J.R. (2013) *The White Racial Frame: Centuries of Racial Framing and Counterframing*, 2nd edn, New York: Routledge.

Garcia, A. (2018) *There are only two owners of color in the NFL*, CNN Money. Online. Available HTTP: <https://money.cnn.com/2018/05/18/news/nfl-nba-mlb-owners-diversity/index.html> (accessed 13 July 2019).

Gearity, B.T. and Henderson Metzger, L. (2017) 'Intersectionality, microaggressions, and microaffirmations: Towards a cultural praxis of sport coaching', *Sociology of Sport Journal*, 34: 160–75.

Hawkins, B. (2010) *The New Plantation: Black Athletes, College Sports, and Predominantly White Institutions*, New York: Palgrave Macmillan.

Hoberman, J. (1996) *Darwin's Athletes: How Sport has Damaged Black America and Preserved the Myth of Race*, Boston: Houghton Mifflin Harcourt.

Ladson-Billings, G. (1995) 'Toward a theory of culturally relevant pedagogy', *American Educational Research Journal*, 32: 465–91.

Leonardo, Z. (2004) 'The color of supremacy: Beyond the discourse of "white privilege"', *Educational Philosophy & Theory*, 36: 137–52.

McDonald, B. (2016) 'Coaching whiteness: Stories of "Pacifica exotica" in Australian high school rugby', *Sport, Education & Society*, 21: 465–82.

McIntosh, P. (1988) 'White privilege: Unpacking the invisible knapsack', in A.M. Filor (ed.) *Multiculturalism, 1992*, pp. 30–6, New York: New York State Council of Educational Associations.

NCAA. (2018) *Coach and student-athlete demographics by sport and title*. Online. Available HTTP: <www.ncaa.org/about/resources/research/ncaa-demographics-database> (accessed 9 July 2019).

Rowe, M. (2008) 'Micro-affirmations and micro-inequities', *Journal of the International Ombudsman Association*, 1: 45–8.

Sanchez, R. (2019) *Another pro sports franchise is doing damage control over racist statements. This time it's the Chicago Cubs*, CNN. Online. Available HTTP: <www.cnn.com/2019/02/06/us/sports-franchises-racist-intolerant-statements/index.html> (accessed 7 June 2019).

Sue, D.W. (2010) *Microaggressions in Everyday Life*, Hoboken: John Wiley & Sons.

Sue, D.W., Alsaidi, S., Awad, M.N., Glaeser, E., Calle, C.Z. and Mendez, N. (2019) 'Disarming racial microaggressions: Microintervention strategies for targets, White allies, and bystanders', *American Psychologist*, 74: 128–42.

Tuhiwai Smith, L. (2012) *Decolonizing Methodologies: Research and Indigenous Peoples*, 2nd edn, London: Zed Books Ltd.

West, C. (1994) *Race Matters*, New York: Vintage Books.

Wise, M. (2017) *Greg Popovich's speech about white privilege felt like a personal value*, The Undefeated. Online. Available HTTP: <https://theundefeated.com/features/nba-gregg-popovich-speech-about-white-privilege-felt-like-a-personal-rebuke/> (accessed 9 July 2019).

21

BECOMING AN AGENT OF CHANGE

Key strategies for the development of coaches in Indigenous Sport for Development contexts

Steven B. Rynne, Tony Rossi, Audrey R. Giles, and Carl Currey

Chapter objectives

By the end of this chapter, the reader should be able to:

1 Identify the backgrounds and educational experiences of Sport for Development (SfD) coaches, highlighting the development of skills related to movement competence rather than developing skills to foster broader social goals.
2 Problematize "traditional" approaches to the preparation of SfD coaches.
3 Propose alternative foci for the preparation and practice of coaches in SfD settings that go beyond the confines of sport itself.

Brief chapter overview

The sporting experience for Indigenous participants within the context of SfD initiatives is contingent upon the educators, their background, experiences, and training relative to the groups with which they are working. Problematically, the preparation of SfD coaches is often inadequate and incomplete. In this chapter, we seek to outline the specific circumstances under which SfD may have positive outcomes. In doing so, we draw upon specific traditions associated with decolonizing approaches, critical reflexivity, and the prioritization of local knowledge systems. The adoption of any of the instructional strategies discussed in this book by coach developers who intend to work, or find themselves working, in SfD environments may be informed by what follows.

Why and when We use Sport for Development

The approaches we advocate have been developed in relation to our own experiences as coaches and in other volunteer roles across a variety of sports (Currey, Giles, Rossi, Rynne) and organizations (Giles, Currey), as well as through experience as former physical education teachers (Rossi, Rynne). Our understandings and convictions have been further strengthened through our careers in physical education teacher education (PETE), coach education, and/or community-based sports organizations.

The essentials of Sport for Development in Indigenous sport

Definitions, essential components, and goals of SfD

Indigenous

The word "Indigenous" is often used to refer to the original inhabitants and traditional custodians of a region. Primarily used in direct contrast to settlers/occupiers/colonizers who originate from other regions or lands, in Australia it is regularly used in reference to Aboriginal peoples and Torres Strait Islanders. The word "Indigenous" is culturally loaded, and there remain significant debates regarding how Indigenous groups self-identify and are identified by others. What seems to be common, however, across all Indigenous peoples, is the almost irreparable damage done to the communities as a consequence of colonization. The legacy of this damage is obvious well into the 21st century and is manifest in poorer health outcomes, lower participation in education and lower educational outcomes, over-representation in incarceration rates, chronic alcohol abuse, and lower life expectancy at the population level for Indigenous peoples (Eversole 2005; Nelson 2009).

Sport for Development

The term Sport for Development (SfD) has a history of use within global research and connects with the common vernacular associated with numerous programs and policy initiatives in a variety of countries. SfD programs occur when efforts are made to address deep-rooted social or health problems using sport as a vehicle for change. Such programs are not solely physical activity interventions focused on increased levels of moderate to vigorous physical activity for purported health gains. SfD programs intend to use sport to deliver a much grander array of outcomes related to what Sen (2010) calls capabilities (e.g. peoples' freedom to achieve a lifestyle they desire). Interestingly in popular understandings of SfD, sport is often valorized to the extent that it is seen to have the capacity to achieve development goals that might appear almost impossible via any other means. For example, the field of sport has been positioned as a way of attracting disconnected youth to social programs, fostering leadership skills, supporting the development of social capital, encouraging self-determination, and promoting a variety of educational and health outcomes (Hayhurst & Giles 2013; Kay & Dudfield 2013; Kidd 2008; Rossi & Jeanes 2016; Rossi & Rynne 2014; Rossi, Rynne & Nelson 2013). Examples include programs using sport and physical activity to raise awareness about HIV/AIDS across Africa (Jeanes 2013), the Football for Peace project in Israel (Schulenkorf & Sugden 2011), and cricket programs aimed at engaging people with disabilities in Fiji (Beckman et al. 2018). Programs are intended to be transformational, and the coaches are intended to be the agents of this change.

Problematizing SfD

There is mounting scholarship serving to temper the often naïve and misleading positivity associated with sport's capacity to contribute to development agendas. Coakley (2015) challenges the largely taken-for-granted view of sport's inherent goodness, suggesting the existence of the Great Sport Myth: (a) sport is pure and good; (b) this purity and goodness is automatically passed on to those involved in sport; and (c) sport inevitably leads to the development of individuals and their communities. Coaches play a key role in the Great Sport Myth, as they are charged with ensuring sport's goodness and participants' development of key attributes. However, critical scholarship in SfD demonstrates that much sporting and developmental practice remains entrenched within traditional, top-down approaches that adhere to dominant neoliberal forces invariably born out of a paternalistic, colonial concern for the "other" rather than providing opportunities to challenge existing power structures and norms (e.g. Darnell & Hayhurst 2011; Giles & Lynch 2012; Spaaij & Jeanes 2012). In other words, programs tend to treat young people who experience marginalization (predominantly) as problems to be solved.

In Australia in particular, SfD programs slip (often unintentionally) into a colonial discourse via the sheer assumption that Indigenous communities need Euro-centric interventions and that sport is a "good fit" for Indigenous communities. As a consequence, SfD programs may give the appearance that the changes they seek to achieve are primarily about ensuring Euro-centric, neoliberal values and behaviors prevail (Adair & Stronach 2011; Maynard 2012; Wane 2008). In addition, the links made between sport and Indigenous peoples have been especially strong with an enduring assumption that Indigenous sportspeople are "naturally talented" and endowed with special gifts related to their sport performances (Adair & Stronach 2011; Tatz 1987). Hence, this "natural fit" of SfD programs (and sport participation more generally) with Indigenous communities is framed by a range of racist discourses that, broadly conceived, promote the idea that some magical natural talent prevails over hard work, intelligence, and endeavor. What remains unclear, however, is how coaches and coach developers for SfD might be able to change problematic practices and beliefs that are deeply entrenched within sport and the links with Indigenous Australians.

Coaches, coaching, and coach education in and for SfD

In spite of challenges, SfD programs present as a potentially viable approach to addressing a variety of areas of disempowerment and disadvantage (Rossi 2015; Rynne 2016; Svensson, Hancock & Hums 2016). To more regularly achieve positive outcomes, community coaches who work on SfD projects need to have a strong grasp of the context of Indigenous politics, as well as an understanding of the needs and wants, but more importantly, the ambitions of the communities with whom they work (Hartmann & Kwauk 2011). An additional challenge is that they need to have the educational training to not only instruct in sport, but somehow connect this to the social change through development that SfD attempts to bring about. Development is, after all, an educative process, albeit one that is also deeply sensitized to the local challenges to which it is responding.

Sport for Development in practice

The nature of the sporting experience for Indigenous participants within the context of SfD initiatives is contingent upon the background, experiences, and training of educators (coaches and coach developers) relative to the groups with which they are working. This presents a serious challenge because of the typical characteristics of these cohorts.

A commonality across virtually all SfD coaches (as well as other key personnel, such as coach developers) is that they have typically had positive, early experiences in sport, often as junior players, through physical education as students and sometimes as high-performing athletes. As such, like coaches in other fields, SfD coaches typically undertake an informal "apprenticeship of observation" (Cassidy & Rossi 2006; Lortie 1975). Understandably, such personnel tend to be imbued with a strong sense of the Great Sport Myth (Coakley 2015). Alongside this, an ethic of volunteerism (Cuskelly 2004; Darnell 2011) and a desire to help disadvantaged groups runs deep for coaches in SfD settings. While positive sporting experiences and a desire to do "good" for the community are in some ways admirable characteristics for coaches to possess, they may present challenges for realizing educational and development goals.

Coaches in SfD settings often see themselves as not just coaching sport, but as "saving" Indigenous people at the same time. In the most extreme cases, there are seemingly few opportunities to challenge the taken-for-granted assumptions of the "evangelical" SfD coach. The consequences of this are that SfD programs may do little to challenge the inequalities that produce the apparent need for programs in Indigenous communities, and they may continue colonial legacies that have been harmful to the communities that SfD coaches and coach developers seek to help.

The difficulty for coach developers in SfD is that the embedded paternalism within the good intentions of SfD coaches makes it challenging to move from a "missionary" perspective of coaching to one that encourages self-determination

264 Rynne, Rossi, Giles, and Currey

and self-reliance for Indigenous participants. While some have written about this as a more sustainable goal of SfD programs (e.g. Rossi & Jeanes 2018), much less has been written about what this could look like as an approach to coaching, and how coaches might be trained and prepared to achieve it within communities.

It is our contention that pedagogy should sit at the center of SfD coach training, and that for the contexts central to this chapter, pedagogy needs to be framed by a development agenda underpinned by decolonizing approaches, critical reflexivity, and the primacy of local knowledge systems.

Ways forward in conceiving and delivering coach education and coaching practices

Decolonizing approaches in SfD settings

Decolonization is a process of removing domination and reinstating self-determination of Indigenous peoples (e.g. Tuhiwai Smith 2012). In our research, we have written about our own processes of becoming aware of some assumptions that might be examples of latent racism (e.g. Rossi, Rynne & Nelson 2013). Rather than the pursuit of a "grievance" discourse, this was more an acknowledgment of our lack of understanding of the communities with which we were working and an acknowledgment of the habitual research practices that perhaps were out of place within the communities with whom we were working.

The challenge of decolonization is exacerbated by the underrepresentation of Indigenous peoples in coaching and, more specifically, in coach education roles (Apoifis, Marlin & Bennie 2018). This means that SfD education is likely to be narrow in focus (i.e. related directly to "sport" broadly rather than the specific "development" needs of Indigenous communities) and narrow in relation to understanding the diversity of Indigenous culture and politics. Broadly, however, in keeping with the foundations of decolonization, we advocate for a paradigm shift in SfD such that dominant deficit models are rejected in favor of programs that promote Indigenous self-determination. This requires that coach developers ensure the central involvement of Indigenous peoples in the design and control of programs that specifically address Indigenous community members' self-identified needs.

This is not without challenge for the predominantly non-Indigenous coaches and coach developers, since it requires a serious questioning of the ways many non-Indigenous people may be complicit in the violence (symbolic and other) perpetrated upon Indigenous peoples the world over – even more so in countries like Australia where the colonizers never left. At the same time, it demands that SfD coaches and coach developers work with Indigenous communities so that SfD initiatives reflect Indigenous ideals of community development and self-development. As Barker (2017) notes, it is difficult to be prescriptive regarding how systematic problematization of non-Indigenous intervention should occur.

Coaches in Indigenous contexts **265**

However, we offer some further principles that may be of some value; namely, a shift to critical reflexivity, and the primacy of local knowledge systems.

Shift to critical reflexivity

Decolonization approaches provide opportunities for SfD coaches and coach developers to change the focus from the pathologization and objectification of Indigenous bodies as ones that must be targeted by SfD programs – bodies to be "saved (from themselves) – to a more inward focus that supports Indigenous peoples' decision-making, self-empowerment, and control of SfD. The notion of critical reflexivity might provide the ground upon which training is conceived and delivered. Critical reflexivity connects well with decolonizing approaches because of its role in unsettling (Pollner 1991). Critical reflexivity, as applied to SfD coaching and coach education, involves employing a critical examination of the assumptions that underpin what we do as coaches and educators. Such a critical examination extends to the impacts of coach actions more broadly and forces a reflection upon what constitutes good coaching practice.

A reflexive approach, according to Bourdieu (1990), is one whereby the contextualized accounts of the analysis of action inform future action. At a practical level, this requires some effort. Coaching notes need to be taken so that a reflective cycle can be developed. How a coach keeps notes that can be reflected upon, challenged, and then used to inform change is a matter of personal preference. Increasingly, coaches are likely to do this digitally; the recording and archiving functions of smartphones allow the retention of real-time observations. No matter the means, the central concern of a critically reflexive approach in SfD is to challenge what was understood to be true such that change, adjustment, and redesign can take place in accordance with the needs, wishes, and ambitions of communities. Often such self-analysis is challenging, and the value of critical friends cannot be overstated. However, perhaps the best way to undertake self-analysis is to involve the very community with which one is working – there will be great wisdom (what we prefer to call expertise) within the community.

Primacy of local knowledge systems

Across a variety of industries, the incorporation of local knowledge, values, and traditions is now considered to be essential in developmental program delivery (Hoppers 2002). Moreover, the significance of Indigenous ways of knowing, being, and doing to delivering culturally responsive coaching (i.e. enabling coaches to be skilled agents of agreed change) has been repeatedly highlighted (Charles, Longerbeam & Miller 2013). For example, in bridging "mainstream" and "Aboriginal" pedagogies, Yunkaporta (2009) provides a framework of common ground comprised of eight interconnected pedagogies, including learning through narrative (story sharing); planning and visualizing explicit processes (learning maps); working non-verbally with self-reflective, hands on methods (non-verbal); learning through images, symbols, and metaphors (symbols and images); learning through place-responsive, environmental practice (land links); using indirect, innovative, and interdisciplinary approaches (non-linear); modeling and scaffolding by working from wholes to parts (deconstruct/reconstruct); and connecting learning to local values, needs, and knowledge (community links).

Accordingly, a foundational aspect of all SfD coach education should be the need to acknowledge and respect cultural knowledge holders. For example, coach developers must emphasize to their SfD coaches that they should seek the views, concerns, and standpoints of locals. This could take the form of involvement in council meetings, the formation of a local advisory group, speaking with existing program operators, recruiting or training local coaches, or seeking perspectives via a range of other face-to-face (e.g. speaking at local events), media (e.g. local radio), and online means (e.g. chat forums). We also recommend giving primacy to local knowledge systems through more formal (e.g. local Indigenous councils) and more informal bodies (e.g. men's or women's groups). We suggest that this be applied before (i.e. prior to committing to the commencement of any program, and in the subsequent planning of programs that meet an agreed need), during (i.e. informing ongoing conduct), and after (i.e. in evaluating the degree to which it achieved agreed goals) any coaching activities.

Coach developers in SfD contexts must ensure that as well as the SfD programs themselves, the programs of education are local and contextually informed, and empower cultural knowledge holders. In several of our projects, we have discussed the need for local "context champions". Ideally, more than one person, these context champions play meaningful roles in informing program design, offering critical and informed feedback, and rallying their communities so that self-determination and sustainability are probable, rather than programs relying on short-term, outside influences. Context champions tend to be self-evident through their initial and ongoing levels of interest, their extensive local connections, and the level of respect they command within their community. It is the role of the coach developer to support such people by including them in meaningful ways, putting their strengths to good use, and expanding their skill set. For example, a context champion could be meaningfully involved in planning activities such as scheduling, adjustment, and promotion of programs. However, perhaps they could be supported in sharing or developing some sport-specific knowledge (e.g. related to technical aspects).

The logical pinnacle of these efforts is that local cultural knowledge holders become the ones delivering professional learning as SfD coach developers. The central involvement of locals also has ongoing value in terms of broadening the cultural dimensions in the "apprenticeship of observation" discussed earlier. Apoifis, Marlin and Bennie (2018) have offered insightful commentary on this in the Australian context. Significant human and financial investment is required for coach education to be authentic and ideally transformative (Burgess 2017).

Coaches in Indigenous contexts **267**

The term "investment" is apt because when education programs commit to giving primacy to local knowledge systems, the return on that investment is SfD coach developers who can support coaching practices that promote Indigenous ways of doing and being. Also, countering existing criticisms, this investment opens up significant programmatic possibilities such as shifts related to conceptions of communication (e.g. oral traditions), time (e.g. non-linearity), and community (e.g. family bonds).

Personal reflections and wishful thinking

Though well-intentioned, many non-Indigenous SfD coaches are underprepared to achieve the lofty goals of the programs in which they work. In becoming agents of change, we envisage a future when SfD coaches can benefit from prolonged and ongoing education facilitated by qualified (ideally Indigenous) coach developers. Such qualifications would involve decolonizing approaches grounded in critical reflexivity. Along with giving primacy to local knowledge systems, this approach would serve to liberate coaches from constrained views on helping ("I'm a good person") and enable more favored approaches like supporting the self-determination of others.

Activities for coach education

Readers might encourage SfD coaches to consider their own backgrounds and contexts with the following questions and activities:

1 Coaches are arranged into small groups (two to three) and engage in a short personal history interview framed around two key questions: What previous experiences have I had in sport and education that frame my practices as a coach? What evidence do I have of the impact of these experiences?
2 Coach developers provide coaches with simple rules for conduct when dealing with sensitive topics. This could include establishment of listening protocols (e.g. talking sticks, respectful listening), room configurations (e.g. yarning circles, debate formation), engagement arrangements (e.g. explicit role playing, including devil's advocate, contrarian, applied advocate).
3 Individuals or small groups of coaches are presented with short case studies of SfD participants (different ages, genders, sporting experience, sporting ability, levels of interest, etc.). They are then asked to explain how well their coaching does or does not yet account for the varied backgrounds of their participants, providing ways to further improve.
4 Coaches are provided with a template for reflective journal and asked to complete it for the first month of practice. Coach developers then reconnect and lead discussions based on questions such as: "Do you have any evidence of deficit- or strengths-based language in your practice"?

Additional resources

1 The platform www.sportanddev.org/ is supported by some of the world's leading SfD organizations, practitioners, and academics. It is primarily an online resource and networking tool.
2 www.clearinghouseforsport.gov.au/knowledge_base/organised_sport/sport_ and_government_policy_objectives/indigenous_australians_and_sport and www.clearinghouseforsport.gov.au/knowledge_base/organised_sport/ value_of_sport/sport_for_community_development
3 The Clearinghouse for Sport is an Australian, member-access resource. The aim is to bring together and coordinate information generated by and through all government agencies in the country around particular topic areas of interest. The two sites above are in relation to Indigenous sport and sport for community development.
4 Hayhurst, L.M., Kay, T. and Chawansky, M. (eds.) (2015) *Beyond Sport for Development and Peace: Transnational Perspectives on Theory, Policy and Practice,* Abingdon: Routledge. This text traces advancements in the rapidly changing geopolitical landscape and provides a collection of specific examples of how theory, policy and practice is changing in SfD.

Bibliography

Adair, D. and Stronach, M. (2011) 'Natural-born athletes? Australian Aboriginal people and the double-edged lure of professional sport', in J. Long and K. Spracklen (eds.) *Sport and Challenges to Racism,* pp. 117–34, London: Palgrave Macmillan.

Apoifis, N., Marlin, D. and Bennie, A. (2018) 'Noble athlete, savage coach: How racialised representations of Aboriginal athletes impede professional sport coaching opportunities for Aboriginal Australians', *International Review for the Sociology of Sport,* 53: 854–68.

Barker, D. (2017) 'In defence of white privilege: Physical education teachers' understandings of their work in culturally diverse schools', *Sport, Education and Society,* 24: 1–13.

Beckman, E., Rossi, T., Hanrahan, S., Rynne, S. and Dorovolomo, J. (2018) 'The effectiveness of a cricket programme for engaging people with a disability in physical activity in Fiji', *International Journal of Disability, Development and Education,* 65: 199–213.

Bourdieu, P. (1990) 'The scholastic point of view', *Cultural Anthropology,* 5: 380–91.

Burgess, C. (2017) 'Beyond cultural competence: Transforming teacher professional learning through Aboriginal community-controlled cultural immersion', *Critical Studies in Education,* 58: 1–19.

Cassidy, T. and Rossi, T. (2006) 'Situating learning: (Re) examining the notion of apprenticeship in coach education', *International Journal of Sports Science & Coaching,* 1: 235–46.

Charles, H., Longerbeam, S.D. and Miller, A.E. (2013) 'Putting old tensions to rest: Integrating multicultural education and global learning to advance student development', *Journal of College and Character,* 14: 47–58.

Coakley, J. (2015) 'Assessing the sociology of sport: On cultural sensibilities and the great sport myth', *International Review for the Sociology of Sport,* 50: 402–406.

Cuskelly, G. (2004) 'Volunteer retention in community sport organisations', *European Sport Management Quarterly,* 4: 59–76.

Darnell, S.C. (2011) 'Identity and learning in international volunteerism: "Sport for development and peace" internships', *Development in Practice*, 21: 974–86.

Darnell, S.C. and Hayhurst, L.M. (2011) 'Sport for decolonization: Exploring a new praxis of sport for development', *Progress in Development Studies*, 11: 183–96.

Eversole, R. (2005) 'Overview: Patterns of indigenous disadvantage worldwide', in R. Eversole, J.A. McNeish and A.D. Cimadamore (eds.) *Indigenous Peoples and Poverty: An International Perspective*, pp. 29–37, London: Zed Books Ltd.

Giles, A.R. and Lynch, M. (2012) 'Postcolonial and feminist critiques of sport for development', in R.J. Schinke and S.J. Hanrahan (eds.) *Sport for Development, Peace, and Social Justice*, pp. 89–104, West Virginia: FiT Publishing.

Hartmann, D. and Kwauk, C. (2011) 'Sport and development: An overview, critique, and reconstruction', *Journal of Sport & Social Issues*, 35: 284–305.

Hayhurst, L.M.C. and Giles, A.R. (2013) 'Private and moral authority, self-determination, and the domestic transfer objective: Foundations for understanding sport for development and peace in Aboriginal communities in Canada', *Sociology of Sport Journal*, 30: 504–19.

Hoppers, C.A.O. (ed.). (2002) *Indigenous Knowledge and the Integration of Knowledge Systems: Towards a Philosophy of Articulation*, Cape Town: New Africa Books.

Jeanes, R. (2013) 'Educating through sport? Examining HIV/AIDS education and sport-for-development through the perspectives of Zambian young people', *Sport, Education and Society*, 18: 388–406.

Kay, T. and Dudfield, O. (2013) *The Commonwealth Guide to Advancing Development through Sport*, London: Commonwealth Secretariat.

Kidd, B. (2008) 'A new social movement: Sport for development and peace', *Sport in Society*, 11: 370–80.

Lortie, D. (1975) *Schoolteacher: A Sociological Study*, Chicago: University of Chicago Press.

Maynard, J. (2012) 'Contested space: The Australian Aboriginal sporting arena', *Sport in Society*, 15: 987–96.

Nelson, A. (2009) 'Sport, physical activity and urban Indigenous young people', *Australian Aboriginal Studies*, 2: 101–11.

Pollner, M. (1991) 'Left of ethnomethodology: The rise and decline of radical reflexivity', *American Sociological Review*, 56: 370–80.

Rossi, T. (2015) 'Expecting too much? Can Indigenous sport programmes in Australia deliver development and social outcomes?', *International Journal of Sport Policy and Politics*, 7: 181–95.

Rossi, T. and Jeanes, R. (2016) 'Education, pedagogy and sport for development: Addressing seldom asked questions', *Sport, Education and Society*, 21: 483–94.

Rossi, T. and Jeanes, R. (2018) 'Is sport for development already an anachronism in the age of austerity or can it be a space of hope?', *International Journal of Sport Policy and Politics*, 10: 185–201.

Rossi, T. and Rynne, S.B. (2014) 'Sport development programmes for Indigenous Australians: Innovation, inclusion and development, or a product of "white guilt"?', *Sport in Society*, 17: 1030–45.

Rossi, A., Rynne, S.B. and Nelson, A. (2013) 'Doing whitefella research in blackfella communities in Australia: Decolonizing method in sports related research', *Quest*, 65: 116–31.

Rynne, S. (2016) 'Exploring the pedagogical possibilities of Indigenous sport-for-development programmes using a socio-personal approach', *Sport, Education and Society*, 21: 605–22.

Schulenkorf, N. and Sugden, J. (2011) 'Sport for development and peace in divided societies: Cooperating for inter-community empowerment in Israel', *European Journal for Sport and Society*, 8: 235–56.

Sen, A. (2010) 'The place of capability in a theory of justice', in H. Brighouse and I. Robeyns (eds.) *Measuring Justice: Primary Goods and Capabilities*, pp. 239–53, Cambridge: Cambridge University Press.

Spaaij, R. and Jeanes, R. (2012) 'Education for social change? A Freirean critique of sport for development and peace', *Physical Education and Sport Pedagogy*, 18: 442–57.

Svensson, P.G., Hancock, M.G. and Hums, M.A. (2016) 'Examining the educative aims and practices of decision-makers in sport for development and peace organizations', *Sport, Education and Society*, 21: 495–512.

Tatz, C. (1987) *Aborigines in Sport*, Adelaide: Australian Society for Sports History.

Tuhiwai Smith, L. (2012) *Decolonizing Methodologies: Research and Indigenous Peoples*, 2nd edn, London: Zed Books Ltd.

Wane, N.N. (2008) 'Mapping the field of indigenous knowledges in anti-colonial discourse: A transformative journey in education', *Race Ethnicity and Education*, 11: 183–97.

Yunkaporta, T. (2009) 'Aboriginal pedagogies at the cultural interface', Doctorate thesis, James Cook University, Queensland, Australia.

INDEX

aboriginal 261, 265, 268–9; pedagogies 265, 270
active learning 7; classrooms 34; methods 10, 35, 44
adapted 59, 130, 135, 160, 216–17, 227–30, 232–5; equipment 231; sport 226–7, 233
adaptive behavior 240
adult learning principles 154, 157, 164, 215–22, 225
aging 224
Amateur Athletic Union (AAU) 227
andragogy 216
antiracist 249, 252–3, 255, 258
anxiety 161, 251
appreciative inquiry 144–5, 153; design phase 145; destiny phase 145; discovery phase 145; dream phase 145
apprenticeship 1, 117, 209, 263, 266–7
assessment: authentic 10, 175, 185; formative 10, 26, 68; peer 10; self 10, 198, 209, 221; strategies 10; summative 27, 68, 184; tools 28, 124
athlete: centered 90–1, 232, 247, 249; control 218, 244; development 90, 230, 232; learning 92, 97; masters (MAs) 215–16, 224; youth 225, 229
autonomy 12, 14, 16, 36, 41, 60, 67, 157–8, 161–2, 218, 230, 232, 256

best practices 2, 12, 44, 119, 121, 153, 208, 214
bias 15, 212, 228, 249, 251
biomechanics 59, 64–5, 67, 105, 193, 196, 199, 257; biomechanical 61, 69, 172, 231

biopsychosocial 241
Bloom's taxonomy 34
Blumberg 7, 9, 11–12, 16, 18; framework 13
Bourdieu, Pierre 265, 268

Canada Games 118
Canadian Association for the Advancement of Women in Sport (CAAWS) 208–10, 213
Canadian Paralympic Committee 119
case study 73, 77, 85, 87, 89–93, 95–7, 236, 249
cerebral palsy 229
certified strength and conditioning coach (CSCS) 191, 193, 196, 198–9
chronic pain 232
classification system 227–8, 231
classroom: -based activity 26; -based work 26
Clearinghouse for Sport 268
coach-controlled environment 90–1, 217
Coach Developer Academy 165, 217
coaching: models 105; philosophy 105, 111, 143, 146, 232; practice 2, 26–7, 32, 46, 48, 53–6, 61, 67, 75, 81, 83, 87, 90–1, 95–8, 100–1, 103–5, 107–11, 118, 121, 138, 141–5, 147, 152, 180–2, 184–8, 215, 222, 224–5, 232–3, 237, 264–5, 267; process 105, 107; research 92, 100–1, 104, 109, 216, 251
Coaching Association of Canada (CAC) 209–10, 213
collaboration 9–10, 31, 46, 51, 53, 60–1, 66, 90–4, 137, 179, 185–6, 217

272 Index

colonial 262–3, 269, 270
colonization 261, 264–5, 269
colorblindness 250–1
community 3, 17–18, 48, 56, 66, 90, 101, 111, 115, 117–20, 122, 125–7, 133, 137, 205–7, 212, 238, 246, 256–7, 261, 263–9; community of practice (CoP) 43, 108, 116–26, 127, 153, 179, 183; links 266; members 118–19, 122, 124–5, 264
competency-based approach 155–61, 163–65
constructivism 10, 112, 177, 179, 204
constructivist learning theories 172
course reflection 16
creativity 109–10, 161, 230, 236
Crenshaw, K. 258
critical: framework 99–101, 103; reflexivity 260, 264–5, 267; thinking 44, 46–8, 58, 75–6, 99–100, 103–4, 109–10, 207
cultural 1–2, 47, 56, 87, 97–8, 100–2, 105, 108–9, 111–12, 162, 164, 199, 204, 135, 248–51, 253, 256–8, 261, 265–6, 268, 270; capital 251; insensitive language 249; values 257

data gathering 48, 51
decision-making matrices (DECMATS) 79, 87
decolonizing 253, 259, 264–5, 267, 269–70
democratic ideals 248; democratic practice 249
developmental patterns (those with impairments) 231
Dewey, John 23, 32, 103–4, 111
differentiated instruction (DI) 191–2, 194, 198–9
discrimination 173, 205, 249, 251, 258
diversity 194, 213, 222, 228, 249, 251, 254, 256–8, 264
docility 91–3, 97
dominance 109

emotional: challenges 56; dimension 49, 56
emotion management 49–50
equitable 69, 209, 238
equity 116, 118–20, 257
ethnicity 227, 249, 270
evaluation 10, 14–16, 35, 40–2, 80, 98, 108, 116, 124–5, 128, 130, 133, 138, 140, 150, 156, 167, 170, 176–7, 185, 188, 191, 206–7, 209–11, 213, 221–3
exam preparation live clinics (EPLCs) 191–6, 198
experience-based analysis 43
experiential learning 20–4, 26–9, 32, 59–60, 67, 74–6, 87, 135, 157, 177,

189; classroom-based 23–4; cycle 20–1, 28, 30; field-based 24; laboratory-based 24; -type activities 20, 21–3
experimentation 21–2, 26–7, 76, 79, 81, 230

face-to-face lectures 50
facilitation skills handbook 165, 217, 225
facilitation strategies 219
facilitator 10, 43, 96, 102, 118, 120–2, 125, 142, 161, 177, 180, 211, 216, 225
fairness 173, 250
Female Coach Mentorship Model (FCMM) 209
Foucault, M. 91–4, 97–8
fragility 229, 251, 258
Freire, Paulo 257, 270

gatekeeper 49
gender 116, 118–20, 191, 204–5, 211, 213, 227, 252, 258, 267
genetics 254, 257
geography 191, 252
globalization 8, 144
governing bodies 4, 9, 50, 52, 62, 69, 142, 167, 172, 249
graduate students 59–61, 77, 90, 152, 216, 234
Great Sport Myth 262
group 2, 4, 8–9, 12–13, 15, 17, 18, 19, 25, 27–9, 32, 34–44, 46, 48, 49, 51, 54, 61, 65–6, 72, 90, 92, 94, 96–7, 104, 108, 112, 117–18, 121–3, 126, 130–1, 133–4, 138, 145, 159, 161–2, 165, 168–70, 176–8, 180–1, 183–7, 193–6, 198, 208, 213, 217, 221–2, 228, 233, 239–40, 248, 251–3, 256–7, 260–1, 263, 266–7; assignment 35; discussion 38, 53, 66, 193, 194, 213, 224
guided systematic assessment 11
guilt 49, 251, 269

Habermas, J. 109, 111
harassment 205
higher order thinking skills 62–3
high-performance (HP) 4, 90, 95–6, 120, 122, 126–7, 129–31, 133, 140, 142–3, 149, 152–3, 168, 184, 220, 227
holism 60, 66
hybrid approach 183

idiosyncratic 108, 130, 140, 151
impairments 226–36, 242
inclusion 11, 133–4, 168–9, 173, 206, 235, 238–9, 246, 254, 256, 258, 269; *see also* inclusivity

inclusivity 212, 249, 251, 253, 257
indigenous 259–70; culture 264; politics 263; ways of knowing 265
inequalities 263
injustice 249, 255
innovation 17, 19, 127, 134–5, 269
inquiry 10, 45–8, 50–1, 56–7, 59–60, 63, 68, 72, 98, 127, 130, 137, 139–40, 144–5, 153, 165, 206; *see also* Social Inquiry (SI)
instructor-centered 7, 10, 180
instrumental rationality 103, 109
intellectual: disabilities 237–8, 240–2, 246; functioning 240
interdependent learning 217
international coach study tour 129
International Council for Coaching Excellence (ICCE) 2, 4, 127, 156, 160, 164–5, 217, 225
International Paralympic Committee (IPC) 228, 235–6
International Paralympic Committee Academy 235
International Stoke Mandeville Games 227
internship 20–3, 27–30, 232, 269
interpersonal: knowledge 156; skills 43, 47, 156, 160, 241
intersectionality 212, 248, 258
intrapersonal: competencies 157; knowledge 156–7, 250, 252
intrinsically motivating environment 10, 217
inventive 230, 233
invisible knapsack 252, 258

King Jr., Martin Luther 257
Knowles, M.S. 216–17, 225
Kolb, D.A. 21, 26, 32, 61, 75–7, 87, 177; experiential learning cycle 20–21; model 21

landscape of practice (LoP) 116–17
latent racism 264
learned helplessness 232
learner-centered 7–11, 18–19, 131, 157, 160; approach 130, 155, 220; assumptions 12; components 11–12; methods 157
learning: activities 4, 13–14, 17, 20, 23–4, 27–8, 31–2, 61, 93, 104, 115, 119, 121, 125–6, 152, 166–8, 170–1, 176, 179–81, 183–4, 187–8; agenda 118, 121; communities 115–16, 118–19, 121, 124, 127; goals 9, 136–7, 170; maps 265; materials 61, 72, 169; objectives 10, 16, 37, 146–7, 176, 184; opportunity 14, 40, 86, 104, 131, 152, 207; outcomes 8, 13, 17, 93, 168–70, 172–3, 176–7, 198, 224; partners 13–14; preferences 13; process 10, 15–16, 35, 46, 53, 74, 162, 171, 199–200
learning style 28, 192–3, 196, 199
literacy 50, 52, 54, 56–7, 241
loafing 35–6, 41
local knowledge systems 264–7
local values 266
logical fallacies 251

macroaggressions 255
macrocycle 64–5
male allies 211
male privilege 252; *see also* privilege
marginalization 4, 251, 257, 262; *see also* marginalized groups
marginalized groups 227, 233, 256
masters coaches 216–23, 225
mentor 1, 3, 43, 54, 85, 118–20, 142, 144, 181, 183, 203, 205, 208–11, 213–14, 232, 257; mentee 208–11, 213–14, 232, 257; mentoring 111, 146, 158, 204–5, 208–10, 213–14, 232, 254; mentorship 92, 116, 167, 176, 203–5, 208–13; programs 208–11
merit 46, 255
meritocracy 250, 255
mesocycle 65, 69
metacognition 66; metacognitive assignment 68
Mezirow, J. 100, 102, 108–9, 111–12
microaffirmations 253–4, 258
microaggressions 253–5, 258
micro-coaching 24, 27, 184, 234, 240
microcycle 64, 67, 69, 150
microintervention 253–4, 258
(micro) political: action 50, 54; competencies 46; dimensions 45–6; features 45; interactions 51; literacy 54; picture 51
minority 256–7
modeling 155, 159, 168–70, 172, 180, 196, 266
multiculturalism 251, 256, 258

narrative-collaborative coaching (NCC) 3, 140–5, 148, 152–3
National Coaching Certification Program (NCCP) 2, 91, 98, 146
National Collegiate Athletic Association (NCAA) 116, 119–20, 125, 206, 212, 214, 249, 258
National Federation of High Schools (NFHS) 167, 247

274 Index

National Football League (NFL) 134, 256, 258
national governing bodies 9, 50, 52, 62, 142, 172, 249
nationalism 250
National Strength and Conditioning Association (NSCA) 62, 65, 191–2
National Wrestling Coaches Association (NWCA) 167
Nationwide Status of Women 118
neoliberal: forces 262; values 262
network 18, 48, 50–1, 115–16, 118–20, 124, 126–7, 132, 140, 153, 158, 162, 187, 205–8, 210–12, 233, 268
Nippon Sport Science University 217, 225
normalization 109, 251
novice coaches 3, 172, 228, 230–4

objectification 265
observation rubrics 80
onboarding 208, 210
operant conditioning 238
oppression 212, 253–5
oral traditions 267
Own The Podium 119

Paralympic Games 227
parasport 116, 118–19, 121–2, 125, 226–30, 232–6
people of color (POC) 248–9, 251, 253, 254, 256–7
personal learning coach (PLC) 3, 141–5, 147–9, 151–3
Personal Value Narratives 125
physical education 8, 15, 27, 30, 32, 57, 87–8, 98, 106–7, 140, 176, 234–5, 251, 261, 263, 268, 270
portfolio 23, 26, 29, 54, 98, 207
positive reinforcement 238, 241
post-positivism 10
power 10, 16, 35, 46, 56, 64, 92, 106, 108, 111, 153, 243, 249, 262
practicum 28, 75, 77, 80–2, 85, 232
prejudice 249, 257
privilege 248–50, 252–5, 257–9, 268
problem-based learning 12, 44, 59, 72–3
problem solving 43, 61, 103, 117, 184, 240
professional development 32, 52, 72, 86, 98, 103, 106, 111, 120, 122–3, 132–3, 137, 162, 188, 206–8, 211, 218–24, 249, 251, 256
Project Based Learning (PBL) 45–8, 50–1, 56–64, 66, 72–3, 98, 249

psychological needs 157; competence 17, 24, 111, 154, 156–7, 218, 220, 240–1, 248, 260, 268; relatedness 157–8, 161; *see also* autonomy

race: as classification 173, 191, 248–54, 256–9, 270; as competition 60, 89, 94–6
racial 53, 173, 248, 250–8
racism 173, 177, 249–50, 254–5, 257, 264, 268
racist discourse 262
RAT 39–40
reflection 12, 16–18, 22, 25–6, 29–32, 52, 57, 60–1, 63–4, 66, 68, 74–8, 80, 82, 85–7, 94–6, 99, 103, 105–6, 108–9, 111–12, 121, 125, 130–1, 137, 139, 142–3, 155–6, 158–64, 169, 171, 175, 180–1, 183–6, 206, 210, 219, 221, 223, 228, 234, 265; -in-action 22; -on-action 22; personal 4, 15, 31, 42, 55, 72, 86, 95, 109, 126, 137, 152, 164, 175, 187, 198, 211, 213, 222, 234, 245, 256, 267
reflective: abilities 75; autobiography 81; conversation 30, 76; cycle 24, 75–7, 80, 265; journaling 15, 86, 267; practice 22, 56, 61, 74–5, 80, 87, 106, 146, 170, 175; practitioner 22, 31–2, 88, 111, 177; process 22, 80, 102, 142–4; storytelling 82–3
reflexivity 16, 99–100, 105, 109, 110–11, 260, 264–5, 267, 269
role frames 76–7
role-playing 54, 86, 180, 193–4, 199, 234, 267

scaffolding 29, 32, 65, 82, 180, 220, 266
self-analysis 265
self-care 241
Self-Determination Theory (SDT) 157
self-directed learner 217
self-esteem 205, 240–1
self-reconnaissance 78
sexual orientation 252
Situated Learning 111, 117, 127, 140, 177, 189
social: actors 51; capital 1, 262; competencies 47; learning 115–19, 124–7, 131, 135, 170; persuasion 173; structure 104; theory 46, 55, 98
social constructionist 99–103, 112
Social Inquiry (SI) 45–8, 50–1, 56, 57
sociocultural 51, 59, 99, 102, 108, 249, 256
socioeconomic status 252
Special Olympics 237–41, 243, 245–7

Sport for Development (SfD) 260–70
stereotypes 204–5, 228, 249
Study Tour 129–40
sustained dialogue 253–4

teaching: approach 7, 9, 13–15, 99–100, 102–5, 110; effectiveness 27–30; experiences 18; practice 28, 53, 87, 199–200; philosophy 12; process 12; strategies 12, 18, 34, 40, 100, 180, 200; techniques 147; unit 15–16
team: assessment 40, 42; assignments 34, 36; -based learning (TBL) 33–44; cohesion 42–3, 81, 146, 239; development 34–6, 43; member 35, 40–1, 238–40
technology 8, 32, 109, 112, 122, 146, 168–9, 174, 177, 179, 182, 188–9, 200, 219–20, 230, 233
Theory of Experiential Education, The 87–8
thinking friend 30–1
training plan 40, 90, 126, 149–50
transformative 44, 100, 103, 105, 108, 111, 124, 131–2, 152, 212, 266, 270
Tucker Center 207–8, 213–14

undergraduate 3, 13, 18–23, 33, 44–6, 50, 59, 172, 234–5, 252; coaching program 20; internships 22
underrepresentation 204–5, 212, 249, 264
unearned assets 249, 252–3, 255
Unified Sports 237–9, 247
unintended consequences 2, 90, 93, 97
United States Paralympic Team 227

United States Professional Tennis Association (USPTA) 227
U.S. Olympic & Paralympic Training Site 232

Value Creation Framework (VCF) 124–5, 127, 131, 133, 137–8, 151
Value Creation Story 125
video self-presentation 145
volunteer coaches 166, 238
volunteerism 263, 269
Vygotsky, L. 116, 127

WeCOACH 206–11, 213, 214
Wenger, E. 108, 115–18, 122, 124–5, 127–8, 131, 140, 151, 153, 179, 183, 188–9
wheelchair: basketball 230, 235–6; curling 116, 119–23, 126; rugby 231, 235–6; simulation 231, 234; techniques 230; tennis 227, 234
White: capital 256; feminism 249; norms 249; people 249–53; privilege (WP) 248–59, 268; racism 249; supremacy 249, 255
Women Coaches Academy (WCA) 206, 208, 212, 214
Women Coaches Symposium (WCS) 207, 211–12
Women in Sport Leadership program 118
working: climate 51–2, 54; environment 51, 160; relationships 45, 56

xenophobia 250

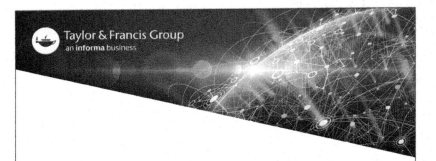

Taylor & Francis eBooks

www.taylorfrancis.com

A single destination for eBooks from Taylor & Francis with increased functionality and an improved user experience to meet the needs of our customers.

90,000+ eBooks of award-winning academic content in Humanities, Social Science, Science, Technology, Engineering, and Medical written by a global network of editors and authors.

TAYLOR & FRANCIS EBOOKS OFFERS:

A streamlined experience for our library customers

A single point of discovery for all of our eBook content

Improved search and discovery of content at both book and chapter level

REQUEST A FREE TRIAL
support@taylorfrancis.com